CW00701581

THE BOOK OF

NEWTOWN

with Porchfield, Locks Green & Shalfleet

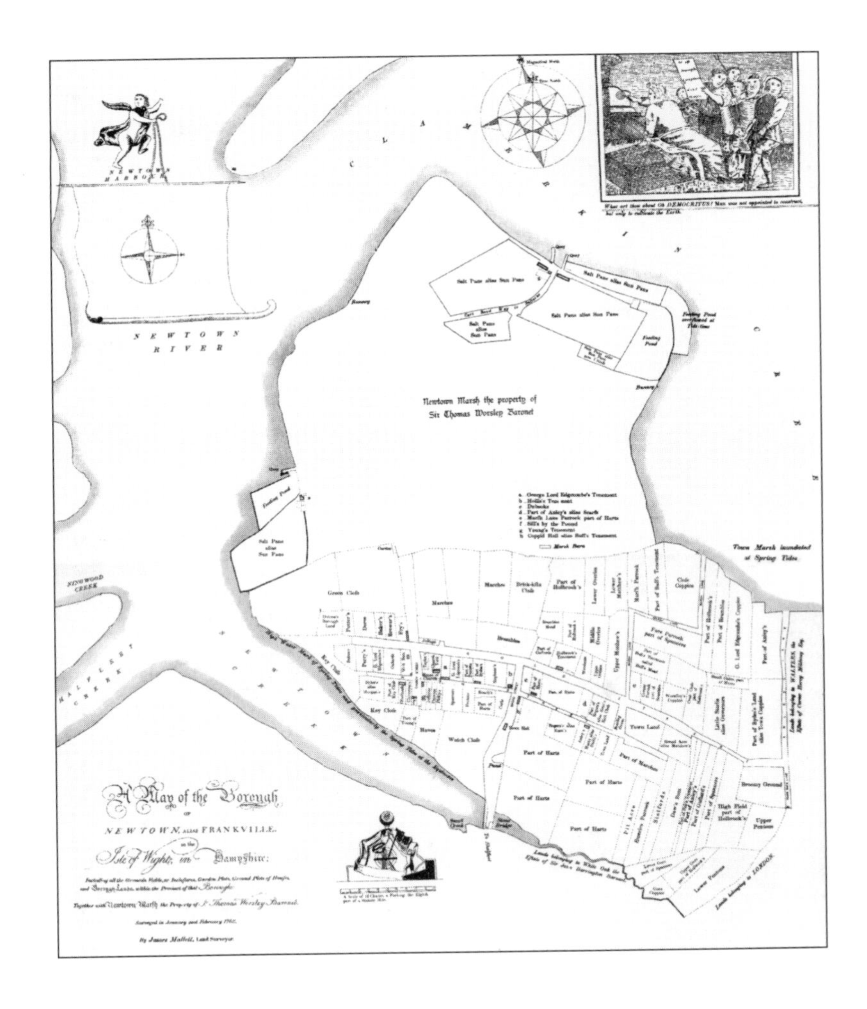

Ancient Capital of the Isle of Wight

KEIR FOSS

HALSGROVE

First published in Great Britain in 2004

Copyright © 2004 Keir Foss

This book is dedicated to my family whose association with the area spans at least 500 years, and especially to my father, a true son of Newtown.

All rights reserved. No part of this publication may be reproduced, stored in a retrieval system, or transmitted in any form or by any means without the prior permission of the copyright holder.

British Library Cataloguing-in-Publication Data.
A CIP record for this title is available from the British Library.

ISBN 1 84114 337 5

HALSGROVE

Halsgrove House
Lower Moor Way
Tiverton, Devon EX16 6SS
Tel: 01884 243242
Fax: 01884 243325
email: sales@halsgrove.com
website: www.halsgrove.com

Frontispiece photograph: *Part of James Mallett's survey of Newtown in 1768.*
REPRODUCED COURTESY OF THE NATIONAL TRUST

Printed and bound in Great Britain by CPI Bath Press, Bath.

Whilst every care has been taken to ensure the accuracy of the information contained in this book, the publisher disclaims responsibility for any mistakes which may have been inadvertently included.

Contents

Acknowledgements

I would like to thank all of the many people who have given freely of their time and expertise to help me turn an idea into reality. Their encouragement, enthusiasm and patience has been invaluable and I hope the book is worthy of their support.

The information contained here has been gleaned from a huge variety of sources over many years, but I am indebted, in particular, to the privileged access which I have enjoyed to the unpublished memoirs of such local nineteenth-century stalwarts as Frederick Fallick, Harry Pritchett and Edwin Holbrook, and to the more recent work of Don Chessell and Frederick James Fallick. In addition I have had invaluable help from my father, Herbert Foss, a true son of Newtown, and from the memories and stories handed down the generations to many of today's residents. In particular, my sincere thanks go to the folk who have kindly loaned me photographic and other materials to include in the book, in particular Barry Angell, Jack Barton, Pat Barton, Doug and Marjorie Chandler, Eileen Fallick, Richard Hawes, Ernie and June Holbrook, Monica Hope-Jones, IOW County Record Office, *IOW County Press*, Brian Manby, Robin McInnes, the National Trust, Hampshire County Record Office, Heather Sanders, Mercia and Richard Seabroke, Roger Smith, Eric Toogood, Shani Watts and Jean Wray. Other specific acknowledgements are provided in the text.

In addition, I would like to make special mention of the help I received from Billy Mustchin, another Newtown 'old-timer', from Robin Barton who worked in the oyster fishery during the 1950s, from Ernie Holbrook who, sadly, did not live to see the book published, and the archivist at the County Record Office in Newport, Richard Smout, and his superb team.

Not least, I would like to thank my mother Elsie, almost 100 years old at the time of going to press, whose enthusiasm for the project and whose knowledge of the area in question has been a great inspiration.

Finally, I would like to thank those organisations and individuals who have helped me with the funding of the project, especially recognising the generous contribution of the Shalfleet Parish Partnership.

I have done my best to check the accuracy of all the material in the book. For any errors or omissions I apologise to those involved. I will be delighted to hear from readers who can add to the area's story, by way of anecdotes or pictures, or who can identify those in the published photographs. (E-mail: keir.foss@btopenworld.com)

Newport Market Place, focal point for Newtown's farmers, c.1908.

INTRODUCTION

The last shop in Newtown finally stopped trading in 1960. In reality, it was the front room of 'Putty' Vincent's bungalow, reached with some difficulty over the obstacles strewn across the floor of his kitchen and hallway. It looked forlornly on to Town Gate Lane along which, perhaps, some 20 casual travellers passed each day. Turnover of stock had slowed to a trickle, and those customers brave enough to trust the durability of the foodstuffs on offer and sufficiently agile to reach the heart of the retail outlet found 'Putty' in his armchair, lovingly caressing an old OXO tin that served as his till. Agitated at the thought of doing business, 'Putty' would ignore the occasional movement of a rat through the gaping cracks in the wall, and press his visitor to take anything that might happen to be available. Whatever the outcome, transaction or not, it would be marked down as a busy day.

Opposite the shop stood Walter's Copse, second home to the woodmen who worked for Sir Barrington Simeon, lord of the manor of Swainston. Spar-maker Ern Seagar, born in 1867, toiled there for most of his working life, alongside George Olden, the hurdle-maker, and brothers Henry and John Ford, all of them leaving a huge legacy of wood-chippings as they turned out perhaps 4,000 spars or 400 faggots each week. Rumour has it that Ern Seagar slept with his pipe still in his mouth. There is no record that he ever set fire to the copse, but mealtimes faced him with a problem. The young Jack Barton, who had gone along to watch the men at work, often sat there like an expectant dog, hoping for titbits to be thrown

Locks Green School Group III and their teachers, 1900. Eva Mary Holbrook, daughter of the local carrier Edwin Holbrook, is third from the left in the second row.

Newtown's former Town Hall, which was rebuilt in 1699, pictured c.1904.

The former Town Hall, with the Noah's Ark beyond, 2003.

his way as the men tucked into their nammet (usually a whole cottage loaf with a knob of butter stored under its crown), and hypnotised by the chance that Ern should make a mistake and try to eat his pipe.

Town Gate Lane was on the route taken by the Island's last horse-drawn carrier van. In 1906, the carrier, Edwin Holbrook, passed that way with a special delivery for Ellen Woolgar, village shopkeeper and purveyor of gossip. A few days earlier she had heard a story she could not bring herself to believe. Vicar and surrogate of Newtown, the Revd Henry Rice Venn, a widower of long standing, had returned from his short holiday, complete with a new wife (Hannah Jessie Cameron Price)! Miss Woolgar could hardly wait for the weekly delivery of the *Isle of Wight County Press* in which she could check the story but, just to make doubly sure, she had ordered two copies.

Across Clamerkin Bridge, Newtown's neighbouring hamlet of Locks Green was home to the local smithy, the school, and the oldest farm in the district. Westmore's steam engine was brought to Locks Farm each year for the threshing but 'Painter' Holbrook, a man of slight build but huge enterprise, scoffed at this newfangled machine, and for a very profitable bet, to have his favourite ginger cake supplied in his nammet every time he worked at Locks Farm, carried a sack of grain weighing three-quarters of a hundredweight on his back from the rick yard to the top of the ladder at the grain bin.

For nearly 1,000 years the fabric of Newtown, that magical place, has been enriched by personalities like these, and this book is about their stories. Initially, they came from all over Southern England to occupy the 70 or so plots in this newly-constructed town. The Bishops of Winchester and the Kings and Queens of England smiled on the place, granting it privileges and establishing markets and fairs, and making it the Island's capital town. It survived invasions by the French and visitations by the Black Death. The first Elizabeth granted it the right to elect two Members of Parliament, thus attracting the attentions of the Worsley and Barrington families who squabbled for land in their quest for political influence. The Town Hall, witness to pomp and power, announced the town to visitors, and the Noah's Ark was mine host to gentry and labourer alike.

For many centuries Newtown folk had fished for oysters, made brine, reclaimed the salt marshes, or gone to sea. Their women kept cows and produced children, and some opened shops and ran schools. Time almost forgot the place. Things were slow to change.

But, as its harbour silted up, Newtown lost its maritime trade and its coastguard station and, in rapid succession, its main shop, its public house, then its school. Its salterns and its brickworks closed. Its farmers declined to embrace modern practices and a silence clung to the land.

Some 70 years ago the last lord of the manor, Sir John Simeon, began to dismantle his holdings and sold them to commoners, bit by bit. Even in the Newtown district the old order was changing and feudal paternalism was overtaken by democracy in the form of the Parish Council.

The area had become supine, a rural backwater lacking investment and enterprise, in some danger of forgetting its proud history.

But what, once, was deemed to be the curse of geographical isolation, cause of stagnation and decay, had, in reality, protected Newtown from the corrosive forces of modern agriculture, transport and urbanisation. Now, its unspoiled landscapes, its riches of flora and fauna, its space and its silence attract a new kind of pilgrim, intent on rediscovering what the men and women of Newtown have always known and enjoyed.

Adela Hole, resident housekeeper at Harts Farm, 1893.

Sir John Simeon (left) *with Maurice Rice, tenant at Elm Farm, c.1930.*

Calbourne Parish Council, c.1968. Left to right: *Doug Chandler, Charlie Smith, Henry Angell, Frank Pragnell, Peter Clark, Eddie Downer.*

Chapter 1

From Capital to Capitulation? Newtown's Changing Fortunes

Picture a medieval seaport with tall-masted ships dwarfing the quayside cottages. Picture the bustling quays with merchandise being unloaded and provisioning going on. See the sailors and longshoremen sweating over their tasks, and the idlers sunning themselves and watching. In the streets adjoining the quay would be business houses, bankers, gold and silver smiths and all the one hundred and one activities surrounding and servicing a seaport.

This evocative passage from Revd E.S. Hayden's 1973 booklet about Newtown is not altogether fanciful. It goes some way to capturing the sights and sounds of Newtown as it was 700 years ago, when it served as the principal town of the Island, bustling with prosperous citizens.

There is little doubt that when Edward I visited Swainston Manor in November 1285 and picked a quarrel with the resident Bishop of Winchester, he had set his sights on the acquisition of Newtown Harbour for the Crown. Amid continuing fears of invasion by France and Spain, Edward had recognised the strategic importance of a deep-water haven for his warships which was capable, according to some authorities, of accommodating 300 vessels at one time!

The main route to Newtown Quay in 1997.

Today, it is difficult to visualise anything on this scale being available on the sluggish shallows of Newtown River, and virtually nothing remains of the harbours, wharves and quays which would have been necessary to support such enterprise. Indeed, the only topographical evidence of this once-thriving medieval seaport and market town is the lingering pattern of thoroughfares bearing such names as Gold Street, Silver Street, Horse Fair, High Street, Quay Street, Market Place (The Green) and Draper's Alley.

The spur of higher land jutting into Newtown Haven between Causeway Creek and Clamerkin River is probably an ancient site of human settlement, and faint traces of ridge-and-furrow cultivation underlie the medieval street patterns, preserved in the modern settlement. Overlooking the sheltered haven, and somewhat drier than the nearby marshy lowland, it was a natural choice for the Bishops of Winchester who, as the abbots of the monastery of St Swithun's, were granted land hereabouts in the year AD735. The whole of the area formed part of the ecclesiastical manor of Calbourne when, in AD827, this was granted to the Bishops by King Egbert. Bearing in mind that Winchester was then the capital of England, successive bishops invested the Newtown area with considerable attention, as their development of the manor of Swainston and construction there of a summer palace confirms.

The south front of Swainston Manor, c.1915. Senior gardener Harry Abblitt is pictured on the right.

At this time, the settlement did not enjoy borough status but, according to Worsley's *History of England*, was already sufficiently prosperous to attract naval raids from pirates and military invaders, the most significant of these being the Dane, Sweyn (father of Canute, who later became the first Danish King of England), who destroyed the town in AD1001 and bequeathed his name to 'Sweyneston' Manor. Recovery seems to have been swift. Soon after the Norman Conquest, the Domesday Survey (AD1086) listed Sweyneston as the largest and richest manor on the Island but did not distinguish Newtown from the manor.

However, by the year 1189, in the reign of Richard I, Newtown had been granted mesne borough status and its citizens already enjoyed certain privileges which relieved them of some of their feudal obligations to the lords of the manor (the bishops). Newtown remained a small settlement within an agricultural manor until, from around AD1218, the bishops formulated plans to 'plant' a newly-constructed town on the site.

Over the next three decades the structure of present-day Newtown was determined, with its classic gridiron pattern of roadways (similar to the contemporary developments in Yarmouth and Newport), together with some 73 burgage plots of land which citizens (burghers) could rent for 1s. each per annum. This was a town fit for the thriving commercial activities of the Haven, and in AD1255 Aymer, Bishop-elect of Winchester, obtained from the Crown a grant for a market and fair at his manor of Swainston. The new settlement was a natural site for such events and in the following year Aymer granted full liberties and free customs to its burgesses (landholders), whilst referring to the town as 'Francheville' (Freetown).

During the next 300 years several monarchs confirmed these rights and privileges in a number of charters. In 1285, Edward I confirmed the charter and in 1318 Edward II confirmed a weekly market to be held on Wednesdays, together with an annual three-day fair (or Rendezvous) to be held in late July at the Feast of St Mary Magdalene. This charter contains the earliest known example of the use of the name 'La Neuton' (Newtown), and the choice of date for the fair seems to imply that the town had already acquired a chapel of ease, although the earliest known direct reference to a chapel is 1407. Further confirmations of the charter were made by Richard II (1393), Henry V (1413), Henry VI (1441) and Elizabeth I (1598). Clearly, Newtown was a place of some substance, already boasting thoroughfares such as Goldstrete (earliest known reference 1441), la Horsfayre (1497) and le Key (1512).

Strangely, the town was not listed among the boroughs of the Isle of Wight in a survey of 1295, yet it elected its own Court Leet, a local council-type body responsible for establishing by-laws, monitoring its citizens and seeing to the fabric of the town. Thus, the town's drains were maintained, its stray animals impounded, its disputes between neighbours settled, and its boundaries protected. The court was also responsible for checking the quality of local beer and bread, but the bishops reserved the right to condemn the baker to the pillory or the brewer to the tumbrel should standards slip! (From 1683 the mayor and burgesses undertook the duties of the Court Leet.)

Newtown's burgesses also sat on the Crown Leet (the manorial court) at Swainston but were not subject to its rulings. However, the town paid various rents to the manor, including, at Michaelmas and Easter, those for the 26 acres of land and the fishery owned by the burgesses as a body, in addition to the rent of assize, and an annual due of 40 eggs as compensation to the bishops for farm produce lost from the land upon which the town was built! Many of these tithes remained payable until the borough's dissolution in 1835.

By permitting citizens of Newtown freedom from feudal duties to the lord of the manor, the bishops attracted to the borough a rich variety of tradespeople from across Southern England, among them weavers, fullers, bakers and smiths of all kinds. The reeve's accounts for 1256 and 1297 show a very high rate of burgage-plot occupation. Newtown's prosperity derived largely from its trading position and from its harbour, and this association is reflected in the borough's Common Seal adopted in the thirteenth century, showing a ship with a leopard of England on the deck and the shield of St George over the rear castle.

In 1285, when the charismatic Edward I coveted the manor for the Crown, its harbour and the wealthy borough of Newtown were his main objectives. Fears of invasion were growing and the secure moorings at Newtown Haven could accept the largest warships afloat. (It is ironic that by 1307 the manor had been given away by the Crown, the first of three such events when monarchs sought to patronise their nobility, although in 1541 Henry VIII had the manor's owner beheaded in order to regain manorial title for the Crown. As a gift from Queen Mary late in the 1550s the manor passed by marriage into the Barrington family and remained with them for almost 300 years before, again as a result of marriage, passing into the hands of the Simeon family who were still resident when the manor was badly damaged by German bombing in 1941.)

By 1305 Newtown was sending shiploads of corn to Berwick to feed King Edward's troops as he warred with the Scots. The port flourished, attracting a host of tradesmen, merchants, smiths and craftspeople to the town. Already, the salt-making and oyster-cultivation industries were well established. By 1344 Newtown was the busiest and safest harbour on the Island, with tax assessed at twice the value of that at Newport. At least 60 families lived in the town, and the borough was probably well represented amongst the 13 ships and 222 seamen which the Island sent to help Edward III capture Calais in 1347. In 1377 almost 200 residents of Newtown were

Above: *Newtown's thirteenth-century Common Seal.*

subject to the poll tax, a measure of the borough's wealth and prestige. Only 22 others paid the tax in the rest of the parish of Calbourne.

Increasingly, however, the Island suffered attacks from the French. By 1334 warning beacons ringed the coastline, including one at Hamstead, and by 1340 each region had its own militia and 'hobblers' (horsemen who carried urgent messages). Fears of invasion were such that the Crown sought to forbid local lords from fleeing the Island.

Despite its prosperity, storm clouds were gathering over Newtown. Four successive disasters were soon to overtake the borough and almost obliterate it. Two were sudden and violent, and took their immediate toll. The others were much slower to develop but probably had a far more lasting influence on the town's future.

In 1348 bubonic plague, the 'Black Death', reached the Island and wiped out a third of the population. Victims of this contagious disease were normally dead within 48 hours, although tradition suggests that Newtown itself escaped the worst effects. (It is thought that Newtown's own Pied Piper tale might reflect the town's good fortune.) But Wight's population as a whole was decimated and when, some 20 years later, renewed fears of French invasion developed, manpower for the defence was in very short supply. Thomas Cheke, Lord of Mottistone Manor, was commanding officer for that area which contained Newtown, but his forces were overrun by the French invasion of 1377 which destroyed the towns of Yarmouth, Newport and Newtown.

Many authorities believe that this marked the end for Newtown as a thriving commercial community, but there is a good deal of evidence to the contrary. The town appears soon to have been rebuilt and its mayor and burgesses persuaded Richard II to confirm its charter as early as 1393; and the 1402 Court Rolls from Swainston confirm that they attended court as free tenants, paying quit rents instead of providing service. The borough survived the unsettled times of the 1400s, its charter confirming its independence from the manor and its chapel showing its independence from the Parish Church at Calbourne. The town's own silver parcel-gilt mace dates from around 1500. In 1541 the lord of the manor lost his head as well as his lands to Henry VIII who was in the process of strengthening the defences of the Solent with a number of forts, including structures at Yarmouth and Cowes. It was Henry's forces which, in 1545, successfully repelled the French, the last invaders ever to set foot on the Island.

Newtown was still thriving but, already, there were signs that the borough would face commercial difficulties. In 1547 the burgesses had relinquished claim to a significant part of the borough lands which became glebe to the Rector of Calbourne in return for his maintenance of a priest who was to live in a cottage next to the chapel in the borough and provide spiritual leadership. A survey in 1559 reported Newtown as having 'streets both of articifers and other cleyn dekeyed... Ther is now nother market nor almost no good howse standing.'

Newtown in 1904, probably looking very similar to how it was in 1750. The Noah's Ark can be seen on the left with the Town Hall in the distance.

Despite this, in 1585 Elizabeth I granted Newtown (and Yarmouth and Newport) parliamentary borough status and the right to elect two Members of Parliament. In 1598 she also re-affirmed Newtown's charter.

But these were hollow victories for the borough. Newtown was poised on the cusp of two distinct phases of its history. Its former commercial prosperity was now in decline, propped artificially by renewed charters and the like. In prospect was its notoriety as a political pawn, a period lasting some 300 years and characterised by inflated property values, absentee landlords and commercial neglect.

As early as 1528 the Worsley family held lands in the borough and, not many years later, the Barringtons married into Swainston Manor. Thereafter, much of the energy of the borough was spent on a continuing political rivalry between these two dynasties and their respective supporters among the burgesses of Newtown. In 1614, a Barrington was elected as the Member of Parliament to serve Newtown for the first time, and from that date an unseemly scramble for landholdings unfolded. Land ownership conferred the franchise, although serious disputes developed over this process which led at one point to the dismissal of the mayor, at another to elections being declared void and, ultimately, to the intervention of Parliament in 1729 to rule upon who had the right to vote.

Well-known families were involved, some still represented in the district including those by the names of Barton, Byde, Meux (Mew), Cheke, Urry, Holbrook, Holmes, Dore and Harvey, in addition to the Worsleys and Barringtons. Property inflation reached the point of absurdity when, in 1772, Sir Richard Worsley paid £3,503 for Marsh Farm and some saltings, and a further £950 for a single tenement in the borough. If this were not corruption enough, a few years later the two families agreed to put forward one candidate each as MP, and to take it in turns annually to nominate the mayor of the borough!

It was probably this concern over land tenure that prompted the production of James Mallett's detailed map of the borough in 1768.

Unfortunately for the borough, this heightened interest and activity rarely led to financial investment in the town, which suffered neglect for some three centuries. Its citizens had survived visitations of the plague and invasions by the French. They had enjoyed royal patronage in their efforts to recover, and some dignitaries had even rebuilt the Town Hall around 1700, although the contributions (from James Worsley, Thomas Hopson, Robert Worsley and John Dillington who each gave £20, from John Leigh and J. Tristram Dillington, £10 each, and also £5 apiece from William Stephens, W.M. Bowerman and Major Holms) were probably designed to reflect the donor's own pomp and circumstance rather than to benefit the town.

The burgesses had been politically astute enough during Cromwell's Commonwealth to have doctored the town mace with a reversible plate ensuring that, as appropriate, either the State Arms or the Royal Arms would be on 'loyal' display. As late as 1781 the harbour could still accommodate 'ships of 500 tons burthen', and the annual fair still took place. This Rendezvous (later corrupted to 'Randy') was still being publicly advertised in the 1850s and J. Redding Ware, writing in 1869, could still report that 'the Haven is the best in the island.'

But the borough had already been in decline for many years and this was reflected in the sorry state of the buildings. By 1636 only 12 houses were occupied and the chapel was dilapidated. The Visitation Books record that by 1663 the chapel was falling down and that no services were held there, and the 1674 Hearth Tax returns listed only 25 hearths in 11 dwellings in Newtown, the occupants of six of which were relieved of the tax due to extreme poverty.

Contemporary surveyors blamed the decline variously on the loss of the wool staple (which had been moved from Winchester to Calais), the enclosure of common lands and the suppression of smallholders. If this were the case, why had Newtown's decline persisted whilst Newport and Yarmouth had each recovered and flourished?

It is highly likely that the Newtown River estuary became victim, over several centuries, to the slow process of silting. Modern hydrographic research reveals that most of the sand and shingle spits which form barriers across the estuaries of Southern England are of relatively recent origin, say 600 years. By severely reducing the ebb and flow of tides through the estuary mouth, they have encouraged the development of mud-flats and salt marsh. As early as 1540 there was a parliamentary Grant of Sewers to drain the marshes at Newtown (although there is no evidence that action was taken), but the reclamation of these marshes was planned as early as 1656 and begun around 1715, soon after the Barringtons took up residence at Swainston. Newtown's maritime commerce was being slowly strangulated, and with it the prosperity of the town. (It is ironic that the storm surges of 1953 and 1954 should have returned Newtown Marsh to the sea and encouraged more tidal scouring of the estuary than it had experienced for some 200 years or more. Many of the saltings, still remembered by some from the early 1900s, have now disappeared.)

As the channel depths decreased, galleons, barques, brigantines and schooners were replaced by barges, luggers, sloops, smacks and cutters which drew less water, and the nature and scale of Newtown's commercial activity gradually changed. Even so, various kinds of trading vessel were able to work the estuary throughout the nineteenth century, some reaching Shalfleet Mill to unload grain whilst others brought coal and stone to Hamstead and Elmsworth and took away salt and bricks. Not until the 1880s did the estuary lose its last trading vessel, although in the later years it is likely that cargoes were transferred at sea into lighters and smaller barges before being brought ashore.

Mallett's map of 1768 shows only a dozen plots containing buildings, 42 plots were vacant, and only vestiges of common fields remained, most having already been enclosed. Yet George Canning, future Prime Minister, was elected MP for Newtown in 1806 and in 1813 patrons of the borough spent £448 restoring the Town Hall. By the 1820s two successful brickworks had been established on the banks of the Haven, the oyster fishery flourished, and there were at least seven working salterns around the estuary. One could almost anticipate revival for the town.

But in 1832 the Reform Act deemed Newtown to be a 'rotten borough'. Three years later a government commission reported that only 39 burgage plots remained, that no burgesses were resident in the borough and that none of the 68 inhabitants, who occupied 14 poorly maintained cottages, possessed sufficient intelligence to hold municipal office. In 1836 Newtown lost its borough status, its mayor, and its right to elect two MPs. Its chapel had fallen down many years previously. Suddenly, there was much less reason to own land in the borough.

Once again Newtown was incorporated into the manor of Swainston, and the corporate property was purchased by the lord of the manor, Sir Richard Godin Simeon, who had inherited the manor through his wife, the daughter of the last Barrington, although it was not until the commission of 1876 that the former borough was deemed to be extinct.

Without delay, Sir Richard invested the corporate assets into the rebuilding of Newtown Church (1837)

Left: *Newtown's former seat of government as it appeared in the 1930s. The furniture was damaged by enemy bombs during the 1940s whilst in storage in the chapel at Swainston. It was restored by E.W. King of Newport and is used at the IOW Council Chambers at the time of writing.* (COPYRIGHT NIGH, SHANKLIN, IW)

View at Newtown in 1799 in an aquatint of a contemporary painting by Francis Jukes.

(REPRODUCED COURTESY OF ROBIN MCINNES)

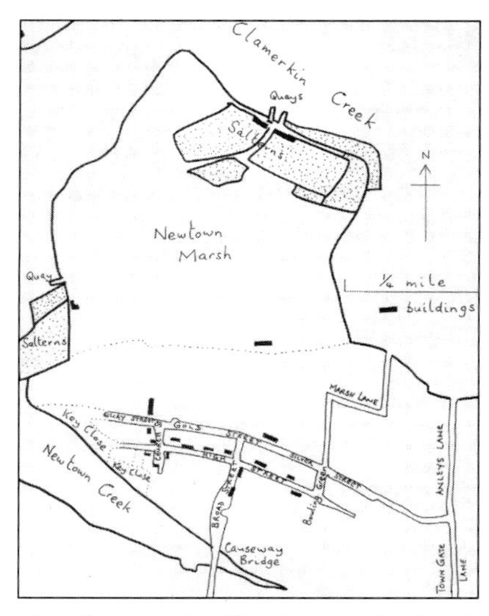

Based upon Mallett's map (below) *of Newtown from 1768.*

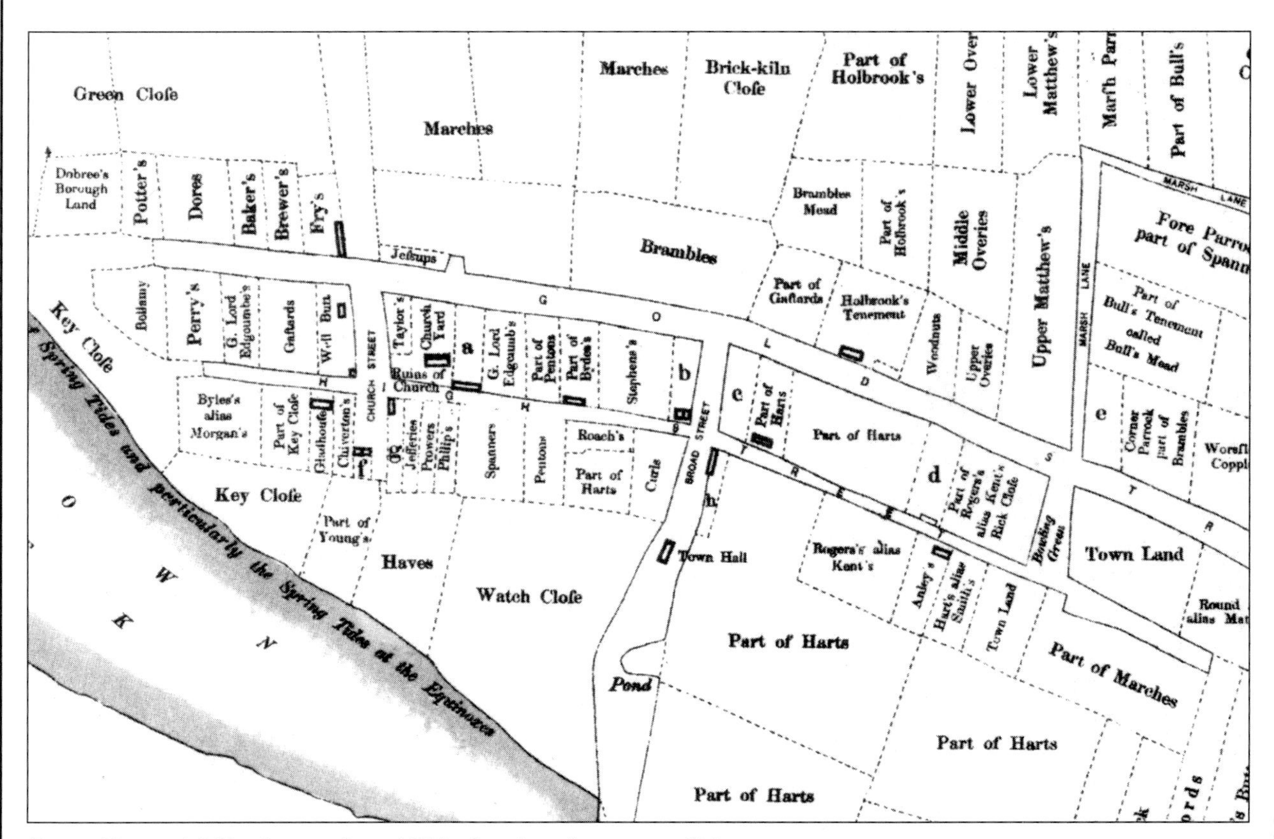

Part of James Mallett's map from 1768, showing the centre of Newtown.

(REPRODUCED COURTESY OF THE NATIONAL TRUST)

Left: *The ivy-clad Town Hall in around 1905.*

Below: *The Newtown Arms in around 1920, soon after its licence had been surrendered.*
(Reproduced courtesy of the County Record Office, Newport)

Right: *Looking east down the main medieval thoroughfare of Gold Street in 1997.*

in an effort to revive the town's fortunes. His son, Sir John Barrington Simeon, was forward-looking and politically active. Standing in the 1868 parliamentary elections as a Liberal, when the adoption of an open-voting system led to rioting and mob rule in both Newport and Cowes, he kept the interests of the manor and Newtown in the public eye. Under his influence, the Church of England opened a new school at Locks Green in 1867, and six years later built a new vicarage in Town Gate Lane. Newtown had its own resident vicar and surrogate for the first time, following its designation in 1871 (with Porchfield) as an ecclesiastical parish. In 1880, the Newtown and Beaulieu Oyster Fishery Company was formed. Yet, once again, the fortunes of the town flattered to deceive.

By 1891, the last vestiges of the town's maritime past were almost gone, the last saltern had closed, one brickworks was gone and the other was living on borrowed time. Newtown's commercial activity was in terminal decline. Almost 25 per cent of its population of 127 was aged over 50, and only a prodigious output of children by the resident coastguards and a couple of indigenous families kept the age profile in reasonable balance.

Only the faintest commercial echoes of Newtown's maritime importance remained. Had the seven coastguard officers not been stationed there, only James 'Jumbo' Woolgar, a naval pensioner, and Henry Jacobs, the last riverman, would have maintained the link, although Jonas Foss and his son Henry did still earn their summer income from shell-fishing. Even the oyster fishery was managed by a man who lived at Cowes.

As the Victorian era drew towards a close Newtown had turned its face inland. With five farms and three dairies located within or near the town, 23 out of a working population of 58 earned their living directly from the land, to which might be added a woodman, a gardener and three farm housekeepers. Apart from the farmers, the only resident business people were the shopkeeper (James Woolgar) and the innkeeper (Maria Prangnell). Nine others worked in domestic service. Newtown had become a quiet place, with limited aspirations and more than a whiff of decay.

In sharp contrast, the neighbouring village of Porchfield (with Locks Green) could boast that, in addition to farmers and dairymen, a third of its working population was in skilled trades, including blacksmithing, carpentry, building, masonry, game-keeping, shopkeeping, innkeeping, dressmaking, baking, shoemaking, brick making and bricklaying. In addition, there was a carrier, a firewood dealer and a fowler, and six women took in washing.

Porchfield enjoyed a significant degree of self-sufficiency with its own inn, two chapels, and a Post Office-cum-shop, and was closer than Newtown to the school at Locks Green. Newtown was beginning to slumber; already it was showing signs of becoming a retreat for more affluent people living off their own means and seeking tranquility and social stability.

Few of the town's original thoroughfares proved suitable for motor cars and many remain today as leafy green lanes. The town's two medieval gateways, Causeway (Cassey) Bridge, rebuilt in the 1730s, and Town Gate, now a barely discernable mound at the roadside near the former vicarage, stand guard on a quiet corner of the Island.

Throughout the twentieth century little happened by way of commercial activity in Newtown. Oyster-fishing continued to wax and wane, salt making had ceased by the 1880s, the last brickworks was abandoned in 1914, small dairies closed, and by 1920 the inn and the shop had each shut; the fabric of the church and its vicarage was close to collapse.

Even the larger farms became less actively agricultural, eventually turning more towards provision for tourism and equestrian sports. Very little residential development took place, the most significant, though perhaps not the most controversial, being the row of bungalows on the outskirts of the village, built by 'Putty' Vincent in Old Vicarage Lane during the 1930s and 1940s.

But in the face of commercial decay there was growing awareness, on the part of local residents and others, that Newtown and its district possessed qualities that were becoming increasingly rare. Large, remote, rich in flora and fauna, steeped in history yet thinly peopled, the area became increasingly attractive to a wide variety of interest groups, not all of them compatible.

Occasionally there were attempts to exploit the area for commercial or strategic gain. As early as 1931 the lord of the manor, Sir John Simeon, sought to obtain planning permission for a major residential building programme on the banks of the river. Another developer was thwarted in 1969. The rifle-range at Locks Hard dates from around 1911, but military activity was expanded considerably during the 1940s as a dummy airfield was constructed on Newtown Marsh and the Haven was used to practise for the D-Day landings. And serious plans were advanced during the 1950s to site a nuclear power station at Hamstead, overlooking the Haven. In 2004 residents nervously await the outcome of oil-drilling exploration near Porchfield.

The sale, generally in small lots, of the Hamstead Manor estate (1926) and much of the Swainston Manor estate (1932 and 1947) provided a greater security to those former tenants who could afford to buy, but it also brought an influx of more affluent people keen to enjoy and preserve Newtown's special qualities. Sometimes with the active support of these incomers, preservation and conservation groups such as the British Trust for Conservation Volunteers, the Nature Conservancy Council, the Isle of Wight County Council Countryside Project and the National Trust became increasingly involved.

The results of voluntary and official efforts are widespread. As early as 1933 the anonymous 'Ferguson Gang' had repaired and refurbished the Town Hall, which had become sadly neglected, and presented it to the National Trust. From its inception in 1964, the Newtown Trust raised funds by public subscription to purchase parts of old Newtown including, in 1965, the Haven itself. That same year the land at Hamstead, previously targeted for a nuclear power station, was gifted to the National Trust. The Newtown Trust has been superceded by the National Trust which owns several ancient plots, together with properties including the Town Hall and the former inn, several copses and an area of pasturage, and is keen to increase its holdings at every opportunity. Wildlife sanctuaries have been established on the marsl lands and spits, and some areas have become designated Sites of Special Scientific Interest (SSSIs). Bird hides have been built, staffed by enthusiastic volunteers. In the 1960s the predecessor of the Isle of Wight Council established a nature reserve and converted a former farm building into a visitor centre. Part of the Haven is now a National Nature Reserve, managed by the National Trust in partnership with English Nature. Ancient roadways, boundaries and woodlands are now managed by the National Trust, whilst this and other bodies have appointed wardens, berthing masters and conservation officers; among the first was Alec Mellor, National Trust warden from 1972.

In modern times a coastal audit has been made by the Island's Archaeological Unit funded by English Heritage, and the Monumental Protection Programme has surveyed the medieval remains in the village. It is all in sharp contrast to the views of 'Jumbo' Woolgar in 1889 when he described 'the dreary swamps of Newtown... now the solitary hunting-grounds of keen winds and hungry seabirds.'

Visitor numbers to the Newtown estuary and its environs have increased sharply on both land and water, threatening the very qualities the people seek. Yachtsmen, walkers, bird-watchers, picnickers, students – all compete for space – and storm and tide continue to threaten and invade. The authorities charged with the conservation of the area have to make difficult decisions in order to improve facilities for public access yet exert controls over that access, and to preserve the existing qualities of the area without stifling its development.

Not since the thirteenth century has demand for a part of Newtown been so great.

Left: *The white admiral butterfly is characteristic of Town Copse and Walter's Copse.* (BARRY ANGELL)

Below: *Newtown in 1908. (Part of the Ordnance Survey's 25 inches: 1 mile map used during the sale in 1946 of parts of the Swainston estate.)*
(REPRODUCED WITH THE KIND PERMISSION OF THE ORDNANCE SURVEY)

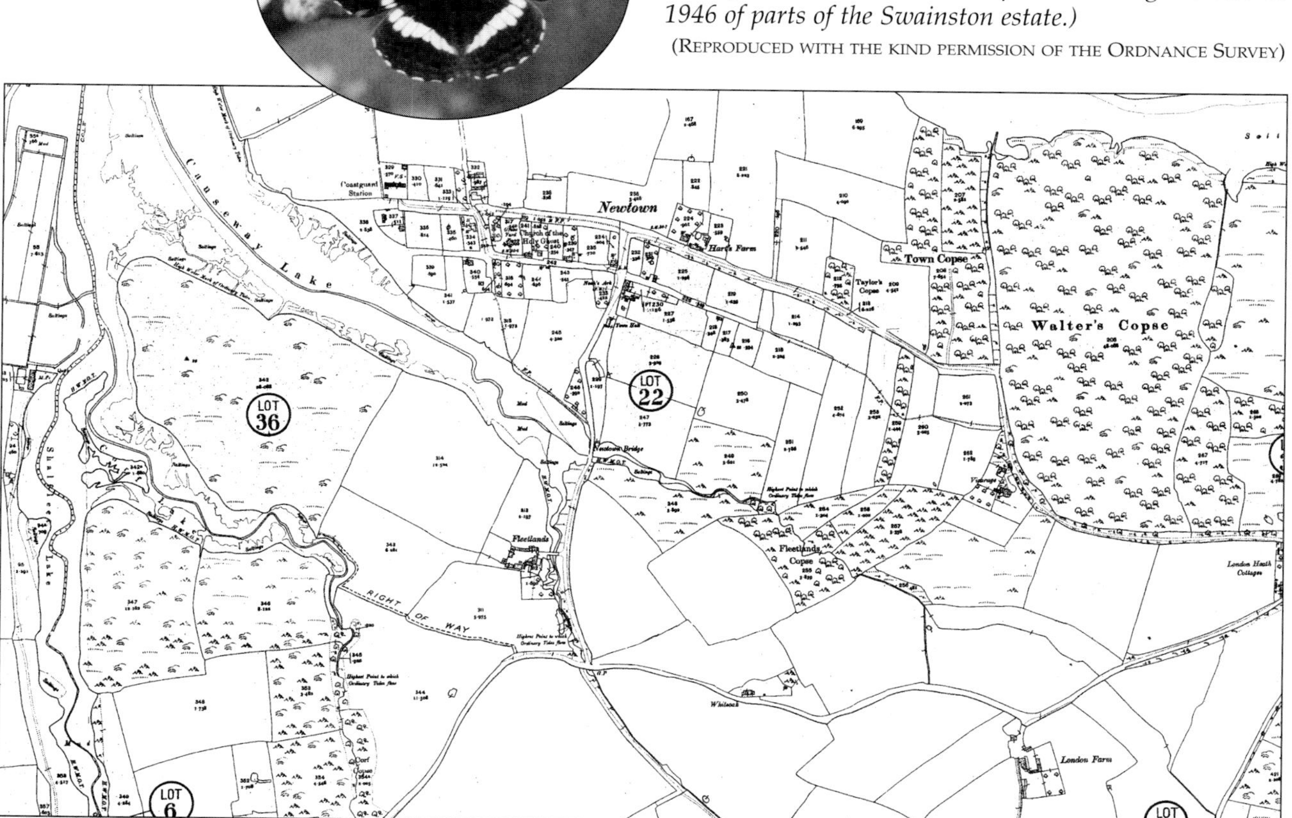

Chapter 2

Just Beyond Memory: Newtown in the Late 1800s

Partly due to its geographical location, and partly thanks to historical accident, Newtown has not been swept along by the tide of change. The pattern of its roadways and green lanes has remained largely the same since the thirteenth century. Land divisions and boundaries still reflect past feudal practices; oysters and grass have remained the staple crops.

The settlement still looks much as it did on the manorial plan of 1636, on Mallett's 1768 map, and on the 1840 Calbourne Tithe Map. Few boundaries have changed. Most new buildings have merely replaced those which have decayed and collapsed. On the 1840 Tithe Map medieval tenement plots and the furlong strips of the feudal farming system contrast sharply with larger fields on the reclaimed marshlands and the few remaining remnants of the open fields as they were before enclosure.

Until the break-up and sale of Swainston's manorial estates, which began in 1932, lifestyles in Newtown had remained entrenched in an earlier century. The main breadwinner in most local families worked for the paternalistic lord of the manor. Virtually all families paid him a rent of one kind or another, even those who had worked to develop their own businesses, like the Prangnells, the Paskinses and the Holbrooks. Only the mariners (and those who chose to emigrate) were relatively free from the embrace of the estate.

Until the end of the nineteenth century there remained a gulf between, on the one hand, the gentry – Sir John Simeon (lord of the manor), the Revd Henry Rice Venn (vicar and surrogate) and, perhaps, John Sweet (farmer at Marsh Farm and Harts Farm) – and on the other hand the farm labourers, estate workers, homeworkers and coastguards who made up the majority of the population. Somewhere in between were those who, despite their higher earnings – men such as James Holbrook the ship owner, Luke Barton the head gamekeeper, and Thomas Paskins the manager of the fishery – would never enjoy membership of the gentry.

The Woolgar family was one of four who had been resident in Newtown since the 1830s, and around 1893 James 'Jumbo' Woolgar, a retired coastguard and mariner who had returned to Newtown to help his elderly mother run the shop, traced the history of the buildings that made up the village. His record, and other contemporary sources, help to build the following picture of Newtown's buildings at that time.

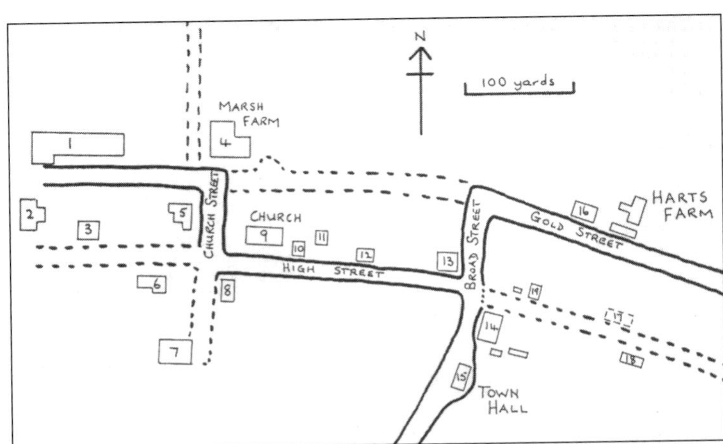

Above: *Newtown's buildings towards the end of the nineteenth century. The numbers on the map correspond with the descriptions of properties on the following pages.*

Left: *Taken from the Calbourne Tithe Map, 1840.*

1. **Coastguard Station:** *A row of five stone-built cottages erected around 1840. The western cottage, with its own toilet and wash-house, was reserved for the coastguard officer, though in 1891 James McGregor had a wife and eight children to squeeze in, so they also occupied the cottage next door. Normally, four other families lived in the adjacent two pairs of cottages. Each pair shared an entrance, and was separated by a passage which contained communal cupboards. Each cottage had two bedrooms and a living-room, with a toilet and coal shed at the end of the garden, but there was a communal wash-house. 'If you stoked up Monday, I had to do it Tuesday', said one elderly resident. Prior to this, the coastguards lived on a wooden hulk berthed in the river. In addition to the purpose-built cottages, several other village properties were leased to the Admiralty to accommodate coastguards until around 1920, notably Rose, Myrtle and Anchor Cottages. In 1901, out of a total population in the village of 105, 21 people belonged to coastguard families.*

Billy Mustchin with his grandmother in the garden of the coastguard cottages where they lived in 1924.

2. **Lamb Cottage:** *This imposing eight-roomed house was built in 1847 for Captain James Holbrook, master mariner, who owned the last trading vessel to work out of Newtown. His relatives, some of whom ran the local salterns, occupied the house for many years. James was a bachelor and rented out many of the rooms, mainly to other mariners, even whilst he was in residence. He died in 1884 and the lease passed initially to his relatives who rented it to the Seagar family for over 15 years. A later owner, Dr Howard Hawkins, bequeathed the property to the Church in 1919 and it became The New Vicarage until the late 1930s.*

3. **Anchor Cottage:** *This brick-and-tile cottage was built for Captain James Holbrook around 1864 on land which he had leased for 99 years. Thomas Holbrook, another mariner and nephew of James, lived there during the 1870s before taking up residence on his boat, which was moored in the Haven. A fisherman, Henry Jacobs, and his family were resident during the 1880s before it was rented to the Admiralty and occupied by coastguards until the early 1900s.*

4. **Marsh Farmhouse**: *The farmhouse was built in around 1850 using stone brought from Street Lane quarries near Newbridge by horse and cart. It incorporates parts of a much earlier farmhouse, including a large oven and a nearby well. The barn and stable are considerably older than the farmhouse. Built of small, distinctive red bricks and roofed with slates, some of the barn's architectural features suggest a Flemish influence, possibly from the eighteenth century. The Earl of Yarborough sold the farm in 1847 when Robert Harvey, one of a long family line of Newtown farmers, was tenant. Later, it was farmed by Robert Lock, then by widower John Sweet who held the lease until his death in 1915, although he resided at Harts Farm. From around 1888 rooms at Marsh Farm were rented to a variety of people including Locks Green schoolmistress Kate Ridett and, later, to the village nurse.*

5. **Rose Cottage and Myrtle Cottage:** *This is a double tenement built over a long period by the Prangnell family of brick makers from Elmsworth. It is possible that the building stands on the site of a 'messuage' built in 1747 by local salt boiler, John Munt. Rose Cottage is the older of the two tenements, probably dating from around 1860, and it incorporates some remnants of a very much older, stone-built dairy owned by Lord Heytesbury, and is fronted by a limestone wall dating from the same period. Myrtle Cottage was built by the Prangnells, almost as a hobby, over many years between 1870 and 1885, and incorporates some of their fine, decorative yellow bricks from the Lower Elmsworth brickyard. Sir John Simeon purchased both cottages from Maria Prangnell, then licensee of Noah's Ark, and leased them to the Admiralty for the use of coastguards. By 1891 the two resident coastguard families consisted of four adults and ten children. At this time there was a pond on the green opposite the cottages, possibly on the site of the Horse Fair mentioned in fifteenth- and sixteenth-century town records.*

6. **Key Close Farm**: *This was one of several 'dairies' in Newtown, for many years occupied by the Holbrooks. From at least 1840 Richard Holbrook, a salt boiler, and*

his wife Ann, who ran the dairy, lived there, survived by their unmarried children Hannah, Reuben and Richard who continued the salt-making business and the dairy. It is a brick-built cottage and occupies the plot known as Gladhouse which, in 1768, contained a building. Widow Elizabeth Stark tended a few cows there during the 1890s, assisted by the son of a neighbour, Herbert Wheeler, who, in turn, became her lodger and husband. The locals then called the place 'Wheeler's'.

7. **Ruins of a double tenement**: *This was demolished during the 1880s, leaving only the east wall standing in 1889. During demolition a medallion dating from 1740 was found. At least partly constructed of stone, it was probably the building used in the eighteenth century as the Parish House. It faced onto The Green, sometimes called the Market Place, on which the village pound, still there in 1696, was sited to pen stray animals.*

8. **Woolgar's Cottage**: *This is possibly one of the oldest properties in the village. The plot contained a building in 1768. It was occupied for many years from the 1830s by Hannah Woolgar (née Holbrook). She founded the town's first school in the Town Hall, was the much-respected church sexton for many years, and ran the village shop. She died in 1884 after which her children James and Ellen ran the shop. James died in 1899 and Ellen, who died in 1918, was still running the shop in 1915. Clem Seagar bought it in 1932 when it still had only one ground-floor room containing a water tap and bucket.*

9. **Church of the Holy Spirit**: *This was constructed in 1837 on the site of an earlier chapel of ease which had lain in ruins for nearly 150 years. It incorporated the south porch of the earlier chapel, together with its font. Following the designation of Newtown as an ecclesiastical parish in 1871 it became the Parish Church. By 1888, the east window contained some fine stained glass, including a section depicting the borough seal. Heated ineffectively by an unsightly coke stove until 1889, then for a year by oil-lamps, parishioners complained until new oil stoves were installed in around 1892 by Upton's ironmongers from Newport. By 1920, the church had been partly destroyed by ivy, and the architect and antiquarian Percy Stone FSA declared it a 'dilapidated wreck' and unsafe for services. Public subscription raised around £1,000 and it took builder James Hall from Calbourne almost two years to effect repairs. Handsome gifts were made to the church upon its restoration, including oak and wrought-iron altar*

Woolgar's Cottage, the village shop, in 1888. Left to right: *Ernest Seagar, James Woolgar, Ellen Woolgar, John Sweet, Thomas Abrook.*

rails (from Mrs Gibson), a brass jewelled altar cross (given by the Gibson sisters), and an altar frontal (donated by Lady Laura Simeon). Sadly, the renovated church no longer contained the stained-glass east window.

Newtown Church interior in 1888.

10. **Church Cottage:** *Almost abutting the road, this stone cottage had been occupied in the 1860s by a cattle dealer, then by a succession of labourers' families. During the 1890s John Wheeler ran a small dairy there, then the Brett family lived there – the two daughters became the village dressmaker and schoolmistress respectively. The cottage fell into disrepair and was demolished during the 1920s. A tenement had stood on this plot for many years. It was probably the site described in sixteenth-century documents as being 'next to the chapple', on which stood the cottage in which the clerical reader lived, who was appointed by the Rector of Calbourne, and Mallett's map of 1768 also shows a tenement on the site. (A more recently built property occupies part of the plot at the time of writing.)*

11. **The Cottage (formerly Oyster Cottage)**: *This substantial brick-built cottage was erected in around 1865 for Thomas Abrook, the foreman of the oyster fishery. His father, Henry, also an oyster fisherman and mariner, had lived in an older building on this site since at least 1840. When Thomas Abrook retired during the 1880s he moved next door. Two of his daughters married local coastguards, and his son Harry became a woodman in Walter's Copse. Thomas Paskins took over the oyster fishery but preferred to live at Cowes, so Oyster Cottage was sublet, initially to Charles Olden, a domestic miller. In some documents from the 1890s Thomas Paskins was referred to as a riverman, one of Newtown's last. His son Henry Paskins took over the oyster fishery when Thomas retired.*

Newtown Church in around 1924, with the end of Church Cottage just visible on the right.

12. **Nobby's Cottage:** *This is another of Newtown's older properties, built of stone with a slate roof. It might even be the tenement shown on the 1768 map. It was reported that a large oven was discovered during refurbishment of the property, together with Australian coral set into a wall, each in its own way a reflection of Newtown's history. Thomas Abrook, who had been foreman of the oyster fishery, had retired in the 1880s and carried out dairy work here. Earlier, the cottage had been let for many years to local fisherman Thomas Henry Foss, whose widow remained the occupier until around 1880.*

13. **Hollis Cottage:** *Henry Jacobs, Newtown's last full-time riverman, rented this cottage until just before he died in 1893. His father, also called Henry, was taken ill and drowned in the pond behind the house in 1880, and his mother Mary died there in 1890, having had many visits from Sir Barrington and Lady Simeon during a long illness. Henry's grandmother, Fanny Jacobs, who was a dairywoman, had moved to Newtown from Whitwell probably during the 1830s, and had occupied Hollis Cottage for some 30 years before John Arnold, a blacksmith, moved in with his family. John then took over the dairy business at the Noah's Ark before handing it on to his son James, who also became the resident publican. The younger Henry Jacobs, a fisherman like his father, had rented Anchor Cottage for many years before moving the family back into Hollis Cottage. By the early 1880s the cottage had become badly overgrown by ivy, but was restored and renovated by the Swainston estate by 1886. In the 1890s Mr Buckler, the baker from Shalfleet, left Newtown's daily supply of bread at Hollis Cottage for individuals to collect, including that given as poor relief. A public postbox was set into the wall from an early date, and in the early-twentieth century a small shelter*

Newtown High Street, c.1888. Hollis Cottage is on the right with Nobby's Cottage in the distance.

stood alongside where the postman waited between morning delivery and afternoon collection.

14. The Newtown Arms: *The village public house was known locally as Noah's Ark for most of the nineteenth century, although the census enumerator described it as the 'Borough Arms' in 1901, and some early documents refer to it as the 'Franchville Arms'. The Venable Guide of 1860 reported that it offered 'humble accommodation'. It is believed that Newtown's 'Town House' existed on this site from 1589. Whilst Thomas Bull was resident, the 1630 survey described the property as 'a dwelling house containing a capped hall with chimney, and two other little rooms, with a loft over the hall', all of which is characteristic of a medieval smallholder's property. The building on the site at the time of writing almost certainly dates from 1727, which is around the same time that the Taylor family and descendants obtained the licence, and makes it the oldest dwelling in the village. From 1852 the licensee was James Taylor, before Henry Prangnell, the brick maker, took over from 1879. In 1896 Henry's widow Maria handed over to her daughter, Sarah Arnold, and her husband James, who were to be the last licence-holders. Sarah survived her husband and remained as licensee until the pub stopped trading as an inn in 1916. She was a direct descendant of the Taylor family who had, therefore, held the licence for some 200 years.*

Part of the building had been used as a dairy for many years, a counterpart lease dated 1873 referring to the 'inn, cottage, stable, outbuildings, land and premises'. At that time William Baron Mew, the Newport brewer, was paying £20 per annum for the lease.

Sarah Arnold died in 1922, but her daughter Mary, who had married James Kingswell from Fleetlands Farm, continued to occupy Noah's Ark for many years, running the dairy-farming activity. From the 1930s, the building was rented to tenants, among them Fran Jupe and Ruby Seagar who sold sundry items from the premises, including cigarettes. The National Trust acquired the building in 1961.

Hollis Cottage in 1904, looking east along the green extension of High Street.

15. The Town Hall: *This building was erected between 1677–99 on the foundations of an earlier town hall. There appears to be a stone undercroft, and some half-timbered walls have been found in the basement, suggesting an Elizabethan origin. In 1933 a seventeenth-century barrel oven was discovered during the refurbishment of the building. Scene of the medieval Court Leet and, later, the parliamentary hustings, the Town Hall witnessed much of Newtown's history. In 1811 Albin's guide noted: '... parties carrying their provisions and liquors may be accommodated at the Town Hall.' The building was restored by the burgesses in 1813 at a cost of £448, but lost its municipal role after 1835 when, after a short time as a dwelling-house, it was used as a pay-school until the 1850s. It then became residential again and two of the lodgers married – Emily Jolliffe (who had been there since 1851) and Richard Godden, whose surname had been linked with Newtown since the fifteenth century. He became a widower and was still resident in the Town Hall at the turn of the century, cared for by a new housekeeper, Mary Skeats, whose own timber cottage had collapsed some years earlier. Used briefly as a youth hostel, by 1930 the building had fallen into severe disrepair when a group of anonymous benefactors, the 'Ferguson Gang', paid £5 for it. Among others, Bill Stickers and Shot Biddy restored it and gifted it to the National Trust in 1933.*

16. Harts Farmhouse: *Harts Farm has existed at least since 1633, farmed from 1651 until the early 1880s by the Harvey family. Mallett's 1768 map shows extensive holdings close to the village, and in 1795 the farmer, William Harvey, was the only burgess resident in the village. A new farmhouse was built here during the 1880s by John Sweet, a widower, who became the tenant farmer, employing a resident housekeeper, Adela Hole, and a resident farm labourer, Herbert Foster. The roadside barn is much older than the farmhouse, as is another smaller residential building to the north of the farmhouse which was part of much earlier accommodation, probably for farm labourers. When*

John Sweet died in 1915 Charles Barton became tenant, followed by his sons Geoff and Ted Barton. The local ploughman, Dickie Fallick, always slept in the smaller building whilst employed at Harts Farm by the Barton brothers. (Stephens Cottage in the High Street was built in 1948 as farm-worker accommodation for Harts Farm. Its neighbouring cottage, Byde Cottage, was built at the same time for farm labourers at London Farm.)

The cows arrive for milking at Harts Farm, Newtown, in 1890.

17. The converted barn: *This former barn, which belonged to Harts Farm, was sited along what local residents called Dirty Lane. It had been converted into a double tenement some time before the new Harts Farmhouse was built in the 1880s. At one time James Woolgar had occupied the eastern end. By the 1890s it had collapsed and been abandoned, but spring bulbs still mark the site of the gardens each year. It became the sixth tenement to collapse in the village since the 1860s.*

18. The wooden cottage: *This was Newtown's last wooden cottage, occupied until its collapse in the mid-1880s by Jenny Skeats with her daughter Mary, who supplemented her pauper's income by taking in the village laundry.*

Looking east along the extension of High Street, c.1904. The wood-and-thatch former cottage belonged to Harts Farm but had been unoccupied since 1890.

19. An unoccupied cottage: *By 1893 this was very dilapidated and collapsed in the early years of the twentieth century.*

Newtown remained the centre for several surrounding farms and cottages despite its shortage of facilities. Henry Rice Venn, Newtown's longest-serving vicar and surrogate, occupied the vicarage along Town Gate Lane, tended by his resident housekeeper, Jane Coleman, and ministering to his flock on a sturdy tricycle. Four cottages at London Heath, constructed around 1863, housed estate workers John Ford (woodcutter), Jonas and Henry Foss (fishermen and general labourers who worked on the banks of the Marsh each winter), George Olden (hurdle-maker) and Charles Hunt (coachman to the Simeons at the manor). Across the fields at St Hubert's Lodge lived the head gamekeeper, Luke Barton, whilst the modest cottages at Whiteoak, part of Fleetlands Farm, housed farm labourers John Hayward (and his 11 children!) and Isaac Merwood.

In addition to the two farms inside the village, three more looked towards Newtown. At the head of Causeway Creek was Fleetlands Farm, occupied for many years by the Kingswell family whose memorials now stand guard in a serried row in the local churchyard. Along another branch of the estuary was Clamerkin Farm where the Sanders family had been long-term tenants, and between the two was London Farm, which housed a frequent turnover of tenants until Enos Whatley moved in during the 1890s.

Perhaps the most unlikely villagers were the Prangnells at Lower Elmsworth brickyard. Rather than face the two-mile trek on foot to Porchfield they counted Newtown as their own, commuting by boat from their isolated home.

Thus, as the twentieth century dawned, Newtown remained a sleepy place, the daily rhythms much the same as they had always been. The social order of things was a recognised and accepted part of life, and dependency on the paternalism of the lord of the manor was endemic. Church or chapel on Sunday, the carriers' vans on Tuesday, Wednesday and Friday, the working day from dawn until dusk, choir practice on Thursday, and the occasional lantern slide show on Saturday, the wait for a doctor who might visit on horseback the next day, the sound of the guns after 3 September, the soda-charged chilblains from laundry on Mondays, and the pram-push to Cowes to sell mushroom ketchup. This was a different world, yet one which is only just beyond living memory.

Above: *The Kingswell memorial stones in Newtown churchyard, 2003.*

Chapter 3

'Hallelujah! Praise the Lord!': Church, Chapel & Ceremony

Aaron Fallick's voice could be heard rising above the general rejoicing and tumult in the crowded little Bible Christian Chapel at Porchfield in 1870... 'Hallelujah! Praise the Lord!' It made an awful impression on the young Edwin Holbrook (1867–1963) who, writing in 1951, described Aaron's certainty about the personality of the devil and his anguished battles with that undesirable character. 'The 'class meetings' were not suitable for a child to attend', wrote Edwin, 'and I remember being quite afraid to go out alone for fear that I might see that terrible, evil personality.'

A century or so ago everyone who could get time off work attended church or chapel, and village life was greatly influenced by these institutions. Much of the fabric of English society developed in such a way that it reflected the interaction between State and Church, a relationship that was not always harmonious. In many ways, the early Church contributed to an orderly social structure based upon the family unit operating within the broader framework of the manorial and borough systems, and the Church also provided a measure of direction and control over contemporary values and lifestyles. Paradoxically, religion, through the Free Church movement, also offered a promise of escape from the economic and social deprivations suffered by the majority of the people within that system. At a more personal level the Church was witness to the joys and sorrows, hopes and fears of ordinary people as they were baptised, betrothed or buried, and it reached out to touch their lives in other ways through its parish responsibilities for things as wide-ranging as poor relief, the upkeep of roads and bridges, the registration of smallpox vaccinations, and the collection of tithes.

Christianity reached the Isle of Wight in the year AD686, when Caedwalla, King of the West Saxons, took the Island by conquest and invited Bishop Wilfred to preach at Brading. The earliest records of religious foundations in the Newtown area refer to the eleventh-century chapel at Swainston built for the summer palace of the Bishops of Winchester, and to the church at Shalfleet, one of the few churches on the Isle of Wight listed in the Domesday Book of 1086.

Newtown Church

Newtown and Porchfield formed part of the large ecclesiastical parish of Calbourne. Residents were somewhat isolated from their Parish Church, and it became quite common in such situations for the mother church to establish chapels of ease in outlying areas. This is the probable origin of Newtown Church, although it is a matter of dispute when, and under whose auspices, this occurred.

The earliest surviving record of a 'chapelle of Calbourne' at Newtown dates from 1407, but other evidence suggests that one existed there well before that time. Some authorities claim that the Benedictine Abbey of Lyre in Normandy, which founded the Priory at Carisbrooke, held six churches on the Island in the mid-thirteenth century, including one at Newtown. Others suggest that even earlier, in 1175, Newtown was a parochial chapel of Carisbrooke and that its residents were expected to attend Carisbrooke for religious festivals.

Some historians believe it to have been a medieval tradition for any local fair to be held on the feast days of the saint of the local church, and Edward II's borough charter for Newtown in 1318 granted such a fair around the feast days of St Mary Magdalene. This implies the pre-existence of a church or chapel. Furthermore, the 1407 document also records that the 'chapelle' was endowed with 40 acres of land, part of which in later documents was called Maudlin (Magdalene) Mead or Parson's Ground. With income from these glebe lands, the Rector of Calbourne was to provide a clerical reader for Newtown Chapel.

Ruins of Newtown Church in 1809, from a contemporary painting by Charles Tomkins.

However, the geographical separation of Newtown from the Rector of Calbourne appears to have encouraged the burgesses to insist upon a level of independence regarding the occupation of their own chapel's lands and the funding of its services.

In 1531 Richard Bower and Robert Wadon were granted powers to:

... enter and take possession of lands belonging to Newton [sic] *on the north side of Boylands called Mary Magdelens now held by force by Raynolde Harwar, clerk, and others* [a clerk being a cleric].

And 23 years later the mayor, bailiff, constables and burgesses of Newtown appointed attorneys 'to settle a dispute with Randoulphe Harwod, parson of Calbourne, concerning lands called Mari Maudlen and the funding of a priest for the chappelle.' This latter dispute occurred despite an earlier agreement (1548) between the borough and the rector for him to hold the glebe land of the chapel ('Longbridge Croft otherwise called Magdalene's Croft') in return for maintaining a priest to reside in the house adjoining the chapel. (The similarity of the names recorded suggests that the same cleric was involved in both disputes.)

The earliest surviving Newtown Borough Registers (1666) confirm that the annual fair was always held on Magdalene's Croft. This might have been the case since the original charter granted in 1318.

From around 1500 Newtown suffered a long period of gradual decline and it seems the church suffered likewise. Corporation Books of the seventeenth century rarely mention the church except in some fund-raising capacity to effect repairs. In 1651 John Harvey was ordered to pay relief 'to the use of the church', and in 1656 the inhabitants were ordered to meet in the churchyard 'for the making of a rate to repair the Pound.'

In a survey of 1663 the church was reportedly dilapidated and by 1686 Henry Dore (churchwarden) could pass an accounts balance of only £2.0s.8d. to his successor John Gustard. However, the church still exerted more than a spiritual influence over the district, the churchwardens' duties including the supervision of mending of roads and bridges, responsibilities towards vagrants, paupers and the militia, and the provision of poor relief as well as church upkeep. The Vestry accounts also contain details of local charities, church rates, cattle owners and tithe payments, and in the sixteenth century churchwardens were also responsible for rat-catching and ensuring that woollen hats were worn on Sundays!

By 1724 the monthly divine service provided by the Rector of Calbourne had ceased. With the town reduced to a few cottages, the chapel, formerly supported by a charge on the inhabitants, was now 'out of repair for many years', although its burial-ground remained in continuous use.

A 1768 map shows the chapel as a ruin, and so it remained until the borough lost its status in 1832 and reverted to the ownership of Swainston Manor. Sir Richard Godin Simeon raised £970 by selling property of the former borough and the new church was built and endowed for £1,608, receiving its first congregation in 1837. Throughout the troubled 1830s Thomas Woodroffe was the Rector of Newtown and J. Wilson was his curate.

The building standing at the time of writing was constructed on the lines of one of the chapels of Salisbury Cathedral in the Early English style with a nave, north porch (used as a vestry), south porch, turret and bell. The plaster-vaulted interior was designed by Augustus Livesay. The font is probably the only surviving relic of the earlier church, and the cream-coloured hexagonal floor tiles probably came

NEWTOWN CHURCH

1300	Robert de Botetourte
1316	Thos. De Fulguardby
1337	Nicholas de Kaerwent
	John de Whyte
	Hugh Atte Oke (died 1375)
1375/6	John Blount
1380	John Grys
1403	John Wykeham
1404	Walter Ande
1547	Randolph Harwarde
1553	Nicholas Udall (Canon of Windsor)
1599	Dr Hamton
1616	Arthur Price
1638	Dr Hopton Sydenham
1652	... Bucker: 1652 Daniel Evans
1671	Neville Heath
1686	Benjamin Heath
1722	Thomas Terrell
1739	Edward Beacon
1766	John Fisher
1788	Edmund Poulter
1808	Mathew Woodford
1808	Hon. Thos. De Grey
1832	Thos. Woodroffe
1845	Robert Sumner
1851	John S. Utterton
1853	Arthur M. Hoare
1863	Cornelius W. Wilson

Vicars of Newtown

1873	Hudleston Stokes
1878	Henry Rice Venn

Rectors of Calbourne who had charge of the Chapelry of Newtown 1300–1871, and some subsequent Vicars of Newtown. (Based on the work of Harry Guy of Yarmouth 1911)

Newtown Church interior in 2003.

from a local brickyard. The new church was dedicated to the Holy Ghost, a great rarity in the Church of England tradition, and prospered in the medium term, although still as an outreach of the Parish Church at Calbourne. The full range of services were conducted here by the rector of the mother church. (On Christmas Day 1859 Amelia Greenen, an agricultural labourer's daughter from Whiteoak Cottages, married Leonard Warne at Newtown Church, and in 1933 celebrated her 100th birthday.) Much of the church's success grew from the enthusiasm and skill of its sextoness, Hannah Woolgar (née Holbrook), who served in that capacity for 34 years.

By an Order of the Queen in Council in 1871, Newtown and Porchfield were declared a separate ecclesiastical parish, and in 1873 Revd John Vicar (Rector of Calbourne) appointed Revd H. Hudlestone Stokes as curate to the new parish. He administered services at the church and also on alternate weeks at the newly-constructed Locks Green School. The school was used in this way until the turn of the century, serving the east of the parish, and among its earliest congregations were Mrs Mew, Mr and Mrs Dore, Samuel Bourne, Jacob and Ann Delderfield, and the Hughes and Scovell families. Until the completion of the new vicarage in Town Gate Lane in 1875, Revd Stokes lodged at Youngwoods Farm with the tenant Henry Kingswell.

In 1878 Revd Henry Rice Venn succeeded Revd Stokes as surrogate and vicar at Newtown, and remained in that capacity until 1919 when, as the oldest incumbent on the Island, ill health enforced his retirement. (A surrogate could issue marriage licences on behalf of the Bishop.) His 14-roomed vicarage was set in three acres along Town Gate Lane in the gift of the Bishop of Winchester and in 1910 had an average tithe rent value of £116 per annum. This provided a good living for the resident vicar who enjoyed an elevated status amongst his parishioners. Revd Venn could afford to fund a special gravel trackway from his home to Clamerkin River, a bridge across an intervening creek, and a pier, alongside which he moored his boat.

In due deference to his status he was chair of managers at Locks Green School, gave public lectures on a variety of social and scientific matters, taught at the school, and hosted musical soirées at the vicarage. But declining health reflected in his work and congregations dwindled sometimes to nil during the last years of his ministry. The vicarage became neglected and by his retirement in 1919 it had fallen into a state of disrepair. It was demolished in 1922 by 'Putty' Vincent, a builder from Ventnor, who used some of the materials in the construction of the bungalows in the vicinity.

The year that Revd Rice Venn retired, Dr Howard Hawkins bequeathed his large Newtown home to the church and Lamb Cottage became the vicarage for Revd Venn's successors, from 1922–24 Revd F.E. Heaton Thomas as curate (a victim, in post, of tuberculosis), Revd Philip T. Glover until 1929, then Father Clark until 1934, probably its last incumbent vicar. The Revd Glover was a very popular appointment and he attracted large congregations from as far away as Porchfield.

Above: *After Sunday-morning service at Locks Green School, c.1881.*

Right: *Revd P.T. Glover in 1927 and Revd Farmer in 1937* (inset).

Not for the first time, the church had undergone major repairs (1920–22). Its reopening for services was marked by the reunification of the ecclesiastical parishes of Newtown and Calbourne, and a little later by a visit from the bishop for the first time in living memory.

Like most institutions during the eighteenth and nineteenth centuries the established Church reflected the social-class divisions that were developing. Increasingly, the Church of England was patronised by the wealthier groups – landowners, tenant farmers, boat owners, craftsmen, and those of independent means – and the surviving memorials in Newtown churchyard reflect the prominence of the Kingswell, Woolgar, Holbrook, Prangnell and Abrook families, for instance.

Pew rents were charged and the seating arrangements in the church reflected the comparative social standing of the squire, then the farmers, the squire's gardeners and coachmen, down to the schoolmistress, the maid servants and eventually the cottagers. Indeed, sermons often dwelt upon 'man's appointed place in society'.

The Annual Meeting of the Newtown P.C.C. and Vestry sitting together was held at Lock's Green School on January 29th, 1929, when the following Officers were elected.

Chairman—The Rector.

Vice Chairman—Rev. C. J. Penrice.

Churchwardens—Mr. A. C. Gibson and Miss I. L. W. Gibson.

Sidesmen—Mr. Hunt and Miss Cousins.

P.C.C. Council—Mrs. Hunt, Mrs. Gray, Miss T. Gibson, Miss Mustchin, Mr. Hunt, Mrs. Sanders.

Hon. Secretary—Rev. C. J. Penrice.

Hon. Treasurer and Diocesan Representative—Miss I. L. W. Gibson.

From the Shalfleet, Calbourne and Newtown Church Messenger, *1929.*

In the late 1920s Newtown Church witnessed a development that disenchanted the majority of its congregation. Several of the talented Gibson sisters had moved from Porchfield into the coastguard cottages at Newtown. Ida, Sybil, Truda and Mamie Gibson were all single and of largely independent means, and quickly became very active in church matters to the extent that some local residents accused them of 'taking over'. They were instrumental in the appointment of two 'high church' vicars (including Father A.J. Clark, who had been seconded from an urban parish where he had suffered a breakdown) to succeed Revd Glover, who had moved to Wroxall. Congregations rapidly dwindled, and it may not have been coincidental that the Salvation Army's mobile church van began to hold services opposite the Town Hall in 1929.

The period 1930–35 was very troubled. Many of the church records were lost, including the roll (a new roll was begun in June 1936). Writing for the *Church Messenger* of 1935 the Rector of Calbourne, who was shortly to resign himself, observed that:

> *Mr Norman Paskins has again been chosen as Churchwarden for Newtown. We cannot give him too much gratitude for the way in which he has done his best to pilot that parish amid the shoals and reefs of a very trying time.*

At about the same time, the church sold its vicarage, Lamb Cottage.

Billy Mustchin, who was born in Woolgar's Cottage opposite the church in 1920 and who (in 2004) is possibly the village's only native-born resident, can recall the chequered history of the church since the Gibson influence waned. He has served several Rectors of Calbourne including Revd Connolly and Revd Seymour, who journeyed by bicycle to take local services. The Revd Connolly was the last Rector of Calbourne to appoint a curate to Newtown. Appointed in June 1935, Revd Farmer's weekly wage of £2.10s.0d. was barely sufficient to cover the cost of his lodgings with the Mussell family in Mill Lane, Shalfleet. After 1945, a former captain in the Isle of Wight artillery at Freshwater was appointed to minister at Calbourne and Newtown and, at the time of writing, the vicar of the neighbouring parish of Shalfleet takes responsibility for Newtown Church services.

In 2004 the church still has a devoted congregation who keep it in good repair. Village resident Dorothy Smith is typical, having organised the Isle of Wight Hospital Broadcasting Association's annual Christmas carol service in the church since the mid-1970s.

The Free Churches

Sadly, the established Church has a long and ugly history of the persecution and torture of Dissenters, at times even burning them at the stake. The Roman traditions imposed by the Normans had been usurped by Henry VIII's creation of the English Church, and Cromwell's Puritan revolution of the seventeenth century had further inflamed religious passions. Following the Act of Uniformity in 1662, the 'Free Church' movement gathered pace and, soon, the first Congregational Church on the Isle of Wight opened at Newport.

Until the Tolerance Act of 1689 the monarchy, the State and the established Church (whether Roman or Anglican) together had repressed dissension, sometimes brutally. Catholics, Jews, Anglicans, Quakers, Presbyterians and others had all suffered in their turn. The demise of Cromwell's Commonwealth in 1660 and the Restoration led to the adoption of a rigid Anglican orthodoxy based on a new Common Book of Prayer. A massive purge of clergy followed, and Dissenters were banned from holding separate services. At the same time land and wealth were concentrated in the hands of an emerging 'squirearchy', and the new alliance of parson and squire dominated village life for the next 250 years.

Nonconformity was born out of this situation. The 1689 Act permitted freedom of worship for the first time, and the Independents and Congregationalists began to flourish on the Island, but it was to be almost 100 years later (1753) that John Wesley arrived at Cowes to bring Methodism to the Islanders, and it was 1787 before the first Methodist minister was appointed.

Religious fervour swept through rural communities during the nineteenth century and many cottagers joined more than one congregation, becoming known locally as 'Devil dodgers'. Evangelical music from the Sankey and Moody hymnal helped the Methodists (often known as 'ranters') attract large congregations who were encouraged to adopt homely precepts within their lifestyles: 'pay your way and fear nobody', 'tell the truth and shame the Devil', or 'know it's a sin to steal a pin'.

Methodism splintered into several evangelical sects and in 1821 Captain Caws of Brading invited some Bible Christians from Cornwall to preach on the Island 'because of the spiritual darkness and destitution of the people.' Mary Toms from Tintagel arrived at Cowes in 1823 and immediately attracted great interest and large crowds, not all of them supportive, for Islanders were reported as being 'notorious for Sabbath breaking, swearing, smuggling and drunkeness.'

Out of this spirit of evangelical commitment many people devoted a lifetime's service to their chapels and communities. As recently as 1935, Local Preacher Awards for 40 years or more of service to Methodism were awarded to David Holbrook of Porchfield (who had begun preaching in 1873) and to Tom Essau Mussell of Shalfleet (local preacher since 1886).

Porchfield Bible Christian Chapel

The first Isle of Wight Bible Christian Society was founded at Arreton in 1823 and by the following year the first meeting at Porchfield had taken place. Many of the early meetings were held in the open beneath a huge tree which stood to the left of the road between the Sportsman's Rest and Locks Farm, and others were held in local cottages.

Children of the Chambers family of Locks Green were among the first to be baptised in 'dwelling houses'. Jacob, who was born in 1829, was baptised in a Porchfield cottage and became a wood sawyer in the village.

Eventually, a little chapel was built in Dirty Lane (since named New Road) in 1852 and attracted a fervent following including such stalwarts as Aaron Fallick, Jonathan Punch, Moses Grist, John and Andrew Chambers, David Holbrook, Thomas Phillips, Robert Bennett, and Charles and Daniel Denness. Hopefully, they were not subjected to the kind of persecution described in a contemporary account recorded in Revd J.B. Dyson's book *Methodism in the Isle of Wight*, published in around 1855:

The 'Great Tree', an early gathering-place for Bible Christians at Locks Green, pictured in around 1904. The cottage opposite was also an early preaching house and later became an informal meeting place for the area's youth.

> *Drums, tin kettles, horns or any discordant thing was brought into requisition to drown the preacher's voice, while a shower of rotten eggs, sticks and stones, with now and then a live animal or any other offensive missile, fell with annoying effect on the preacher and his audience. The dresses of the audience were fastened together, that they might be torn when they separated; ferocious animals were turned into the worshiping assemblies; and sparrows were let loose to put out the lights; the top of the chimney covered with a lid and the door tied to suffocate with smoke those who were imprisoned.*

For many years the chapel was packed but by 1895 younger people were already leaving the district in search of work and the gathering had dwindled to 29, most of whom were:

> *... homely, hearty, unpretending persons and blessed with the life and power of Godliness, much interested in missionary work, which they support to the utmost of their means.*

But five years later they still managed to replace their chapel with a new building on the same site.

Their zeal for missions, especially the Women's China Missionary League, was no doubt fired by the fact that W.A. Grist, a grandson of Moses Grist, had recently won a language scholarship to Oxford University and subsequently had become a famous missionary in China in charge of the T'ong Chuan

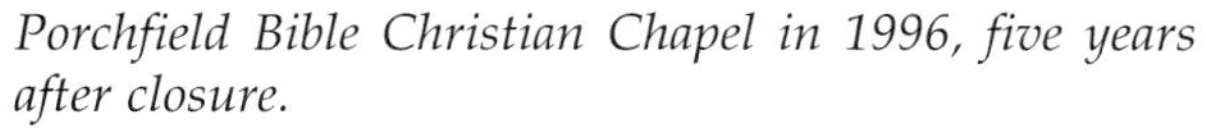

Porchfield Bible Christian Chapel in 1996, five years after closure.

Barton's Corner Bible Christian Chapel, built 1864–69.

Above: *Laying the foundation-stones at Porchfield Bible Christian Sunday School, c.1919.* Left to right: *Mrs K. Whillier, Mrs E. Holbrook, Charles Holbrook, George Hayward, David Holbrook, Fred Morris, Robert Flux. Fanny and Fred Fallick are pictured far right.*

BARTON'S CORNER
CHAPEL
1869

Left: *The original keystone.*

Right: *Herbert Foss received a 1904 edition of the Methodist hymn book.*

Presented

TO

Master HERBERT A. H. FOSS

ON THE OCCASION OF THE

FOUNDATION STONE-LAYING

OF THE

SHALFLEET

Wesleyan Chapel.

THURSDAY, MAY 10th, 1911.

mission station. That such a man, whose family had spent hard times at Forest Side Workhouse as paupers, could achieve this distinction, must have been a great inspiration.

The Bible Christians always monitored their membership and attendance carefully. The Porchfield and Newtown Society's earliest records survive from 1823 and show attendances at that time varying from 3–20 each week. In 1905, Fred Fallick, head gamekeeper at Swainston, joined the chapel when he moved into St Hubert's Lodge. Some years later he gave some land to the chapel (bequeathed to him by Aaron Fallick) for the building of a Sunday School room at the back.

But as the twentieth century unfolded Porchfield's membership began to decline. In 1948, Mr G.S. Hayward of The Moorings, Newtown, who was the Methodist Society Steward for Porchfield, presented the final quarter accounts for 1947 which showed a membership of 34 at Porchfield, and only 12 at Shalfleet. By the late 1980s, the only remaining members were Roger and Pamela Smith and Roland and Eileen Wells, and the last devotional service before closure took place on Sunday 24 March 1991. The chapel building is a private residence at the time of writing.

Barton's Corner Bible Christian Chapel

On 19 May 1783 a licence for a Dissenters' meeting-place was obtained for the house of John Fry. This was almost certainly the tenement at Newtown standing on the plot called Fry's on the map of 1768, adjacent to the Marsh Farmhouse in 2004. In 1790 John Fry, 'husbandman', leased further tenements and land nearby at Key Close and Bellamy's.

Later, various members of the Bible Christian movement preached for some time in Newtown in the period 1825–40 but 'could not get a settled position' and gave it up in favour of more suitable places. These 'more suitable places' might have included another plot and tenement bearing John Fry's name situated at Barton's Corner at Shalfleet. This plot, later occupied by Alby Jupe, is situated opposite the earliest known 'preaching house' in Shalfleet. The Barton's Corner Society met for many years during the mid-1800s in the cottage of Luke Barton, an early convert, later to become the head gamekeeper at the Swainston estate, 'a dear, quaint, enthusiastic, intelligent old saint... of strong and striking personality', according to one of the contemporary ministers. The cottage witnessed many baptisms including that of Andrew Barton in 1866 who later became steward of the Swainston estate. Eventually, the little meeting could afford to build their own chapel alongside in Long Mead, which they leased for 1,000 years. Using bricks from Lower Elmsworth brickyard, building work started in 1864 and was completed five years later.

The chapel was supported by the well-known local preachers Mr Bubb (who visited on his penny-farthing bicycle) and Mr Young. It attracted folk from as far away as London Heath. Margaret Foss made her way there each week from 1863 until 1914, dressed in her fox-fur collars and ankle skirts and clutching her handbag, magnifying glass and Bible.

From the 1880s Fred and Fanny Fallick became pillars of this society and, writing in the 1960s, their son Frederick James Fallick recollected with great warmth his attendance at the Sunday School with the other two pupils! Before the purchase of an harmonium there was no instrumental accompaniment for the singing at the chapel. Later organists included Nora Mussell and Doris Smith. Ministers, such as Matthew Hoare and Josiah Datson (who signed Frederick's first missionary box), and lay preachers walked many miles to preach every Sunday, enjoying a roast lunch with Mr and Mrs Fallick (senr) at their cottage ('Stitches') on the Ningwood road. After the meal:

> *... a word of prayer would be suggested and we would all, children included, kneel down around the settees while the minister or layman, followed by my father, would pray aloud.*

Apparently, the 'intrigue of another denomination' (probably Shalfleet Methodist Chapel) threatened attendances, but the little Society survived until well into the twentieth century, fed by the enthusiasm of families such as the Fallicks who, after their move to Lower Hamstead, walked a total of 12 miles in all weathers to attend the two services each Sunday. The little Society ceased to function around 1930 and, not without irony, the building was purchased by Andrew Barton who, in 1866, had been baptised in the 'preaching house' next door. In 1936 Andrew's son Jack bought it from his father for £10 and demolished it.

Shalfleet Methodist Chapel

Shalfleet Methodists first met in the home of Mr Hollis. The chapel was built in 1861 on land donated by Sir John Barrington, and the Sunday-School room was added in 1911. By then, the chapel was packed full each week, many paying a pew rent to obtain a favoured seat. A long line of local young men, including Dave Angell, always waited for the service to begin before filing into the rear pews, among the last to enter being Ern Seagar who reluctantly knocked out his perpetual pipe on the porch wall.

There tended to be a marked division of loyalties, with those of a Liberal persuasion attending the Methodist meeting whilst the local Tories worshipped at the Parish Church down the road, discharging into the public house opposite after the service.

Porchfield Independent (Congregational) Chapels

One of the earliest alternatives to Anglican worship in the district was provided by the meetings of the 'Independents' in Porchfield, where the first services were held in 1804. A little later, the farmer at Lambsleaze, John Ridett, provided the land and appealed for funds, and in 1810 a small thatched chapel was built, called Bethel Chapel. It flourished, and in 1835 Revd Thomas Mann from Cowes founded a Congregational church there.

Among the founder members were Barnabus Arnold (superintendent), Mr and Mrs Rice of Locks Farm, and the Porchfield residents Mr Attrill, Mr and Mrs Robert Atkins, Henry Damp, Mrs Saunders, Mrs Cooper and Leah Arnold. A little later Mr and Mrs Benjamin Ford and Moses Grist (whose father of the same name was a Bible Christian) joined the chapel. Attendances swelled to over 200 and an appeal for funds raised 200 guineas towards the cost of a larger chapel, built on the same site in 1846 for £440. Mr Maurice Dear of Cowes, Guardian of the Poor and founder of grocers Dear and Morgan, who preached at Porchfield for 50 years, made generous donations and again he contributed in 1859 to help clear outstanding debts. The chapel enjoyed the loyalty of prominent local families for many years. From 1866 until 1903 Henry Mew (the local builder) was church secretary, succeeded by his son Edward Mew until his sudden death in 1927. Henry achieved a lifetime ambition when he built the Sunday School adjoining the chapel in 1902. The local carrier, Edwin Holbrook, and his wife, who lived next door to the chapel in Bethel Cottage, were stalwarts for over half a century.

The chapel had to fight for its existence in the mid-1860s when the grandson of John Ridett attempted to reclaim the land on which the chapel stood, serving a 'notice of ejectment' on the trustees. Although successful at Winchester Crown Court, the chapel was not awarded costs which amounted to a near-crippling £300.

An American organ, installed to mark the jubilee of the chapel in 1896, was symptomatic of a strong musical tradition developing there. Its choir gave many concerts at Locks Green School and the surrounding chapels but, like so many rural chapels, it faced gradual decline throughout the twentieth century and eventually closed in the 1980s. The building was demolished in around 1988 but the little graveyard remains as testimony to a thriving meeting.

The demise of the village chapel is a comparatively modern phenomenon, and inevitably closure has a negative impact on rural communities and adds to the problems brought about by the closure of other village institutions such as the school, the shop or the Post Office.

Edward Mew, c.1923.

Porchfield Congregational Chapel and Sunday School, c.1920.

In 2004 there is no 'Free Church' presence in the Newtown or Porchfield area. Only the two Anglican churches at Shalfleet and Newtown survive. Yet, until recently, church and chapel played an integral role in the lives of local residents, administering to their spiritual, social and civil needs. Even for those who were not regularly in attendance at devotional services, the church or the chapel played host to those momentous family events surrounding birth, marriage and death, and also provided a setting for regular social occasions involving the community at large, be it a musical evening, a harvest festival, or a jumble sale.

Courtships & Marriages

The 'nuclear family' has been the bedrock on which almost all human societies have been built, and betrothal of the partners in marriage has a very long history. The State, the community and the individual all had a vested interest in the concept of marriage for it provided a socially stable basis for the provision of labour, the raising of tithes, taxes and militia service, and legal protection of assets. Marriage became enshrined in civil and ecclesiastical law and the established Church was charged with its administration. Where such laws were broken heavy penalties were meted out by the consistory courts such as those, recorded in the Shalfleet Visitation Books dated 1606, imposed upon Thomas Chiverton and Aelce Upton for adultery.

The Anglican Church jealously guarded its right to perform the ceremony, and even as late as 1753 the Hardwick Act confirmed the illegality of other forms of marriage except for Jews and Quakers. Only comparatively recently have Roman Catholic, Nonconformist and (from 1837) civil marriages become more common. The 1753 Act also frowned upon the practice of marrying off children as young as two years old in order to protect or gain family wealth, decreeing a minimum age of 14 years for boys and 12 years for girls, a situation that remained unchanged until 1928.

At that time parents had a greater influence over their children's choice of friends. Elsie Lock recollects 'tagging along', at the age of 13 in 1920, with her cousin Sally Lock on their way home to Elmsworth Farm from chapel in Porchfield and being sworn to secrecy as Sally walked with her favourite, Georgie Mullett, as far as the Sportsman's Rest before she then 'permitted' Reg Hayward (later to become her husband) to see her the rest of the way in case her father should be working his fields! At around the same time, Herbert Foss and his friend Ted Barton could be found each Sunday 'loitering with intent' as the young women spilled from the chapel, and so began their friendships with Elsie Lock and Aggie Mew. Celebrated brick maker Harry Pritchett (born 1876) recorded that:

> *It was an old village custom for a suitor to hang his hat on the 'byllis' (bellows hung behind the cottage door) when calling on his lady love. If the visit was not welcomed the girl threw the hat out through the open door, as a hint for its owner to follow.*

When geographical and social mobility was more limited, the choice of marriage partner was often restricted to members of the local community, who might well also be a distant relative. In Newtown and Porchfield there were many links by marriage between families such as the Fallicks, Holbrooks, Mews, Haywards, Angells and Arnolds, and it was quite common for first cousins to marry.

For centuries, intermarriage between farming families was common. The marriage registers of Newtown Church are sprinkled with examples. In 1877 Mary Alford Kingswell from Fleetlands Farm married a farmer's son, Henry Bull from Gatcombe. In 1900 Walter Hillier Lock of Elmsworth Farm married Elizabeth Hayward from Locks Farm, barely one mile away. Alec Whatley, of London Farm, married Ella Hawkins of Lambsleaze Farm in 1913, and in 1926 Sarah (Sally) Lock from Elmsworth married Reg Hayward of Little Thorness Farm. More recently, in 1969, Arthur Attrill (Durrant's Farm) and Janet Cool (Coleman's Farm) married at Newtown Church. Of course, chance and necessity also played major roles in the mating game. Herbert Foster was a humble cowboy working for John Sweet and living-in at Harts Farm in the 1890s. Farmer Sweet also employed a resident housekeeper, Adela Hole, whose sister Ruth was a frequent visitor. Herbert and Ruth were married in 1896.

Some associations were brought about more by the force of necessity, particularly when husband or wife died prematurely and there were young children to look after. Thomas Henry Foss of Newtown drowned in 1870 leaving a widow, Emma Jane, already aged 41 and still with five of their ten children on hand. They lived in Nobby's Cottage in Newtown High Street and the loss of the family breadwinner could have proved disastrous. But by 1872 Emma Jane was again married, this time to a young gamekeeper, Samuel Bourne, who claimed at the ceremony to be four years older than his 21 years. However, they added further to the family, and later moved into Whiteoak Cottages near Fleetlands Corner. Probably, similar marriages of convenience took place when, in 1873, Richard Godden aged 26, who lodged at the Town Hall, married another lodger, Emily Jolliffe who was 17 years his senior, and in 1901, when Elizabeth Stark who ran a small dairy from Key Close, married Herbert Wheeler, a near neighbour and ten years her junior. Most fleet of foot was Jonathan Punch, the local cobbler who, between 1838 and the mid-1850s, married in succession three Woodford sisters, skirting the law by using different chapels and even once changing his name!

Baptisms

From the fifteenth century the Book of Common Prayer required that every child should be baptised into the Church fellowship, but it was not until Thomas Cromwell's injunctions (1538) that a system of registration was applied to make it easier to prove ages and to establish lines of descent. Thus it became more straightforward for local blacksmith, William Fosse, to pre-arrange the distribution of his worldly possessions in 1555. After bequeathing his 'soul to Almighty God, to His Blessed Mother our Lady Saint Mary, and to all the holy company in heaven' (the

Above: *Wedding reception at Rodgebrook Farm of Herbert Foss and Elsie Lock, 1926.* Left to right, back row: *Henry Foss, Charlie Goddard, Herbert Foster, Robbie Lock, Walter Lock, Herbert Foss, Bob Lock, Elizabeth Lock, Agnes Mew, Robert Lock, Gertie Cousins, Fan Dawkins, Revd Glover, Mrs Glover, Minnie Cousins;* front row: *Adela Foss, Kitty Lock, Elsie Lock, Florrie Dawkins, Jane Lock, Dick Lock, Ms Hunt.*

Left: *Sarah ('Sally') Lock, Elmsworth Farm, 1921.*

The marriage of Sarah Lock and Reginald Hayward, 9 January 1926. Left to right, standing: *Mrs Glover, Revd Glover, Jane Lock, ?, Frances Flux, Agnes Mew, Flo Jones, Walter Lock, Elsie Lock, Mary Mew, Reg Hayward, Ernest Flux, groom's sister, Bob Lock, Jack Arnold, Walter John Lock, ?, Simeon Hayward, ?, ?, ?;* seated: *Carrie Mew, Elizabeth Lock, Sarah Lock, ?, Matilda Hayward, ?.*

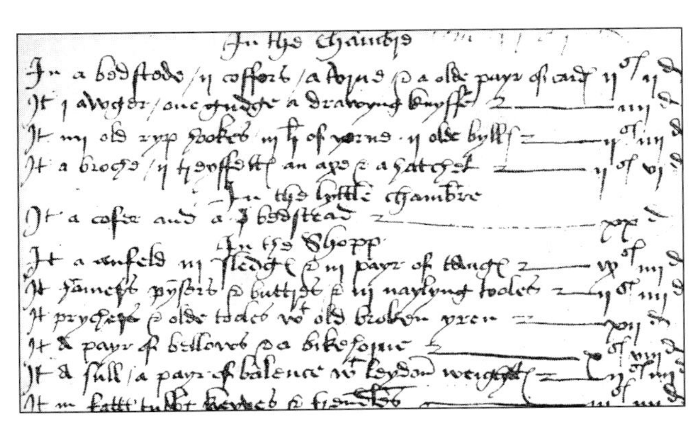

Part of the inventory to the will of William Fosse, 1555.

(PART OF MANUSCRIPT 1555U/26 REPRODUCED COURTESY OF HAMPSHIRE RECORD OFFICE)

established Church had temporarily reverted to Rome!), he left 54s. to the poorest people of the parish and the remainder of his estate variously to his wife Anys and children, John and Isobel (the latter receiving a cow, four ewes and, for two years, 'an acre of wheat sown'). Part of the inventory of his will reads (translation courtesy of David Pedgley):

In the chamber

a bedstede/ two coffers/ a torne & a olde payr of cards
two shillings and tuppence
one awger/ one gudge / a drawyng knyffe
four pence
four old ryp hookes/ three pounds of yrne. two old bylls
two shillings and fourpence
a broche/ two treysells/ an axe and a hatchet
two shillings and sixpence

In the little chamber

cofer and a bedstead
twenty pence

In the shop

a anfele three sledgs and three payr of tongs
nine shillings and fourpence
harness pysers and buttres and three naylyng tooles
two shillings and fourpence
Prychers and olde tooles with old broken yren
thirteen pence
a payr of bellowes and a bikehorn
ten shillings and fourpence
a sull/ a payr of balece with leyden weights
two shillings and fourpence
Three? fatts tubbs keyves & trendles
three shillings and fourpence

NB: coffer = storage chest; torne = spinning-wheel; cards = wool combs; gudge = iron pin in a wheel axle; pysers = pincers; buttres/prychers/bikehorn = probably blacksmith's tools; sull = plough; fatts = vats; keyves = ?; trendles = low bed on wheels kept under a high bed.

From the outset (and despite a system of fines) many people tried to avoid Cromwell's registration, fearing that it might be used to impose taxes. Illegitimacy and illiteracy were also very common, which meant contemporary records were often incomplete. Even where records were kept spellings varied wildly, and were often given in the vernacular (Faws, Faulse, Fawse; Osbon, Osbourne, Osborne; and Greenen, Greenham). The very practical difficulties involved in rural travel and the reluctance of employers to grant time off work made it difficult for families to have their children baptised. Sometimes, families 'saved up' and had several children baptised at the same ceremony, especially if they lived in a remote spot. Jonas and Margaret Foss occupied the remote Elmsworth Saltern at Fish House Point alongside Jonas' brother, Thomas Henry Foss, and his family. In 1859 the two families seem to have arranged a special 'day-trip' to get their latest offspring baptised. Such a journey by small boat, especially in the depths of winter, held its own perils, bearing in mind the large families involved and the nature of clothing available.

Baptism was a significant social occasion which merited the use of the family's 'Sunday best'. The attire of Herbert Foss pictured here in February 1903 for his own baptism reflects, perhaps, the elderly nature of his parents and the slow pace of change in fashions at Newtown.

Burials

The Church held responsibility for burials in consecrated ground. For at least 350 years the churchyard at Newtown has been in continuous use, serving a widely scattered population. Until around 1900 it was not uncommon to see an upright coffin standing in a dinghy as a corpse was brought from a remote spot to the hard at Causeway Bridge and delivered to the undertaker Frank Long (established 1764 at Calbourne) or John Gustar from Sun Hill (in the 1880s), before interment.

Newtown's churchyard reflects the town's more recent history, especially that of the nineteenth century when memorials were more commonly used as an expression of family grief. The 16 Kingswell family memorials are prominent, sometimes referred to as 'the plague stones' because several mark premature deaths due to tuberculosis. Other groups of memorials belong to the brick-making Prangnells (nine memorials) and the Holbrooks (nine memorials), variously mariners, salt boilers and farmers. As in many small communities, stories persist long after a given event, and one such tale, unverified, relates to the layout of the memorials to the Holbrooks and the Abrooks. Unusually, they face in opposite directions and it is suggested that following family quarrels one branch of the Holbrooks assumed the name Abrook and remained aloof even in death!

Large family sizes, combined with a high rate of infant mortality, placed increasing pressure on space in Anglican churchyards, and the established Church, whose power was enshrined within an Act of Parliament, was not always sympathetic towards the burial of the poor, especially if they were also Nonconformists. As a result, many were given a pauper's funeral at the Newport workhouse, or were even buried locally without record.

Soon after the opening of the new Congregational Chapel at Porchfield in 1846, the chapel community obtained the freehold of some adjacent land. The chapel records show that:

> *... more instances of refusal to bury the poor having occurred a piece of ground has been bought to ensure that the villagers shall be laid to rest independent of the consent of the parish church incumbent.*

The little graveyard remains as a monument to Nonconformity in the village.

Such was the control of the Anglican Church that it was not until after the Burials Act of 1880 that non-Anglican services were permitted in Church of England graveyards.

The Broader Community Roles

Even though church and chapel disputed control of the formal ceremonies affecting family life, each made broad and important contributions to the community in terms of education, welfare and cultural activity, in addition to their spiritual provision.

By 1829 the Congregational Chapel at Porchfield had a thriving Sunday School organised by a Mr Haines, and by 1856 the Island's Bible Christian movement had 635 scholars and 104 teachers (growing to 1,859 and 288 respectively by the year 1896).

In the early-nineteenth century these schools were the only alternative to dame-schools, and bearing in mind that until the 1890s parents were required to pay for day-school attendance by their children, and that school attendance during the week denied young children gainful employment or the opportunity to help out at home, Sunday Schools became the preferred choice.

William Holbrook (born 1828) attended day-school for only two days, refusing to return after being stood in a corner wearing a dunce's cap! Later, his wife painstakingly taught him to read (and to write in capital letters) to give him the access to the scriptures he craved. Writing in 1951, his son Edwin recalled the exclusively religious reading matter in his childhood home, including the Holy Bible, John Bunyan's *Pilgrim's Progress*, the Chapel Hymn Book and the *Bible Christian Magazine*. In addition, William's wife often read to him from Fox's *Book of Martyrs*.

The school at Locks Green was consecrated and used for services and Holy Communion until around 1900. In the 1870s Revd Stokes visited the school each Thursday morning and Edwin recollected the talks he gave 'on the wonderful deliverance of the children of Israel from Egyptian bondage.' Revd Henry Rice Venn continued this tradition well into the twentieth century. In addition to the cane, the school made use of the vicar and the policeman to bear witness to the 'awful consequences' if children did not mend their ways!

Sunday Schools owed much to the devotion of personalities such as Henry Mew, superintendent of Porchfield Congregational School from 1860–1903, and of Mrs Caroline Hayward, a teacher at the Bible Christian Sunday School for over 40 years spanning the turn of the century. Mrs Eva Holbrook, wife of Edwin, served in a similar capacity for many years at the Congregational Sunday School before her premature death in 1930. Sunday-School membership was still growing as late as 1919 when the Lock siblings and others laid foundation-stones at the new Bible Christian schoolroom in Dirty Lane, Porchfield. Many local names are inscribed on the stones.

It was here that Elsie Lock learned to collect funds for overseas missions, something she continued for many years alongside her zeal for raising funds for the National Children's Homes. Despite their own impoverished circumstances, chapel members were often generous towards those they believed to be in greater need. Wight's Bible Christians raised what was then the enormous sum of £384 for missionary work in 1896.

Mrs Caroline Hayward, Porchfield Sunday-School teacher, in a photograph taken in c.1922 to commemorate 40 years of service.

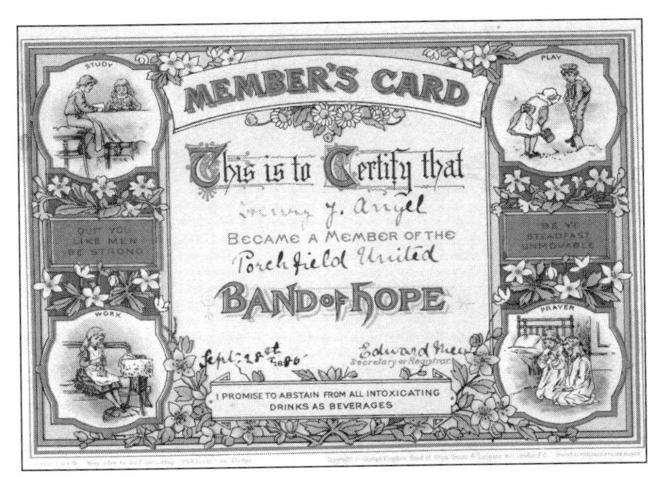

MEMBER'S CARD

This is to Certify that

Henry J. Angel

BECAME A MEMBER OF THE

Porchfield United

BAND of HOPE

Sept. 28th 1880

Edward Mew
Secretary or Registrar

I PROMISE TO ABSTAIN FROM ALL INTOXICATING DRINKS AS BEVERAGES

Henry Angell's first Band of Hope membership card, 1880.

Church funds were also used to help local folk who had fallen on hard times, an echo of the relief provided by the Church since the Middle Ages. Such charitable attitudes were extended into various kinds of personal service to the local community, as members of the Board of Guardians (Henry Mew 1870–1900) or as school managers (Edwin Holbrook 1930–45).

Chapel choirs gave concerts and members arranged socials, jumble sales and garden parties. Children looked forward to Sunday-School outings in the carrier's van, those from Shalfleet Methodist Chapel always making for Stone Steps for tea whilst Porchfield children's horizons extended as far as Freshwater or Sandown. Church and chapel also played a significant part in the cultivation of Victorian values in the community. Public houses had few licencing limitations and home-brewed beer and wine were freely available in cottage larders. In spite of his very meagre income, Henry Foss always kept a two-gallon barrel of light ale on a stool in the pantry at London Heath, together with a ready supply of cider and a bottle of port. Much greater abuse of alcohol was common, adding to the problems of poverty and the ill-treatment of children. In 1870 a local branch of the Band of Hope Temperance Society was formed in Porchfield, holding regular meetings with lantern slides to publicise the 'evils of drink'. Henry Mew was its first president and Mr F. Sheath its secretary. From the age of six children were encouraged to 'sign the pledge', and received prizes for attendance, like the book awarded to Bertie G. Bennett, the village baker's son, in 1900. The branch thrived until its eventual closure in 1942.

The Salvation Army toured the area in the latter years of the nineteenth century, preaching about the evils of drink, and this led to very public altercations via the press between local personality Alfred Prangnell, the champion brick maker, and the Army captain. Defending the pleasures of wine, Alfred quoted liberally from the Bible, announcing that 'If God does not condemn us, who can be against us?'

Devoted Salvationists, the Flux family of Porchfield in 1910. Left to right: *Ernest, Winnie, Frances (née Lock) and Daisy.*

Personalities

Such intimate involvement of church and chapel in village life inevitably produced some larger-than-life personalities. Edwin Holbrook, the highly respected local carrier from 1903–26, was a gentle, devout man, steeped in Porchfield's Congregational activities. But, as a carrier, he also came into contact with the seamier side of life. In his own words:

> *When stopped at the Noah's Ark one evening I went inside to settle up an account. When I came out and went to chain up the tailboard, instead of the board I grasped a man's foot. The customers in the tap room had laid him into the van knowing perfectly well I should see him home. After that I adopted a different plan, and delivered the goods for the Landlady on the way to the village, and when returning home drove full trot past the pub.*

The Revd Henry Rice Venn, a tall, solemn Irishman, became an institution in Newtown between 1878 and 1919. As a widower, man of substance, sailor and local dignitary, he invoked a feeling of awe amongst villagers as, dressed in flowing black robes, he toured his parish on a tricycle. One might imagine local reaction when, following a visit to the mainland, he returned with a new bride, a fair lady many years his junior. Cosseted at times by a young domestic servant, aged 21, and a 15-year-old housemaid, Revd Rice Venn's image rather outweighed his competence, and the management of both church and school suffered.

Most rural nineteenth-century communities had their own religious eccentric, and cutting an altogether different image to that of Revd Rice Venn was 'Holy Joe', otherwise known as Alexander Grey. He wore very long hair and shabby clothes, moving from house to house preaching, always carrying a huge umbrella. He claimed to be God's special messenger, warning people of their sins and at the same time enjoying their food and hospitality. Poor Aaron Fallick, who was superintendent of the local Sunday School, was particularly vulnerable to such 'tidings' and took Holy Joe into his home for several weeks until his brother Philip Fallick declared him an imposter and forcibly ejected him from the cottage in Dirty Lane, Porchfield, only to hear him singing lustily as he left, 'When the Roll is called up yonder, I'll be there!' Aaron was a noisily devout Bible Christian and a man of immense physical strength, but himself also rather eccentric. For many years towards the end of the nineteenth century he was a familiar figure, riding his tricycle very slowly between Porchfield and Cowes delivering goods, always dressed in corduroy trousers, heavy hobnailed boots, a white canvas smock and a large mushroom-shaped hat. Almost inevitably, he became the the butt of many jokes amongst the younger fraternity.

Holy Joe in the early 1900s.
(Reproduced courtesy of the Isle of Wight County Record Office)

In 1870 Dr J.E.B. Gibson moved his large and talented family, complete with live-in nurse and governess, from Cowes to 'The Homestead', a specially constructed house at Porchfield. He practiced medicine in Cowes, followed by his son Dr Percy Gibson – this service lasting for a period in excess of 50 years. Some of the family members became pillars of Newtown Church and great patrons and organisers of social and cultural events in the community. Daughter Louisa ('Lisa') became a concert singer, performing at the Royal Albert Hall, and the youngest son Isham Edward Gibson became an admiral in the Royal Navy. Ida Gibson, one of three pairs of twins in the family, was a professional violinist, and provided instrumental lessons at Locks Green School. She and her sisters were expert horsewomen, often riding with the hounds. Ida was the last surviving sibling and for many years before her death in 1954 (aged 83) she was actively involved at Newtown Church as organist, churchwarden and bell-ringer, in addition to indulging her passion for sailing with the Royal Solent Yacht Club.

Of all the church and chapel personalities, perhaps Hannah Woolgar holds pride of place. Born in 1808 at Cowes as Hannah Holbrook, granddaughter of one of Newtown's salt boilers, her family had returned to Newtown by the time her father Thomas died in 1814, when Hannah was only six years old. In 1834 she married James Woolgar, a Yarmouth man, and they probably moved immediately into the cottage opposite Newtown Church, bestowing their name upon it. They had three children, Henry James ('Jumbo'), Ellen Elizabeth and Frances Sarah, none of whom married. Before 1845 Hannah had become sextoness of the church, possibly its first, a position she held almost until her death in 1884. By 1840 she had opened Newtown's first school, probably a dame-school, in the Town Hall. Soon it became a branch of the National School, still with Hannah as teacher until the 1850s. By 1861 she had opened Newtown's only shop, selling small groceries and general provisions. At different times each of her daughters assisted in the shop, as did her son after his retirement in around 1885. Ellen was the last survivor, eventually closing the little shop in around 1916, by which time she was almost 80 years old.

Hannah Woolgar did not live to witness the decline of Newtown Church as the vicar's health failed, nor the troubled times of the 1930s. Despite many efforts – including the regular 'sales of work' by the Newtown and Porchfield working party (sponsored by Lady Laura Simeon and organised by the Misses Gibson and by Mrs Clements of Locks Green) – and the renewed optimism expressed by the rector in 1935 when he wrote in the *Church Messenger* that the refurbished Town Hall was to be available for church-sponsored social events, the role of the church in village life was in decline.

At the time of writing, for a variety of reasons, church and chapel are no longer so vital a part of village life. Younger generations, the lifeblood of any organisation, have moved towards the towns and, like the village school, the Post Office and the village shop before it, the village church and chapel have declined towards closure. Now, only the Anglican meetings at Newtown and Shalfleet survive, and a once-vibrant part of village life is in some danger of being lost for ever.

The Porchfield Chapel outing to Sandown, c.1922. Adults standing, left to right, include: *?, Mr Aldridge ('Natty Whiskers' to the kids), Mrs Aldridge, ?, Mrs Pettit, Mr Pettit, Charlie Holbrook (chimney-sweep), ?, Edwin Holbrook, Mrs Holbrook, Mrs Carrie Mew, Edward Mew (farmer, builder and undertaker);* on the back seat: *Elsie Lock, Minnie Cousins, Miss Rice, Alan Mew;* others include: *Mrs (blacksmith) Heal (in the dark coat seated in the charabanc) and Joe Osbourn (the child in front with his hands in his pockets).*

Chapter 4

From Shanks' Pony & Back: The Story of Local Transport

A modestly-priced motorcycle made an early appearance, in c.1919, at Locks Green. Charlie Heal, son of blacksmith Fred Heal, obtained one which quickly became a focus for village attention at the smithy. Fred, very nervous even on his push-bike, looked aghast when invited to ride pillion on the motorbike, especially with an audience anticipating entertainment. Neither Charlie nor Fred disappointed them! Fred, his face ashen, sat gingerly on the pillion but refused to lift both feet at the same time. Charlie, no doubt intent on making an impression, roared away leaving Fred standing bow-legged in a cloud of blue-grey smoke, much to the amusement of onlookers.

Herbie Foss on Bert Cutler's BSA motorbike in 1924.

Motorised transport was beginning to stretch the imagination of the local youth. Today personal mobility is taken for granted. Motor cars and public transport extend horizons almost without limit. In little more than a single lifespan there has been a revolution in the ways people move from place to place.

Prior to the coming of the railways to the Island in the latter part of the nineteenth century, most people had to rely on shanks' pony. The stagecoach was expensive and uncomfortable. The farm cart and the carrier's van were slower, and even more uncomfortable. The more affluent and the farmers rode their own horses or carriages, but, for the vast majority, walking was the only realistic option.

Perhaps there was less need to travel far. Communities tended to be more self-sufficient and, in earlier times, local and national laws of settlement inhibited movement. Parishes sought to limit calls upon their Poor Law funds by discouraging 'incomers'. Travel was physically difficult. In 1610 no fewer than 52 field gates needed to be negotiated between Yarmouth and Newport. From 1773, toll-gates became increasingly common on main routes. Similar tolls might have been charged at Newtown's two 'gates' – one in Town Gate Lane and the other at Causeway Bridge.

Daylight travel was the norm. Gravel trackways and muddy footpaths linked rural communities whilst, from 1813, the Highway Commissioners tried to maintain the roadways between larger towns, handing over to the newly established Isle of Wight County Council in 1890, which raised a highways rate to fund road maintenance. For many centuries, 'rights of way' were established in Britain by common usage of routes which circumnavigated boundaries and landholdings, giving rise to the characteristic twists and turns of the nation's tracks, paths and bridle-ways. Until the twentieth century most residents in the Newtown area tramped distances along these routes that only the more enthusiastic rambler would undertake for leisure in the twenty-first century.

Edwin Holbrook, carter, in Dirty Lane, Porchfield, c.1890.

In the 1880s Edwin Holbrook and Fred Fallick walked great distances during the mowing season. Fred, as a 12-year-old, jobbed for his grandfather who was in a mowing gang. They were often employed to cut corn on Apes Down, some four miles from home in Porchfield. Similarly, for a while, Edwin and his four brothers worked as a gang of grass mowers. They were paid at a rate per acre commensurate with the weight of the crop, and often worked five miles from home, starting out at 5a.m. and getting home at 8p.m.

Right: *The nineteenth-century pram belonging to Adela Foss, pictured in 1940.*

Below: *Edwin Holbrook, carrier, at Locks Green, c.1904.*

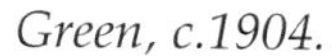

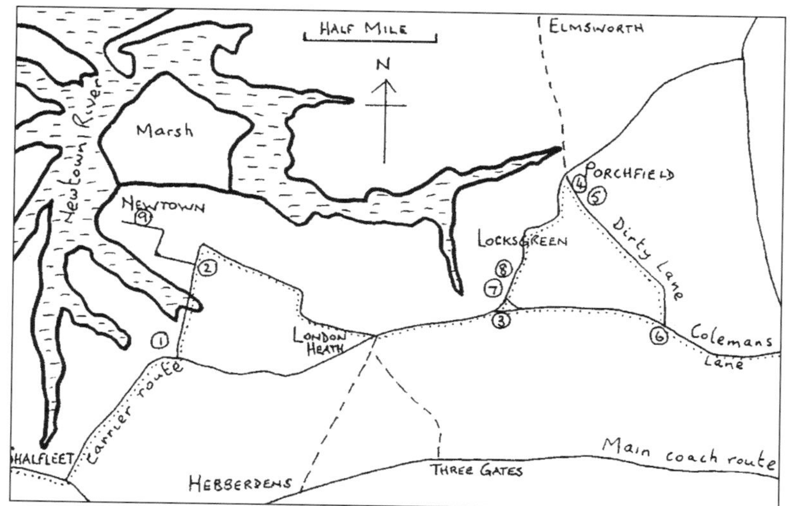

Carriers' routes and locations near Newtown. Indicated are: *1. Fleetlands Corner, 2. Noah's Ark, 3. Three Cocked Hat, 4. Sportsman's Rest, 5. Holbrook's garage, 6. Broomfield's Corner, 7. Locks Green smithy, 8. Wheeler's garage, 9. Huggins' garage.*

Edwin and Eva Holbrook, c.1917.

or rode horseback. Each kept a grand office and toured the district with pony and trap, in their capacities as rate collectors and Guardians.

Admirably, Pat Barton, who farms Harts Farm at Newtown at the time of writing, has, until very recently, maintained the tradition of the horse, occasionally using her palamino pony to take her trap along the lanes. She still grazes horses on her land.

Just as the coaches had bypassed the Newtown area, so, inevitably, did the railway. The Freshwater–Newport line, which opened in 1889 and closed in 1953, paid its closest call to Newtown at 'Calbourne and Shalfleet' Station, some two miles away from the village. A little further away, and available mainly for residents and visitors at Swainston, was Watchingwell Halt, where the train driver stopped only by prior arrangement. Mrs Cooper was clerk at Watchingwell, where the station was kept spotlessly clean for the local lord of the manor, and where candle lanterns from the station cottage were provided for late arrivals to light their lonely journeys home.

Watchingwell Station, originally built to serve Swainston Manor, as it was around 1950.

The bright, apple-green livery of the engines marked them out as belonging to the Isle of Wight Central Railway Company which, in 1902, was offering cheap return tickets to Newport Market each Wednesday and Saturday afternoon, and could boast that passengers leaving London Victoria on the 11.35a.m. express could connect to Calbourne and Shalfleet Station by 3.15p.m. For many years early in the twentieth century the stationmaster at Calbourne and Shalfleet Station was William Henley who was stone-deaf and relied heavily upon his wife to run the station efficiently. His successor in 1914 was Henry Bell.

The optimism of early railway pioneers was almost boundless. Whether or not the Central Railway Company, or its successor in 1923, the Southern Railway, managed to attract much trade from Newtown is left unrecorded, but at least one local family made use of the train to visit relations across Southern England. One trip took them to West Pennard, in the deepest part of rural Somerset, and involved changes of train and boat at Yarmouth, Lymington, Brockenhurst, Salisbury and Templecombe, before they joined their last connection at Evercreech Junction. Such determination matched that of the pioneers. Perhaps unkindly, it might be said that Newtown's closest contact with the railway age was the purchase, by a local resident in 1938, of coach 6369, a four-wheeled saloon carriage built in 1887 and used on the Island railways from 1924. Until the 1980s it stood in the grounds of Myrtle Cottage, near Newtown Church, and was used as a holiday cottage as well as an office for the river committee.

Not surprisingly, the relatively convenient alternative of travel by road became a great attraction. The 1920s marked the beginning of the golden age of motorised public transport, and many of the initiatives sprang from the ranks of existing carriers or from military drivers recently demobilised from the Forces following the First World War. A typical example involved the Freshwater–Newport omnibus route which, at first, was the nearest serving those Newtown residents willing and able to walk the lanes and fields to Three Gates.

Henry Hall, a Dorset man, was already involved in the West Wight carrier business by the early 1870s, and he was succeeded by his son Herbert. When Herbert's son, Hilton, learned the motor trade at Cheverton's in Newport (supplier of most Ford vans to the carriers), it was not long before his business became motorised, in around 1920. Fitted with fold-up seats, his carrier vans had developed a significant passenger business and soon Hilton had established a fully-fledged omnibus service, including the Freshwater–Newport route. His vans and buses all had a distinctive yellow livery, and former residents of the Newtown area still recall the bitter and sometimes dangerous competition that developed along this route between this and the rival red bus service of Captain Brown and his son Cecil, which began in 1925, as they quite literally raced for passenger business. Brown's buses were bought out by Southern Vectis in 1935 for almost £11,000.

With the release of suitable chassis after the First World War the rather more luxurious charabanc became very popular, hired for special occasions by clubs, societies, chapels and visitors alike. Round-the-Island charabancs from Fountain Garage at Cowes, the white 'Sandown Belle', and the coaches of the Coombes Brothers of Ventnor, regularly navigated the lanes through Locks Green and Porchfield. Few bus services to Newtown have ever been commercially viable, yet for some residents they have been a vital link with the rest of the Island. Run more for social benefit than as a profitable operation, Southern Vectis Service 19 served Porchfield and Newtown until around 1970. It was replaced successfully by the Post Bus for several years after 1974 and then by the Red Squirrel Community Bus, but a decision by Southern Vectis in the late 1980s to

The engine 'Freshwater' at Havenstreet Station in 1995. It is now owned by the Isle of Wight Steam Railway.

Calbourne and Shalfleet Station in 1951.

Newtown's Post Bus in the High Street in 1979.

(REPRODUCED WITH ACKNOWLEDGEMENT TO G.W. WATTS)

St James Square, Newport, c.1928.

Miss E. Sergeant outside her shop in Shalfleet, c.1890.

Shalfleet shop and Post Office, c.1950s.

reopen a service to Newtown using a double-decker bus, advertising it as a sight-seeing tour, met with considerable indignation and concern from local residents, not least due to the serious lopping of tree laterals that was required. At the time of writing, bus route No. 35 keeps Newtown in touch with Newport (via Thorness Bay), joined during the summer months by route 47 which picks up day-trippers from the Lymington–Yarmouth ferry as well.

Newtown's tenuous relationship with public transport is nothing new. Until well into the 1930s villagers found travel so difficult that it remained more common for tradesmen to come to the village than for villagers to travel to them. A combination of village 'all-sorts' shops and delivery services mitigated the problems of isolation. Rural communities have always relied to some extent on the 'travelling salesman' in one form or another, ranging from the pedlars and entertainers of the Middle Ages, through to the gypsies, the tallymen, and latterly the carters, carriers and delivery vans. Until the 1940s, Harold Higginbotham and, later, Harold Shepherd, were still serving the Newtown area as tallymen.

As early as 1318 the town was granted the right to hold a weekly market on Wednesdays and:

... a fair at the same place every year to last three days to wit... on the eve, on the day and on the morrow of St Mary Magdalene, unless such market and fair should be hurtful to neighbouring markets and neighbouring fairs.

The annual fair (or 'Newtown Randy') was held certainly until around 1781, possibly until the 1850s, and weekly markets continued until well into the nineteenth century, providing villagers with access to all manner of goods, services and entertainment, as well as a sales point for their own produce.

At one time the commercially thriving capital of the Island, Newtown's taxation list of 1379 (only two years after the French raids) still boasted three butchers, two tailors, two weavers, a baker and a smith in High Street alone. But such levels of prosperity were comparatively short-lived, and by the eighteenth century it is likely that Newtown had no more than a single shop.

Until the beginning of the twentieth century this tended to be the common pattern for most villages the size of Porchfield, Newtown or Shalfleet. From around 1840 Newtown's only shop (apart from the public house) was run by Hannah Woolgar in her cottage opposite the church. After her death her children, firstly James and then Ellen, ran it until its closure in 1915. The commercial risks surrounding such enterprises bore heavily on 'Jumbo' Woolgar in 1890, who was moved to write to the *County Press*, bemoaning the fact that he had laid in a special stock of ginger beer and ginger ale in anticipation of doing good business with members of the Hampshire Field Club who were visiting the area, but 'not one of the party patronised his establishment.'

For a few years during the 1920s, some very basic goods were sold from the Noah's Ark, the former public house (sugar, milk, cigarettes and the like), then 'Putty' Vincent, the Ventnor builder who had been engaged to demolish the former vicarage, and then built several bungalows in Old Vicarage Lane, himself opened Newtown's last shop from the front room of the bungalow facing on to Town Gate Lane. Like its predecessor, it was a small grocery store that sold 'other things', and probably generated little turnover until its demise in around 1960.

For many years from 1842, the Drake family ran the little village shop in Shalfleet in addition to their carrier's van. Built on fourteenth-century foundations, the shop seemed to cower behind the low parapet of the bridge over the Caul Bourne. Down a couple of steps from street level, and quaintly squashed into a tiny room, the shop sold a range of groceries, sweets, magazines and haberdashery. Miss Hillier and Miss E. Sergeant took over from the Drake family and they, in turn, passed the business on to Frank and Florence Gray, formerly of the Sportman's Rest at Porchfield. After Frank's death his wife ran the business until 1949. A jolly, rotund lady, Mrs Gray is reported to have had some difficulty wedging herself behind the counter. Miss Fletcher then took over the shop until its eventual closure in 1970. For some years around 1900, the little shop faced competition from another just around the corner in Mill Lane, especially when the latter obtained the Post Office contract. Although relocated, in 2004 Shalfleet still has a village stores and Post Office, the only one in the district, which is open several days each week.

Porchfield's only shop and Post Office closed in 1994. One of its earlier locations, Brook Cottage, somewhat predictably got washed away in storms in 1875 as Rodge Brook turned into a raging torrent. It was run in the 1850s by Isaac Arnold (who later built the Sportsman's Rest), and then from the 1860s by Luke 'Posky' Saunders and his wife Hannah, who were there at the time of the flood. They then moved 'up the hill' to a newly constructed shop on the other side of the brook, built by the Mew family builders and later called Port Vale.

Luke was a turnip hoer for much of the year, but also kept a donkey and a small cart which he took each week to Newport to replenish the shop's supplies. By 1901, Frank Bennett and his wife Hannah were there as bakers and grocers, and E.W. Mew had taken it over by 1915, still running it as a bakery and grocery, calling it 'Kirkees Stores' and publishing postcards of the area. The district's first public telephone was installed at the shop in 1919.

The village has recently regained its Post Office services, available part of each week from a private residence.

Porchfield's village shop (Port Vale) in 1930. The Congregational Church can be seen in the distance.

The 'all-sorts' shops tried to provide for most everyday needs, but increasingly sophisticated demands and choices outstripped their ability to compete. In a booklet he wrote in the mid-1890s, just before he died, 'Jumbo' Woolgar bemoaned the competition in Newtown:

> *Some visitors tell me I have no opposition, there being no other shop in the place, but I can tell them they are mistaken; men come from Newport and take orders, and every fortnight a grocer's van, well loaded, comes into the place from Newport. I keep my shop-board up all the same, and if my trade is small... why, then I keep the board up, like some poultry dealers say, just for a hobby.*

In all probability the van he referred to belonged either to Jordan & Stanley or to Upward and Rich (later to become Wray & Sons), each of them large provisions merchants. During the 1920s Newtown residents also made use of the delivery services of Mundon (Newport) and Dear & Morgan (Cowes) for their groceries. Many also bought a ton of coal each August from Weeks, the coal merchants of Calbourne. All delivery vans were initially horse-drawn, but from around 1910 they were increasingly motorised, much like those of Wray & Sons. These specialised 'carriers' were in direct competition with the country carriers, and it is no surprise that Fred Wray was instrumental in trying to move the carriers out of St Thomas Square, Newport, in 1933.

Jordan & Stanley also delivered to Shalfleet, as did Hibberds of Carisbrooke, whilst Fryer's meat and Mills' bakery products came from Yarmouth.

In nineteenth-century Newtown, animal supplies such as meal and corn feed were delivered by Guy's of Newport, and carters sometimes delivered the likes of stone, hurdles, hay and firewood faggots. Several other horse-drawn vans delivered in the area soon after the turn of the century. The Porchfield baker, Mr Bennett, delivered bread and flour at least twice each week and Mr Whillier from Newbridge had a bread-delivery round in the area. Mr Buckler delivered from the Shalfleet bakery which was opposite the mill, up to which the wheat-laden barges used to sail. He was the Sunday-School superintendent at Shalfleet, and often delivered bread to poor people despite their inability to pay.

Mains electricity did not reach Newtown until 1960, and only then due to the initiatives of the farmer at London Farm. (Mains gas is still not available there in 2004.) Before that people relied on candles and oil-lamps. Almost from its inception in 1883, Walter Neat's shop, of Lower St James Street in Newport, sent its horse and van around the area delivering paraffin and ironmongery, and the Wednesday-morning round (by then motorised) was still running during the 1940s. In 1936, one resident purchased a large lamp from the van for 13s.6d., and the following year bought a Beatrice stove for 7s.3d.

Once each week Reynolds, a butcher in Newport, delivered to Newtown. There was also a Newport fishmonger who visited the area weekly, often bartering bloaters for rabbits which he hung all the way around his van. In addition, until the 1950s, the villagers relied heavily on the all-purpose country carrier to bring in their shopping needs. But already, in the early years of the twentieth century, the seeds of a more independent existence for many families were being sown. As early as 1905, Frank Cheverton had seen it coming and, despite there being only 17 motor vehicles on the Island at the time, had opened a motor department at his cycle stores in Lugley Street in Newport. The motor car and the motorcycle were soon to provide villagers with much more frequent access to the towns and much less dependence on deliveries.

When Daimler and Benz invented their petrol-driven internal-combustion engines in the mid-1880s and fitted them, respectively, to a bicycle and to a four-wheeled carriage, they can have had little idea of their potential impact on people's lives. Around 30 years later the mass production of the motor car and motor bike was under way.

The advantages of speed, convenience, access and mobility all caught the public's imagination. Many people returned from the First World War with driving skills, and others soon bought their own private vehicles. Until the Road Traffic Act of 1930 no driving test was required for persons aged 18 years or over and motor licences could be purchased for 5s. But during the war years young men were in short supply, and it was this condition that led Herbert Foss to his first driving job. Wray & Sons was short of drivers, and their female driver had lost her nerve when she overturned the delivery vehicle near Whitecroft. Herbert, 15 years old and an apprentice at the firm, was drafted in illegally. At first, Fred Wray drove the van to the edge of Newport before sending Herbert on his delivery rounds into the

Wray's delivery driver, Herbert Foss, aged 15, 1917.

The motorised van of Neat Brothers Ironmongery, c.1928.

countryside, but this precaution was soon abandoned. Within a few weeks, a jilted girlfriend reported Herbert's activities to the police and he and his employers were duly fined 5s. but, on special pleading, he was allowed to continue driving the delivery van!

One day, with his pal Bill Price lying flat on the floor of the Model T Ford trying to focus on the wavering needle of the speedometer (which was set into the floor near the gear change), they roared and shook down Blackwater Shute, near Newport and, with the engine complaining loudly and the body threatening to part company with the chassis, they managed to top 32 miles per hour!

The expense of motor cars and the cost of petrol, which was 4s.3½d. a gallon in 1920, allied to rural conservatism, probably delayed their arrival in the Newtown area. One of the first, in the late 1920s, was the magnificent bull-nosed Morris Cowley owned by Walter Lock of Elmsworth Farm. The registration plate (DL 2577) indicated the growing popularity of motoring on the Island. A few years later Sir Hanson Rowbotham garaged his Model T at Marsh Farm.

The difficulties of travel persisted in the Newtown area much later than in most other places. This was a mixed blessing; access to choice places of employment, entertainment and social interaction were restricted, but at the same time the Newtown area was protected from rapid change. Home-grown social and communal activities survived here longer than in many other places and deep into the twentieth century many people continued to be reared, married and buried a short distance from their birthplace. For centuries Newtown's residents could be said to have suffered as a result of their isolation. In a peculiar reversal of fortunes, local residents and bodies such as the National Trust now seek to limit access to and from the area in order to protect it from the more damaging effects that motor transport might inflict.

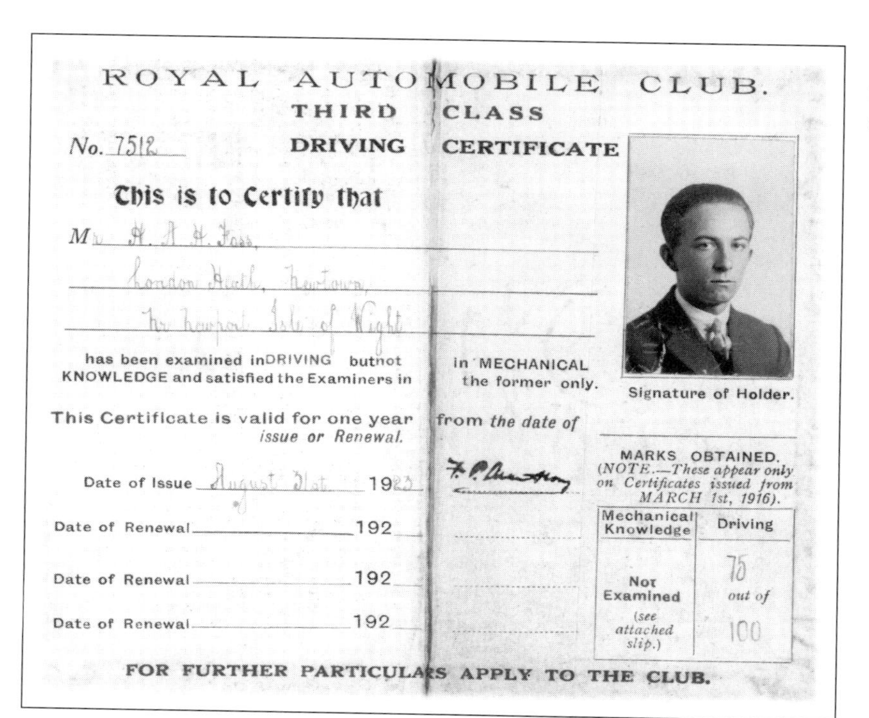

ROYAL AUTOMOBILE CLUB.
THIRD CLASS
No. 7512 DRIVING CERTIFICATE

This is to Certify that

Mr H. A. H. Foss
London Heath, Newtown,
Nr Newport Isle of Wight

has been examined in DRIVING but not in MECHANICAL KNOWLEDGE and satisfied the Examiners in the former only.

Signature of Holder.

This Certificate is valid for one year from the date of issue or Renewal.

Date of Issue August 31st 1923

Date of Renewal 192

Date of Renewal 192

Date of Renewal 192

MARKS OBTAINED.
(NOTE.—These appear only on Certificates issued from MARCH 1st, 1916).

Mechanical Knowledge	Driving
Not Examined (see attached slip.)	75 out of 100

FOR FURTHER PARTICULARS APPLY TO THE CLUB.

This 1923 RAC test and certificate was not compulsory but could assist job applications.

Sarah 'Sally' Lock at Elmsworth Farm, c.1926.

Chapter 5

'Look, Duck & Vanish': Seafarers & Military Men

Robert Lock's sadly prophetic note *(below)*, written hastily in pencil in September 1939 to his employer James Ball, placed him among a long tradition of young men from the Newtown district who have sought adventure in naval or military service. Over the years, many looked towards the sea as a source of employment, whether directly, as crew on trading vessels or as fishermen in local waters, or more indirectly, as stevedores, shipwrights, coastguards, or in a myriad other supportive roles. Some used the proximity of Portsmouth and Southampton to enroll into the Merchant Marine or the Royal Navy. Others viewed these places as ports of emigration.

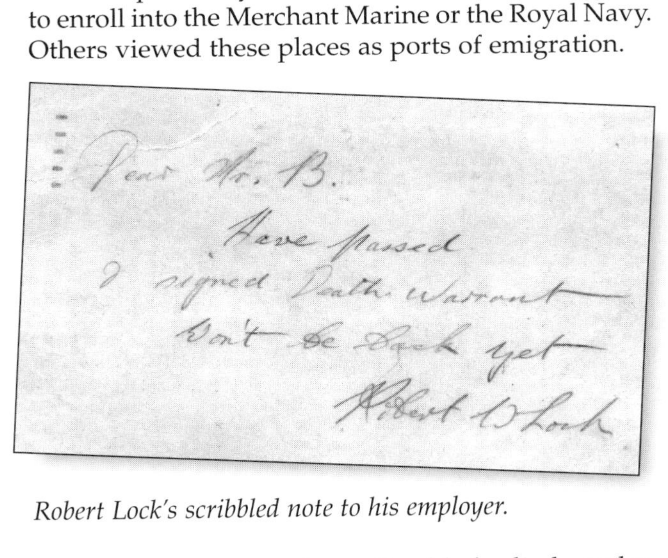

Dear Mr. B.
Have passed
& signed Death Warrant
Don't be back yet
Robert W Lock

Robert Lock's scribbled note to his employer.

For many centuries, all able-bodied males, especially those living near the sea, were vulnerable to the attentions of the press-gang, particularly during the wars with France and Spain. Before 1836, when the press-gang was replaced with the offer of bounties, victims disappeared without trace, impressed to serve in the Army or Navy, and only occasionally to return to their families many years later.

Many others joined the armed services voluntarily, each for their own reasons, whether that was loss of other employment, sense of adventure, or perhaps, as in the case of Robert Lock, to escape a family dispute. Robert Woodman Lock was born in 1875, the eldest child of Robert 'Peter' Lock, tenant-farmer at Calbourne Lodge Farm, then, for many years, at Elmsworth Farm. Robert 'Peter' Lock had always seemed to favour his younger son, Walter Hillier Lock, and this was a source of friction in the family. Following a particularly fierce argument and a thrashing from his father, Robert Woodman Lock left home and took lodgings with Mrs Ridett in Porchfield, odd-jobbing for a year before, at the age of 19, joining the Royal Marines at Eastney Barracks, Portsmouth – probably a 'bolt-hole' for many young men from Newtown and Porchfield over the years.

HM Yacht Osborne *passing along the Suez Canal, c.1904.*

After training in field combat, musketry and sea gunnery, Robert soon found himself aboard HMS *Powerful* en route to the Boer War in South Africa, where he landed on 19 October 1899 with the naval brigade attached to the Kimberley Relief Force. He took part in all four actions fought by that brigade, including Belmont, Modder River and Mogersfontein, and, transferring to headquarters ship HMS *Doris*, saw further action at Paardeburg, Driefontein, Johannesburg and Diamond Hill.

The return to England took two months aboard the SS *Lake Erie* and in 1901 Robert received the first of many service medals, the South African Medal and seven clasps, together with the princely grant of £5. He soon became batman to an officer serving on board the Royal Yachts *Osborne* (1901–08) and *Alexandra* (1908–14), and sailed to the far corners of the Empire. Then, after a year aboard HMS *Amethyst*, Robert was posted to Deal (Kent) to instruct Royal Marine recruits until 1919 when he was demobilised.

Unlike his son who died in the Second World War, Robert survived his service years unscathed with the exception of an accident which left him with a deformed finger. He could boast a distinguished career in the armed services which lasted 23 years, somewhat longer than the naval career of the man whose son was to marry Robert's eldest daughter!

Henry Foss was born in 1859 at a saltern cottage which stood at the mouth of Newtown River. Like his forefathers he was, at first, employed in the

HM Yacht Alexandra, *on which Robert Lock served.*

Robert Woodman Lock, RM, 1904, in Malta.

orchards on the Swainston estate. Later he maintained the banks around Newtown Marsh.

It is not clear what made him enlist into the Royal Navy in 1884. His eldest sibling, Thomas, had volunteered for the Isle of Wight Volunteer Artillery Militia in 1871, at the age of 17, so he must have had some idea of the military opportunities open to him. The mix of self-employed shell-fishing each summer and uncertain estate work each winter was always a precarious source of income, and Henry might have sought greater security. The estate was facing economic difficulties during the 1880s and employment may have been restricted. Or he may have been influenced by his cousin Ambrose Foss who, in 1883, had returned to Newtown having been invalided out of the Navy after serving only half of a ten-year engagement.

Ambrose had served as a stoker on several ships, including two brief periods on HMS *Asia*, the same ship that Henry joined as a stoker in March 1884. Ambrose had been aged only 16 when he enlisted, so he had lied about his age in order to obtain a man's rate of pay. He probably advised Henry to do the same, except that in his case he was too old to enlist, so he provided an easily remembered false date of birth, 1 April 1862.

Henry, a thick-set man of five feet seven inches, with a ruddy complexion, red hair and piercing blue eyes, thus became Stoker Foss aboard the 3,594 gross tons HMS *Asia* of the Guard Ship Reserve, the flagship to the Admiral Superintendent, Portsmouth. Gone was the salty, fresh air of Newtown Marsh, the wide-open spaces, the cry of the seabirds, and the self-determined lifestyle. In its place were the cramped conditions of the engine-room, the heat, dirt and howling din, deep in the bowels of an iron-clad warship where he shovelled coal. Who was the April Fool now?

Henry did not find it to his liking. In desperation, and using a classic military escape method, he consumed large quantities of soap which not only caused violent sickness but also gave him a deathly pallor. He was moved to Haslar Hospital at Gosport and was soon discharged from the service as medically unfit, barely six months after his enlistment. He was even given a small pension!

Henry returned to spend the rest of his life at London Heath, but in some ways he was an exception. Military service was always available as an alternative to local employment, and the nineteenth century saw an enormous growth in Britain's naval power and the development of its colonies. These opportunities for employment, travel and resettlement appealed to more than one young resident of the area. For example, the period 1852–72 saw several younger members of the parish volunteer to join the Isle of Wight Volunteer Artillery Militia, each enlisting at a particular centre. These included:

1852	*William Christmas, 19*	*Calbourne*
1858	*Henry Manning, 23*	*Calbourne*
1860	*Jacob Parsons, 17*	*Newtown*
1861	*Andrew Barton, 18*	*Calbourne*
1861	*George Barton, 18*	*Calbourne*
1863	*John Hayward, 17*	*Calbourne*
1865	*Henry Harding, 17*	*Calbourne*
1866	*Edward Rogers, 24*	*Calbourne*
1866	*Frank Greenen, 17*	*Calbourne*
1866	*Robert Burt, 19*	*Calbourne*
1869	*Henry Saunders, 26*	*Calbourne*
1869	*William Holbrook, 17*	*Porchfield*

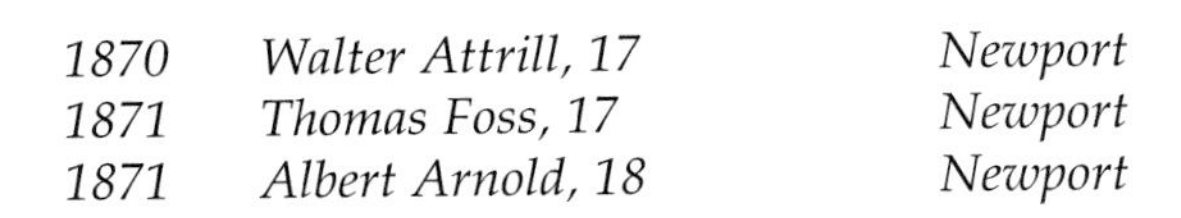

1870	*Walter Attrill, 17*	*Newport*
1871	*Thomas Foss, 17*	*Newport*
1871	*Albert Arnold, 18*	*Newport*

Henry Ford spent many years in the Royal Marines, seeing active service in Russia and Crimea before returning to act as farmer for the widowed Mrs Rice at Locks Farm prior his retirement to London Heath around 1896. He used to amuse the local children on their way to school by feigning the role of sergeant-major and getting them to march up the lane. William Holbrook, from Porchfield, joined at the age of 19 in 1869 and was soon posted overseas. He eventually returned home 16 years later, after taking part in various actions in Egypt and the Sudan, including the failed attempt to relieve General Gordon at Khartoum.

Others left for good. Arthur Foss found his first employment as a cowboy at Elmsworth Farm, but during the depressed years of the 1880s he left London Heath to emigrate to Sydney, Australia, and never contacted his family again. As job opportunities became scarcer, many local young men were attracted by the exciting prospects of emigration, including several of the Fallick family who went, variously, to Australia and South Africa. At home fewer trading and fishing vessels were based at Newtown, the salt industry was declining, and mechanisation was taking its toll on the agricultural workforce. But Newtown still provided a living from the sea for a significant number of its residents.

The main town quay was originally located just inside Causeway Creek, directly accessible from High Street through Key Close and from Gold Street through Silver Street, and it remained in use until the latter years of the nineteenth century. The *Post Office Directory* of 1852 records that ships of up to 50 tons could still berth there. Little evidence of the quays now remains, although there is a distinct shingle 'hard' on the beach, and elderly residents can remember the rotting timbers of a large vessel beached near the spot in the early 1900s. Among the last using the quay was the *Wellington*, the last trading vessel working out of Newtown. It was a smack, a fore and aft-rigged, one-masted vessel, carrying a jib, fore-staysail, mainsail, and gaff topsail, and was moored opposite Newtown Saltern. Other trading vessels carrying stone, salt, bricks, corn, timber, animal feed-stuffs and coal included the *Dove*, the *Weevil*, the *Houghton* and the SS *Arrow*.

In addition to the trading vessels and fishing smacks, the Haven was alive with 'rivermen' going about their business. The Swainston estate operated a number of barges and lighters (shallow draught, flat-bottomed boats often used for transferring goods from ship to wharf). Estate books of 1878 record the payment of 1s. per ton to Henry Foss and Ernie Seagar for unloading six tons of shingle at Shalfleet Quay. In 1873 Jonas Foss received £1.1s.8d. for ten days' work tarring a lighter. One lighter was also used to transport materials for maintaining the banks around Newtown Marsh, and was moored at the Marsh Saltern Quay. A similar lighter was used by the Prangnells well into the twentieth century to transport supplies from Causeway Bridge to their remote home at Lower Elmsworth.

In addition to the main quays at Newtown and Shalfleet, smaller quays were scattered all around the estuary. Where neither quays nor hards were available smaller boats were moored on 'whips' – running lines reaching from the bank to a post and pulley offshore. A few people went to the expense of building their own pier. The Revd Henry Rice Venn, Newtown's vicar from 1878, had one constructed at the bottom of Anley's Lane. The piles on which the pier was built are still visible daily in 2004 at low tides.

Nineteenth-century Newtown still tended to look seawards for much of its livelihood. Civil and ecclesiastical returns for the period are full of references to fishermen, mariners and coastguards. The following are some sample extracts from the census returns:

1851 *Mariners included Thomas Abrook, Henry Abrook, Henry Jacobs, Thomas Henry Foss, William Abrook, George Abrook, William Abrook (junr), Alford Prince, John Millmore, John Millmore (junr) and James Millmore. Fishermen included Jonas and James Foss.*

1881 *Mariners included William Abrook, Thomas Abrook, Harry Abrook, Albert Southcott, James Holbrook and Harry Hollins. Fishermen included Jonas Foss, Henry Foss, Henry Jacobs. Others included Thomas Holbrook (ship's mate), George Lock (ship's boy), Edwin Mursell (manager of oyster fishery) and James Roach (ship's mate).*

Also, in 1881, many other local men (listed here with their ages, places of origin, job and vessel) were at sea or in foreign ports with the Royal Navy, including:

John Hodge, 17 (Newtown)	*boy 1st class on* Achilles
Charles H. Cornish, 20 (Shalfleet)	*carpenter's crew on* Bacchante
Ambrose Foss, 24 (Newtown)	*stoker on* Gannet
Charles William Ford, 23 (Portsfield) [sic]	*stoker on* Gannet
William A. Snook, 25 (Newtown)	*sick-bay attendant on* Malabar
John G. Levers, 21 (Newtown)	*able-bodied seaman on* Minotaur
Frederick Bennett, 22 (Shalfleet)	*able-seaman on* Superb
Frederick Hire, 36 (Newtown)	*navigating Lt on* Tyne
G. Collins, 36 (Shalfleet)	*ship's cook on* Warrior

A London barge (known as a yawl), common in Newtown Haven.

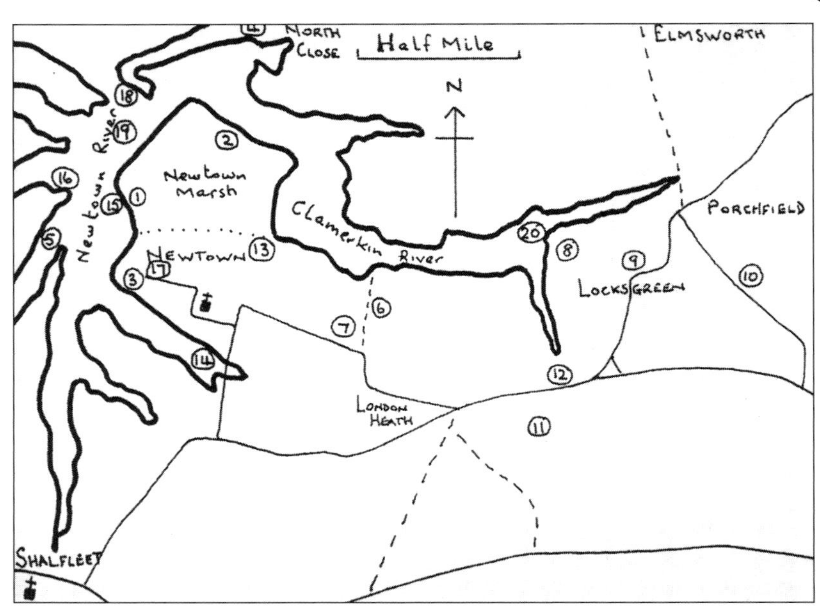

Locations influenced by the military presence around Newtown Haven. Indicated are: *1. Newtown Saltern, 2. Marsh Saltern, 3. original Town Quay, 4. brickyard, 5. Ningwood River, 6. Anley's Lane, 7. Town Copse, 8. rifle-range, 9. Locks Farm, 10. Bible Christian Chapel, 11. St Hubert's Lodge, 12. Clamerkin Bridge, 13. Promised Land, 14. Causeway Hard, 15. present Town Quay, 16. Lower Hamstead Quay, 17. the coastguard station, 18. Elmsworth Saltern Quay, 19. oyster pond, 20. Locks Hard.*

The Prangnells' lighter at Causeway Hard, c.1890.

Nineteenth-century coastguards. (Reproduced courtesy of the Isle of Wight County Record Office)

In the 1830s Newtown could boast only 14 inhabited residences and a population of 68. By 1871 the population had risen to 113 (in 28 dwellings) with many of the men shown as having an association with the sea (albeit several being retired or unemployed mariners). But by the 1890s, quite suddenly, this strong association with the sea as a source of employment had been lost. Future use of the Haven was increasingly for leisure, though Colonel Kindersley and Jack Boswell kept the maritime traditions going by running the Shalfleet Sea Scouts well into the 1920s.

The location of a strong force of coastguards at Newtown, who also acted as preventive officers, reflected the amount of trading and fishing traffic in the Haven. It also addressed the problem of smuggling, which had become big business along the South Coast since the seventeenth century. In 1804 a tub-boat was seized off Newtown attempting to smuggle 270 four-gallon casks of alcohol.

The view in 1995 south-west from Newtown's former quay – a poignant reminder of maritime decline.

A favoured craft for smuggling was the galley, a rowing-boat taking up to 40 men, which could often escape pursuit by naval cutters or luggers by heading into the wind. (A law of 1721 limited rowing-boats to six oars in an attempt to reduce the trade!) The Coastguard Service was formed in 1831 and, significantly, adopted the galley as their favoured craft. The local galley was moored off the Newtown Saltern. By 1836 nine new coastguard stations had been built or planned on the Island, ending the smugglers' heyday. Newtown's station was completed by 1840, providing accommodation for five families. With as many as seven officers (in addition to the chief boatman) still in service as late as 1916, numbers had outgrown the purpose-built station and several coastguards had to be tenanted with their families in nearby cottages. When the station closed in the early 1920s the Mustchin and Huggins families were among the first residents of the cottages, followed by the Gibson sisters.

The coastguards had a big impact on the area, not only in curbing the smuggling trade but also in keeping the local school open. Up to 22 coastguards' children attended Locks Green School at any one time out of a school roll that varied from 40 to around 100.

They also made their marks in other ways. The *Isle of Wight Observer* newspaper carried a report on 11 June 1864 which read as follows:

Serious Accident: On Thursday a Coastguardsman named Westlake residing at Newtown, who had been on duty at a place called Sticlet [sic], *when on his return home a loaded pistol which he carried in the waist of his trousers, accidentally went off, and the ball which the weapon contained entered the thick part of his left leg, going in on one side and out of the other. No one being near, the poor fellow tore off a portion of his clothes in an endeavour to stop the bleeding, and walked across two fields for assistance. Fortunately, two brothers named Foss were cruising in the river, and noticing the poor fellow staggering went to his assistance. They put him in the boat and conveyed him at once to the Station, and after some delay succeeded in obtaining the services of Dr Gibson. Although he is very seriously injured great hopes are entertained that his life will be spared.*

Dr Gibson had to travel from Cowes to attend to the wounded man. One of the brothers, Thomas Henry Foss, a riverman, was drowned in the Haven in 1870.

Local mariners, among them Henry Foss, were not altogether impressed with the seamanship of the coastguards, referring to them as 'gobbies' (short for 'gobbaloon', a somewhat less-than-complimentary term for American sailors). The origin of Henry's contempt dated back to around 1908 when the residents of Newtown organised a regatta and he was invited to join the crew of the coastguard galley, which was pitted against several other nominally slower craft. The galley contrived to come in last, much to Henry's disgust. In later years he was constantly reminded of this ignominy by the local wits as he tried to manoeuvre the same galley single-handedly whilst working on the banks. His Swainston employers had bought it from the coastguards as a replacement for their ageing lighter!

Like many places around the Island's coast, Newtown had its share of smugglers. In the later years of the eighteenth century a primary route for contraband passed through Three Gates. No doubt some local miscreants finished up serving time in the Fleet Prison for running contraband goods, as did Thomas Willis of Shalfleet in 1823. But a custodial sentence was preferable to the fate that befell others, related by Paul Hyland in his book *Wight: Biography of an Island*. The coastguard preventive men once ambushed a group of smugglers at Clamerkin Bridge and shot two dead; another two, who ran, were caught at Newtown and sentenced to be transported; others escaped, but returned to murder their informer!

It was not a particularly violent community but gun ownership was widespread and most families had at least a shotgun, mainly for shooting birds or rabbits to augment their larders. In addition to the formal 'shoots' for pheasants arranged on the lands of the Swainston estate, there were regular pigeon-shoots for local farmers and others. One such day of sport in 1910 was arranged near his home (St Hubert's Lodge) by the head gamekeeper Fred Fallick who bought in 200 birds from a dealer in Charlotte Street, Portsmouth. In an account written in 1955 Fred recalled:

Of course there were quite a few people staggering home that evening as there were quite a few old-stagers that had a wonderful sense of smell when there were certain drinks going free. I remember that one of those was a coastguard from Newtown. Someone came after him because he was supposed to be on duty, and when going across the fields towards London Heath he got down and held on to the grass. Someone else had to do his duty that night!

But these breaches of the peace were slight compared to the upheavals that afflicted the area in earlier times. Newtown Haven was a natural point of attack for all marauding forces, whether pirates or foreign invaders. Indeed, the Island itself was always vulnerable to such intrusions, so from very early times some form of local militia was organised.

From around 1100 the Norman feudal system was based around the notion of 'service', whereby each tenant-in-chief had to provide a specified number of armed and mounted knights equipped to serve the king for 40 days each year. Even when this system was replaced by a professional army, the local militia was mobilised at times of emergency like that in 1335 (in anticipation of the Hundred Years War with France) when all Islanders between the ages of 15 and 60 were called to arms.

The first English system of warning beacons was established around the Island in 1324 (almost certainly including one at the mouth of Newtown Haven), and by 1370 Thomas Cheke of Mottistone was in command of a local defence force for an area that included Newtown. Its failure to protect the town from the devastation wrought by the French in 1377, and subsequent fears of further invasion, no doubt led to attempts to strengthen defences. Almost 200 years later, fearful of Spanish aggression, Richard Worsley, Captain of the Island, armed the militia and reorganised it into ten 'centons' each with 150–200 men, and equipped every parish with a cannon. Newtown's nearest protection was the cannon at Shalfleet Church!

By the 1580s, fear of an invasion by the Spanish had reached such a level that out of an Island population of around 10,000 no fewer than 1,856 were listed as armed officers and men, among them 1,158 musketeers, 109 archers, 116 pikemen and 473 men with halberds or bills. The Island Captain, Sir George Carey, was offering prizes for skills with muskets, bows, pikes and halberds. Even after the scuttling of the Armada (1588) rumours of invasion persisted, with wild stories of armed Persian elephants and poisoned bullets!

From 1757 until 1829, Parliament required each parish constable to draw up lists of able-bodied men between the ages of 18 and 45. From this list ballots were drawn by the Lieutenant Governor of the Island to identify those who should serve in the parish militia. A similar list for the parish of Calbourne has survived, dated 1803, and Arthur Barker's analysis shows that out of a total population of 741 there were five officers and 130 other ranks eligible for service. The officers were:

Sir John Barrington, Lieutenant of Division (in overall command)
Fitzwilliam Barrington, Central Commissary (supply officer)
John Blake, Captain of Volunteers
Richard Dalimore, Captain of Waggoners
Lieutenant Thomas Wingate, Royal Navy

Other ranks included 76 volunteers (foot-soldiers), 9 pioneers, 5 pikemen, 5 horsemen, 6 wagoners, 2 bargemen, 3 cattle drivers, and 24 drivers (of pack-horses). Only 21 men had firearms. William Heal, the blacksmith, had to make do with a billhook! There were four aged 15 – Andrew Pragnell, Isaac Urry, John Pitman and James Blanchard.

After 1829, service in these militias became truly voluntary, and they eventually took the form of the Territorial Army. The Isle of Wight Rifles Battalion was formed as a volunteer force in 1859, specifically for the defence of the Island. A small group of its members saw some service in the Boer War. The Territorial Army was formed in 1907 and the Island's volunteer force took the title 'Princess Beatrice's Isle of Wight Rifles, 8th Battalion the Hampshire Regiment'. From around 1911 the volunteers attended weekend camps under canvas at Newtown Rifle Range, each man receiving an annual bounty of £5, a very welcome addition to their income. The battalion served with distinction at Gallipoli and in Egypt and Palestine during the First World War, later (in 1937) being transformed into a heavy artillery brigade. The Newport-based section, which included men from Newtown, manned the Island's western coastal batteries during the Second World War, including that at Bouldnor. The battalion was eventually disbanded in 1967.

The Hampshire Territorial Forces Association bought 'the soil of Clamerkin and the land of North Close, excepting the oyster rights' from the Swainston estate in around 1910, for £6,700, and the Army made a big impact on the Newtown and Porchfield area from this time requisitioning the field at Locks Green known as Seaclose and developing on it a rifle-range, taking in also all the land at the

Newtown Rifle Range in 1912.

Isle of Wight Rifles in camp at Locks Green, 1913.

seaward side of Clamerkin River. As a result, the tenant farmers in the area – the Locks at Elmsworth, the Prangnells at Lower Elmsworth brickyard, and the Hawkins family at Lambsleaze – enjoyed reduced rents as compensation for the disruption caused whilst firing took place, although the Smiths at North Close had to abandon their farmstead altogether. (The Ministry of Defence still owns some 800 acres at North Close at the time of writing.)

A permanent camp was established in huts and tents, and various regiments – Regulars and Territorials – spent time in residence. The warden's house was soon built and Captain Pirie became first warden, succeeded by Mr Williams.

There were two targets (A and B), one on each bank of the river, with a wooden bridge linking them near Locks Hard. Warning flags were flown at various locations from Shepherds Hill, East Point and Hummet Wood. Nearby was the ominously named Coffin Copse! Local residents recollect that stray bullets whistled overhead at the end of Anley's Lane, some 90 degrees off target!

Such a large influx of men was bound to influence this quiet corner of the Island. Mrs Heal, the blacksmith's wife, did a roaring trade in the provision of cream teas. Porchfield residents faced disruption to their traditional journeys to go shell-fishing at Slinks Bay. And more than one innocent delivery-boy had the fright of his life when challenged with a rifle to state whether he was friend or foe!

A local farmer's daughter, Elsie Lock, recollected the time when the household was woken by a forlorn Irishman who had become lost on his way back to camp after experiencing the social delights of Newport. 'I came up the road and I didn't!' he lamented.

A few of the soldiers added to the problems of Fred Fallick, head gamekeeper for the Swainston estate. The temptation to enrich their diet with pheasant or rabbit sometimes proved too great and there were several confrontations and not a little enterprise from both sides. On one occasion Fred confiscated a gun from a soldier at Clamerkin Bridge and invited him to collect it the day he was posted. This he duly did, and was promptly invited in for tea! The two men regularly corresponded for many years following the incident! On another occasion Dave Angell, Fred's assistant, stumbled across an ingenious military poacher in the very act of inspecting his traps. At this time, around 1914, the estate bought in large loads of barley rakings and left mounds of it in the woods for the pheasants to rake over. Fred later recounted the story:

The soldier had made five or six little paper frockets (stiff brown paper) the shape of a spin top, only longer, and inside he had quite a bit of bird lime or a similar sticky make-up, and well rubbed on around the inside of the little paper, and a few corns put in the bottom, the idea being that when the bird put his head in after the corns the paper bag, which was just the right size, would stick on its head and the bird would be like a cat with its head in a lobster tin.

A military band at Newtown Camp in June 1912.
(Reproduced courtesy of Isle of Wight County Record Office)

Fred was also the unwitting reason for a marked increase in the size of the congregations at the Porchfield Bible Christian Chapel where he worshipped. A few soldiers attended the services regularly and one day Fred and his wife Fanny invited some home to St Hubert's Lodge for a meal. Inevitably, the story spread rapidly around the camp and dozens of young hopefuls descended on the chapel in the succeeding weeks!

The camp also provided some level of additional civilian employment, although not always involving the local residents. At Christmas in 1909 Fred Fallick and his assistant keepers, John Summerfield, Harry Smith and Jim Barton, caught two night-time poachers, Walter Reynard and Charley Harvey, and frog-marched them to Newport police station arriving at 3.30a.m. Because of their previous records for poaching they were each sentenced to six months in prison, but almost immediately upon their release they obtained work at the rifle-range, lodging at Locks Farm. Sure enough, within weeks they were disturbed by farmer Walter Smith's three sons whilst using ferrets and long nets to poach rabbits at North Close, and soon began a new six-month term of imprisonment.

The camp also accommodated young cadets in training, a welcome source of recruitment and local employment. Sending a picture postcard to his sister in Ventnor in 1912, one young recruit observed: 'i am sorry i keep you wating so long with at righing i have been to bessy i have not had time. i have got Sir little poney to look hafter.'

Red Cross nurses learn semaphor at Locks Green Camp, 1915.

During the war years in particular, groups such as the Red Cross used the camp to prepare staff for service on the Western Front where, as well as making the most of their nursing skills, they were expected to complete other tasks such as driving and signalling.

Inevitably, there was a darker side to the area's involvement with the military. The memorials at Porchfield and Shalfleet bear witness to the terrible toll on these little communities taken at the killing fields of Flanders, Gallipoli and elsewhere. Young, innocent men rushed to join the Forces. Soldiers like Frederick James Fallick survived the First World War, as did Charlie Heal, son of the local blacksmith, who joined the Navy and saw service at Scapa Flow before establishing his gunsmithing business in Newport. But recently-married Henry Prangnell from Lower Elmsworth brickyard perished, as did 'Harry' Sanders of London Heath who died at Arras, and comrades-in-arms in the Isle of Wight Rifles Charles Barton of Shalfleet and O.C. Harding of Watchingwell, each a victim of the disastrous engagement at Gallipoli in August 1915. Newtown Church contains a brass memorial to Major Howard Graeme Gibson RAMC, son of a sea captain who lived at Anchor Cottage, who died from his wounds at Abbeville a few months after the war ended. At least nine other local men died in the hostilities, including Leonard Punch, grandson of Porchfield's cobbler, and Bertie Bennett, son of the village baker and grocer.

Many returned from their war experiences as broken men, damaged for life. Others sought peace in quiet places like Newtown Haven. Ernest Sowerbutts was one such man, who came to be known as the 'Crusoe' of Shalfleet Creek. Witness to the most appalling events in his role as spy behind enemy lines, he chose to live most of the time in a small dinghy moored in the shadow of a maple tree. A gentle, thoughtful soul, he was befriended by local folk like Tom Mussell and the young Jack Barton, until his sudden death in 1930.

Ernest Sowerbutts at his home on Shalfleet Creek during the 1920s.

A large crowd gathered in early 1919 to dedicate the Porchfield war memorial. Set onto a plinth made of local stone, a block of timber from HMS *Thunderer* (one of Nelson's warships at Trafalgar) was carved with the names of those who fell during the war, and inscribed 'In grateful memory of the men from Porchfield and Newtown who fell in the Great War 1914–1919.' Above that the cross itself was made of Island oak.

The carnage of the First World War did not deter many of the young men of the district from continuing to volunteer, especially when times became hard during the 1920s. Charlie Pocock, of London Heath, joined the 'terriers' and Robert Lock's two sons followed in their father's fine tradition. The elder of the two, also Robert, became Rifleman No. 5493734 in 1927, winning stripes and the cup as best recruit. His brother Richard's main contribution to local lore was his performance as a 17-year-old 'back-man', trudging behind the parade of Territorials holding the warning lantern, wearing wellingtons, and smoking a clay pipe!

Frederick James Fallick with his mother in 1916.

Horace 'Harry' Sanders, Royal Field Artillery, who died at Arras in 1917 at the age of 21.

Dedication ceremony in 1919 of the original First World War memorial at Porchfield.

Porchfield's original First World War memorial in 1920, viewed from the west.

Above: *Charlie Pocock, 1927.*

Above left: *Robert Lock (Home Guard), formerly of Elmsworth Farm, with his son Robbie (RAOC) in 1941 shortly before the younger man was drowned.*

Left: *Ida Olden, 1941.*

Fate was to treat them differently when they served in the regular forces during the Second World War. Robert was drowned whilst training for overseas duty, whilst Richard served on the only vessel to survive unscathed on convoy duties across the Atlantic between America and Northern Russia.

Most of Newtown Creek and the surrounding land was requisitioned by the War Office during the Second World War. Even the house at Swainston Manor was commandeered, with Sir John Simeon's living quarters reduced to two rooms in the stable block, where he was looked after by his housekeeper Mrs Hooker. Newtown Marsh was converted into a dummy airfield complete with searchlights, thus attracting several enemy bombing raids. Some Air Force personnel were billeted locally in a former railway carriage in the grounds of Myrtle Cottage and two naval petty officers, billeted with Mrs Mustchin at Rose Cottage, were employed to man the searchlight generator which was located in a blockhouse (at the time of writing partly demolished) near the landward end of the footbridge to the quay.

In 1944, far more significant military use was made of the area. Tank landing-stages were built, especially on the Hamstead side of the estuary, and many moorings were sunk in the Haven for landing barges. Lower Elmsworth and adjacent areas were 'invaded' in dress-rehearsals for D-Day and the river teemed with invasion barges.

During each world war the nation almost reached crisis point and looked towards the older generations for active service. At the age of 48 Fred Fallick was required to report for pre-service medicals at Southampton in 1918, and in 1940, aged 38, Herbert Foss was required to register for national service.

Site of the searchlight generator on Newtown Marsh, 2000. Appropriately, another viewing medium, the modern bird hide, stands beyond.

But Newtown had its own last line of defence. In May 1940 the Local Defence Volunteer Corps was formed, unkindly dubbed the 'Look, Duck and Vanish Brigade', and the following July it was renamed the Home Guard. Some of No. 203 Section Home Guards, based at Newtown, were selected for undercover special duties, among them local farmer Ted Barton, and the section was made generally responsible for guarding munitions dumps, including that in the copse near Elm Farm.

Throughout the war, until their standing-down parade in December 1944, the Home Guard Sections from across the Island had firing practices each Sunday at Newtown's rifle-range, now known as Jersey Camp, which is still in use as a training centre for the Volunteer Reserve and Cadet Forces (Eastern Wessex) at the time of writing.

Others were involved in different ways during wartime. Ida Olden, of London Heath, volunteered for overseas nursing duties in 1941, and when 'Digging for Victory' became a slogan in each world war, local responses came from, among others, Henry Foss and Ernie Seagar who broke new growing ground in 1914 on the site of the Elmsworth Saltern where the productive soil was turned rich red from the boiler cinders. In the 1940s farmers in the area were required to plant up former grazing land, and Edwin Holbrook recollected that it cost him more to harvest the wheat and oats from his Porchfield smallholding in 1944 than he obtained for the crops. Likewise, Mr Spalding ploughed up part of Newtown Marsh and the pastureland known as Promised Land.

During and after each war everyone had to cope with strict rationing of certain foodstuffs and clothing, although country dwellers were better placed than

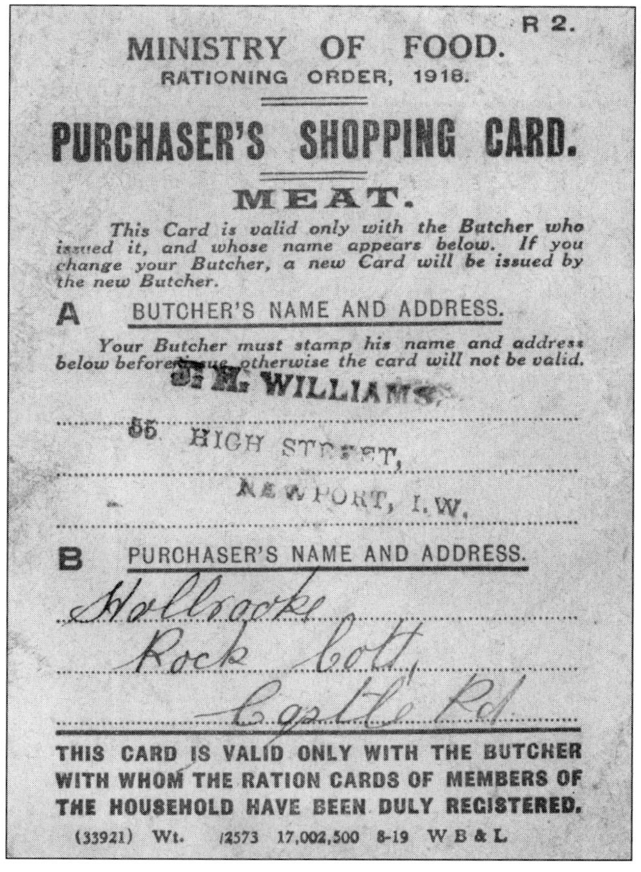

R 2.

MINISTRY OF FOOD.
RATIONING ORDER, 1918.

PURCHASER'S SHOPPING CARD.

MEAT.

This Card is valid only with the Butcher who issued it, and whose name appears below. If you change your Butcher, a new Card will be issued by the new Butcher.

A BUTCHER'S NAME AND ADDRESS.

Your Butcher must stamp his name and address below before [illegible] otherwise the card will not be valid.

[illegible] WILLIAMS,
55 HIGH STREET,
NEWPORT, I.W.

B PURCHASER'S NAME AND ADDRESS.

Hollbrooke
Rock Cott,
Castle Rd.

THIS CARD IS VALID ONLY WITH THE BUTCHER WITH WHOM THE RATION CARDS OF MEMBERS OF THE HOUSEHOLD HAVE BEEN DULY REGISTERED.

(33921) Wt. 12573 17,002,500 8-19 W B & L.

Eva Holbrook's meat-ration book, 1918.

some to overcome these difficulties. Sadly, in these stressful times not everyone put nation before self, and some of the more affluent residents horded far more than they needed, only to expect the shops to accept it back, unused and out of date, when hostilities ceased.

Generally, the sacrifices of Forces personnel and public alike were widely respected and recognised. Parades, celebrations, memorials and church services proclaimed the peace. The members of the Porchfield and Newtown Women's Institute, among others, were determined to maintain the right spirit and produced their own clarion call in 1946.

Over the centuries, a good many residents of Newtown and district reached out and touched the world. For many others the world looked in and involved them in matters of national significance. Wherever they roamed in the service of their country their roots were firmly embedded in the Newtown area, and many of those who could, did eventually return home.

The discovery of a medallion in the 1880s, concealed under the floor of an ancient double tenement being demolished alongside The Green at Newtown, poignantly illustrates this homing instinct. The medallion had been awarded to a former resident of the borough who had crewed on one of Captain Edward Vernon's galleons which, in November 1739, had famously captured Porto Bello in Panama, Central America, then regarded as a favourite nest of the hated Spanish 'guarda costas'. There was national rejoicing, and Captain Vernon was granted the freedom of London. At least one of Captain Vernon's crewmen had chosen to return home to Newtown.

The Women's Institute banner.

(REPRODUCED WITH ACKNOWLEDGEMENT TO JOHN OWEN)

Chapter 6

'For Every Child a Chance': The Rise & Demise of Schooling

Less than 200 years ago very few people were literate, especially in rural districts like Newtown. Schools, as we know them, did not exist, and apart from Sunday School a child's opportunities were limited to the possibility that a dame-school might be provided, usually by a benevolent lady in her front parlour. Benjamin Ford's daughter was such a woman and from around 1850 until 1865 she taught many of Porchfield's children to read and write in the front room of her home, Bethel Cottage. The teaching methods adopted in such establishments were not always palatable as William Holbrook (born 1828) found out. He lasted only two days at school and never returned.

Bethel Cottage, Porchfield, c.1906. Eva Mary Holbrook is pictured with her mother, Eva Holbrook (née Mew).

There was no guarantee that Newtown's first dame-school was any more sympathetic to children's sensitivities, despite the fact that it was opened by a gentle person who was the church sexton. Hannah Woolgar, later to become the village shopkeeper, set up Newtown's first recorded pay-school in the Town Hall in around 1840 and was its first schoolmistress. It was probably a form of dame-school at first, but when the Shalfleet National School was established at Ningwood in 1850 the Town Hall school was swiftly declared to be the Newtown branch of the National School. By 1852 Mrs Ann Johnson and Miss Mary Gardner were the teachers there, providing rudimentary lessons in reading, writing, arithmetic, Bible study and needlework for those children whose parents could afford to pay. By 1859 Miss Ann Attwood was the mistress.

Until these developments, Newtown children had no formal schooling. Even then, attendance was not compulsory and standards of provision in these early days were variable at best. Funding came partly from the children's payments, but relied heavily on legacies like that of Lady Constance Lucy whose will made provision for a salary of £10 a year for a schoolmistress for 12 poor children of Newtown.

It is doubtful that some children attended the school at all. Thomas, William and Mary, the older children of Jonas Foss, were born during the 1850s at Fish House Point on the eastern side of the Haven estuary, and school at Newtown or Porchfield would have involved a major journey, let alone the fees! Not until the family was driven from its home by tidal flooding in 1863 and rehoused at London Heath were the children likely to attend the Town Hall school.

Common ailments of the day (scarlet fever, measles, whooping cough, influenza and neuralgia) also reduced attendances and, without sufficient footwear, many children found attendance difficult in poor weather. For many years yet to come, other further-flung families such as the Prangnells at the Lower Elmsworth brickyard, the Calloways at Northclose Farm and the Hilliers at Coleman's Farm had little incentive to make the effort to attend.

In the 1860s the Government introduced a major initiative to make schooling compulsory for younger children and began a huge building programme to establish a network of council schools. The Church of England, fearful of losing its influence, responded with its own building initiative and, starting in 1867 as part of this initiative, Locks Green School was constructed to accommodate up to 100 children, supported by local subscription and Government grants. A year earlier, Sir John Simeon had purchased Locks Farm from Lord Heytesbury and had given to the Church of England that part of the farm formerly used as the rick yard.

Much of the school's funding came from a legacy of Miss Ward of Northwood House in Cowes, from Sir John Simeon, Member of Parliament for the Island, and from H. Hughes of Thorness Farm. Henry Mew, of Porchfield House, gave most of the building stone from his land at Quarry Field near the village. For almost 80 years Locks Green School provided education for local children and became a focal point for the community. Divine service was held there each Sunday for many years, alternating morning and afternoon with Newtown Church, and it was used as the venue for numerous social occasions.

The school attendance roll varied and, with it, significantly, the Government grant. In 1871 there

Locks Green School, c.1877, after divine service. Pictured on the left is Mr Hughes of Thorness Farm and Joseph Dore of Porchfield, and on the right is Mrs Mew, grandmother of Fred Mew, and his two aunts Gertrude and Hellie.

were 60 pupils, in 1886 47, in 1906 78, dropping during a troubled time to 62 in 1910 before peaking in 1913 at 100 pupils. Until 1895 children paid 2d. a week for their schooling, which many parents were loathe to afford, especially for the girls, who were often kept back to help in the home. The rule was strictly enforced and Edwin Holbrook wrote about being sent home one day when he forgot to take his 'fee'. However, after 1872 schooling had become compulsory. The level of school funding depended on attendances and teachers were paid according to the performances of their pupils in the six 'standards'. The anguish of the teachers as their remuneration varied from year to year can only be imagined, but the pressure was now placed upon parents and children to ensure attendance.

In the early years conditions at the school were rather basic. All the children, from age five to eleven, were taught in one room by a teacher and perhaps a couple of monitors. Teachers were rarely trained thoroughly. Those with certificates received between £20 and £40 a year, whilst assistants (known as 'supplementaries') were paid £15. Monitors, often recent school-leavers, might have got as little as £1.10s. for a year's work cleaning slates and giving out books and pencils.

For many years the school had no water-supply, pupils obtaining water to drink or wash with from the tubs which caught rainwater from the roof of Locks Farm next door, where Miss Grace White, the teacher, and her younger sister Louisa (aged 17, the pupil-teacher), lodged with farmer Mrs Rice. Both Newport-born, the two women were the school's first teachers. When they left, Miss Sarah Amey was appointed and taught there from around 1877 until 1888, much of the time with Georgina Arnold, daughter of the local blacksmith, as pupil-teacher. Around 1888, Miss Darlington was appointed to teach alongside Miss Kate Ridett, daughter of the Lambsleaze farmer, who lodged at Marsh Farm.

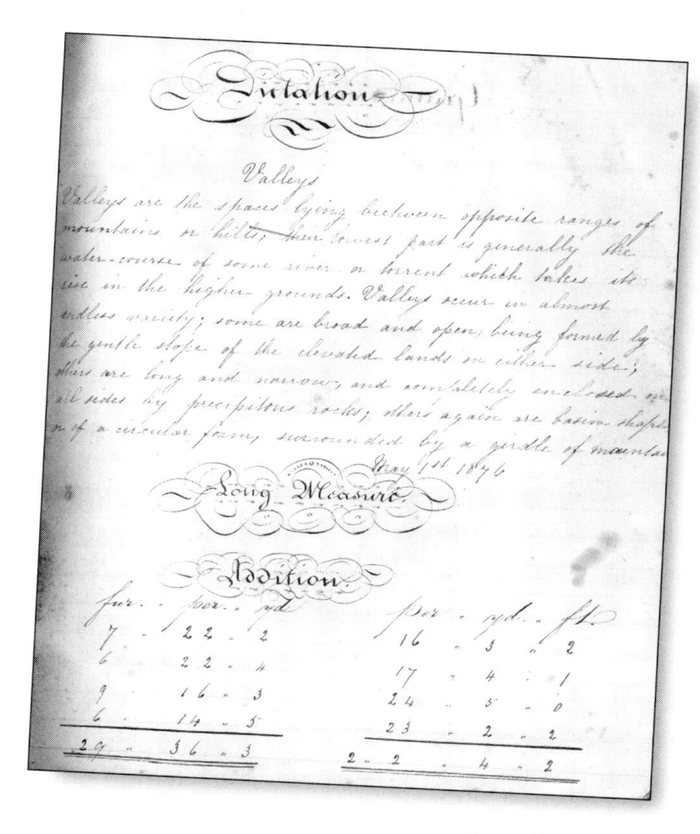

Dictation

Valleys

Valleys are the spaces lying between opposite ranges of mountains or hills; ~~their~~ lowest part is generally the water-course of some river or torrent which takes its rise in the higher grounds. Valleys occur in almost endless variety; some are broad and open, being formed by the gentle slope of the elevated lands on either side; others are long and narrow, and completely enclosed on all sides by precipitous rocks; others again are basin-shaped or of a circular form, surrounded by a girdle of mountains

May 1st 1876

Long Measure

Addition

fur.	po.	yd.
7	22	2
6	22	4
9	16	3
6	14	5
29	36	3

	po.	yd.	ft.
	16	3	2
	17	4	1
	24	5	0
	23	2	2
2	2	4	2

A page from a school book of a 13-year-old pupil in 1876.

Many of the teachers appointed were unmarried women in their twenties. Often, the pupil-teachers were even younger. Without formal training, they learned their tasks through a kind of apprenticeship system, known as 'sitting by Nellie'. Thus, when Worcester-born Miss Marianne Whitehouse was appointed to the headship in 1891 she soon installed her 14-year-old niece Leilah as a pupil-teacher, and by 1901 she had appointed 20-year-old Louisa Brett from Church Cottage in Newtown, and 15-year-old Amy Arnold from Bunts Hill Farm as pupil-teachers.

Edwin Holbrook, a pupil at the school during the 1870s, later described the regimented manner of the school day:

> *Before entering the school in the morning all children lined up on the path outside, the boys on the right and the girls on the left. When all was in order, the Head Teacher entered the school and stood by her desk. At the command of the Under Teacher the girls entered first and curtseyed as they passed the Head Teacher. The boys followed and saluted as they passed. When all were in their place at the desks we all sang a Morning Hymn, repeated the General Confession and (recited) the Lord's Prayer.*

Most of the time was given to reading, writing and arithmetic, reading aloud the same books over and over again. The local vicar, Revd H. Stokes, visited every Thursday to give talks about 'the wonderful deliverance of the 'Children of Israel' from Egyptian bondage', or to admonish children for bad behaviour and warn them of the 'awful consequences'. Materials were in short supply. Slates and pencils were used for arithmetic, and exercise books only for writing.

Locks Green School infant group, 1901. Edwin Holbrook's daughter, Eva Mary, is second from the left at the front.

The whole fabric of financial support for these elementary schools was very fragile, being partly dependent on the raising of local taxes and the provision of grants and legacies. The 1899 balance sheet for the Shalfleet Church of England School illustrates it well:

Income

	£.	s.	d.
Education Dept grant	80	11	6
Fee grant	25	10	0
Aid grant	14	0	0
Legacy	5	14	8
Subscriptions	8	11	0
Voluntary rate	25	9	3
Church collection		18	6
Parish council meeting	1	5	0
Total	161	19	11

Expenditure

	£.	s.	d.
Overdraft	4	3	5
Teachers' salaries	132	15	9
Monitor's salary	1	6	0
Books and stationery	6	2	5
Fuel, lighting, cleaning	5	8	6
Repairs	9	14	8
Bank charges		7	6
Balance in hand	2	1	8
Total	161	19	11

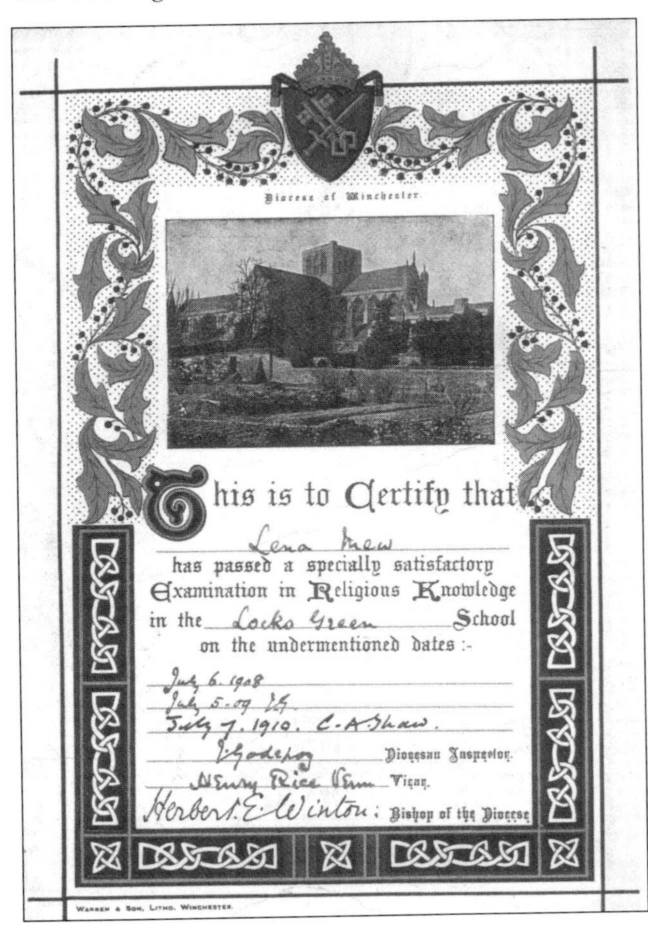

Diocese of Winchester

This is to Certify that Lena Mew
has passed a specially satisfactory Examination in Religious Knowledge in the Locks Green School on the undermentioned dates :-
July 6. 1908
July 5-09
July 7. 1910. C. A. Shaw.
Diocesan Inspector.
Vicar.
Herbert E. Winton: Bishop of the Diocese

Warren & Son, Litho. Winchester

Left: *Lena Mew's Religious Knowledge certificate from Locks Green School, first issued in 1908.*

In November 1893 the Newtown and Porchfield Parochial Committee raised a voluntary rate of threepence in the pound to meet the increased expenses of the parish school after the abolition of pupil fees. In 1895 the school was enlarged to provide an extra classroom, a lobby, and some offices at a cost of £250. Around the same time lessons were also introduced in the district on Sundays by Revd M. Hoare at the Bible Christian Chapel at Barton's Corner.

The extra classroom was next to the playing-fields and provided separate accommodation for the infants. It was endowed with a proper fireplace rather than the traditional coke-burning boiler. The 'offices' consisted of two cloakrooms (one for girls and infants, the other for junior boys) and two earth toilets, little more than a trench over which was placed a long wooden seat with holes at respectable intervals. By this date, on-site accommodation had been provided for the head teacher.

For those children who did attend school regularly in the nineteenth century, great stress was laid on the production of copperplate writing, mental arithmetic, memorisation of Bible passages, and reading competence. Those children who could actually read and write were 'employed' by their elders, most of whom were illiterate, to read and write their correspondence.

A 12-year-old's school exercise book begun in December 1875 contains entries headed 'Grammar', 'Simple Subtraction', 'Scripture Text', 'Geography', 'Welsh Counties', 'Compound Addition', 'Dictation', 'Reduction', 'Addition of Weights and Measures', 'Troy Weight Multiplication', 'Time Addition' and 'Cloth Measure'.

Fred Fallick, the celebrated gamekeeper who worked on the Swainston estate for 52 years, attended Locks Green School during the 1870s. He experienced the harsh methods of Victorian schooling when he was repeatedly caned for stammering whilst reading aloud to the class. He became so nervous that he learned to truant every day that such an activity was in prospect, before eventually passing Standard IV which permitted him to leave school at the age of 11 and earn 6d. a day working at Locks Farm next door. His contemporary, Edwin Holbrook, described how over-use of the cane for petty misdemeanors led to rebellion by some boys. The head teacher was giving one of the bigger boys, Henry Harding, a good thrashing one day when he made a dive for the coal scuttle and 'her ladyship' found herself being pelted with lumps of coal. When she eventually put away the cane her face was blackened and tear-stained. Some 30 years later, when Herbert Foss was at Locks Green School (1907–16) he witnessed a similar incident. Pandemonium broke out when a boy refused to be caned on his hands. The head teacher, Frank Cooper, started thrashing his legs only to receive kicks to his own backside

A class at Locks Green School in 1906, with their teacher Miss Gaill. Note that some attempt has been made to establish a school uniform.

Top and above: *Handicraft lessons at Locks Green School, c.1917.*

from the furious pupil. The two of them whirled around the floor together as cane pursued hobnail boot! Herbert's opinion of school could not have been enhanced by the fact that Mr Cooper took lodgings with Mr and Mrs Hunt at No. 1, London Heath Cottages, right next door to the poor boy!

There were around 19 children in the 'juniors' class, and they were taught by Mr Cooper who always sat at his desk, which was on a raised platform at the front of the classroom alongside a coke-fired boiler. He was always ready to make liberal use of the cane and barely a day went by without several children becoming victim of his wrath, sometimes not without cause! A thrashing was commonly meted out for failing to pay attention, or for laughing or talking or, more deservedly perhaps, for placing live frogs in the master's desk! The children soaped their hands before a caning in order to reduce the effect, or pushed horsehair inside the rod causing it to split when used.

In the late-nineteenth century the school faced a crisis as discipline collapsed. Miss Marianne Whitehouse had been head teacher since 1891 and had lost control. The managers of the school, characteristically drawn from the local dignitaries and clergy, met in closed session to consider their response. The Rector of Calbourne, Revd John Vicars, and the vicar and surrogate at Newtown, Revd Henry Rice Venn, alternately chairman and correspondent, together with farmers George Kingswell (Fleetlands) and Ernest Hawkins (Lambsleaze), and Calbourne businessman F. Long, decided to publicly expel four troublemakers who lived outside the parish. Thus Harry Long and Harry Cosh from Thorness together with Victor Buckett and Arthur Flux took leave of the school for good, Arthur, apparently, just for being 'sulky and defiant'. At the same time the parents of Fred Mew, Ernest Mew and Frank Osbourn were sent warning letters about the conduct of their children. Miss Whitehouse was pressed to resign and in March 1907 Frank Cooper was appointed head teacher, with a Shalfleet man, W.R. Lock, held in reserve in case the new appointment failed. (A 'Harry' Lock was appointed as teacher at Shalfleet School in 1913 and became a much-loved and respected headmaster at the school – and spin bowler for the local cricket team – until his sudden death at the age of 47 in 1935.)

Conditions at Locks Green School remained stressful and in September 1909 Miss Cantelope, the assistant mistress, resigned. Mabel Parsons replaced her on one month's trial to teach the younger juniors. Little could she have imagined that, before long, she would be headmistress. With an open remit to improve discipline, Frank Cooper was so liberal with his use of the cane that, eventually, he was suspended by the managers and Miss Parsons took over. Sadly, she also suffered problems of control, the children often puncturing the tyres of her bicycle.

Not all teachers at the school experienced such problems. Hilda Abblitt, a local person, taught there from 1910 until 1930 under several head teachers, including Miss Dorothy Wakely who was appointed in 1916 at a salary of £85.0s.0d. per annum.

Many pupils missed much of their schooling due to repeated bouts of illness, especially in the winter months. The damp living conditions and cold stone floors in labourers' cottages contributed to regular cases of influenza and bronchitis. Other children often missed school at harvest times, and those from more remote areas rarely attended in bad weather due to lack of suitable waterproof clothing and footwear. Many children also suffered the indignity of head lice, or were disabled by rickets.

Emmie Stevens, the school cleaner and caretaker, had an unenviable task cleaning the mud from the floor brought in daily by so many pairs of boots, and keeping the dust from the Beastove boilers under control.

The school served a large rural area and children were expected to bring a packed lunch every day. Many did not, and endured a long and hungry day. Some children from remote farms had rarely met other people before they attended school and were quite terrified of strangers. Sadly, they were often the target for bullying at school. One particularly withdrawn child was Ted Prangnell, from Lower Elmsworth brickyard. In 1985, Herbert Foss, who was at school with Ted, described how he never brought food with him, nor did he join in playground

Locks Green School pageant, c.1908. Lena Mew is second from left in the middle row, Ellen Heal is extreme right in the back row and Ms Hawkins from Lambsleaze Farm is on the right of the front row.

Right: *Artwork by 13-year-old pupil Herbert Foss.*

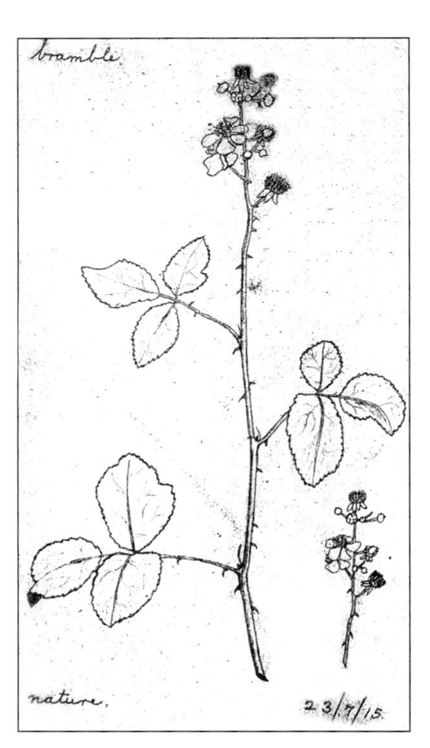

The class of juniors at Locks Green School in 1911. Left to right, back row: *Hughie Wells, Godfrey Buckett, Jack Arnold, Reg Hayward, ? Pragnell;* middle row: *Herbie Wheeler, Sally Lock, Daisy ?, Mabel Cosh, Edie Fallick, Dorothy Cosh, Jim Angell;* front row: *Allan Mew, Jerry Humber, Vi Cosh, Emma Sloper, Betty Masterton, ? Lathey, ? Lathey, Herbert Foss.*

games at lunchtime. Rather, he stood motionless against a wall clasping his hands behind his back. One bitterly cold winter day he turned blue and the children were ordered to march him around until he recovered. Thinking he was about to be hurt he screamed until he foamed at the mouth.

Around 98 children attended Locks Green School at this time, some 33 infants with Miss Gaill, the lower juniors with Miss Parsons and the older pupils with the head teacher. Sometimes the vicar, Revd Henry Rice Venn, taught religious instruction, and other visitors, mainly gentry, sometimes lectured the children about their travels or the reasons to be honest and upright. The morning sessions usually consisted of religious instruction, arithmetic and English (reading, writing and spelling), and in the afternoons children learnt about history, geography, art, nature and geometry. Children were seen but rarely heard. They copied from the blackboard, or they conjugated verbs, or they drew carefully from still objects. Every morning they chanted their multiplication tables. School was hardly an experience in self-expression! Drill, which consisted mainly of marching, epitomised the regimented nature of most schooling. This was particularly popular during the period of the Boer Wars, around the turn of the century, as patriotic fervour gripped the nation.

There was not much equipment despite grants from the Ward estate at Cowes. The infants sat in rows on long benches, whilst the juniors sat in pairs at iron-framed wooden desks facing the teacher. Paper was always in short supply and rough work often had to be done in chalk on slates. Sometimes green canvas was pinned to the wall for art class, and pupils used chalk which could then be rubbed off. Many of the activities were notably practical, not only in preparation for the jobs to follow school, but also to save money, or indeed make money towards the school's running costs. The girls made pillowcases and handkerchiefs in needlework lessons to sell later to buy fresh materials; the boys had gardening classes and their garden became self-sufficient. The school's gardening plot was in Porchfield, with access through the farmyard opposite the village shop up towards Coffin Copse, where each boy had a 12-foot-square plot.

Being raised in such a tight-knit community led to the establishment of lifelong friendships. People followed the progress of their peers with great interest. Few moved far away from their birthplace, and in old age most could give a potted history of the lives of their school contemporaries. In 1992 a nonagenarian recalled his school chums of 1911:

Hughie Wells was the youngest of a family at Locks Farm and later at Porchfield Farm. As an adult he emigrated to Canada.

Joe Osbourn came from Porchfield where some relations are still resident.

Alan Mew lived at Porchfield House. His father was a farmer, builder and undertaker, a pillar of the community. Alan became something of a black sheep of the family with his far-left politics.

Gerry Humber of Fleetlands Farm went with his family to a farm near Ventnor. He always wore a blue woollen jumper.

Sarah 'Sally' Lock lived and later worked at Elmsworth Farm and her father, Walter Hillier Lock, became the first owner in the area of a bull-nose Morris motor car, giving rise to much tittle-tattle.

Mabel, Dorothy and Vi Cosh lived at Thorness Cross. Vi later worked at Forest Farm on washdays for 2s.6d. a day.

Edie Fallick was the gamekeeper's daughter at St Hubert's Lodge on the Swainston estate. She was the sweetheart of Herbert Foss and used her brother as courier to exchange messages of endearment! She worked for a milliner at Newport, cycling to work every day, but died of tuberculosis at the age of 21.

Emma Sloper lived in a cottage at Whitehouse Corner, and later married a blacksmith, whose smithy was at the bottom of Hunnyhill, Newport.

Godfrey 'Buck' Buckett lived opposite the blacksmith's shop in Locks Green. He and a friend were fishing in Clamerkin Brook one lunchtime when the school bell sounded. They were late and were severely caned.

Jack 'Kruger' Arnold lived at Bunts Hill Farm. He was terrified of fire, and as an adult would not have a fire in the farm even in the depths of winter.

Jim Angell later worked for Captain Hudson whose home was on the site of the present Gurnard Pines holiday camp. He then got work with Ball, the builders at Cowes, and died in an accident when he backed a lorry into a sandpit near Dukes Farm, Rew Street, Gurnard.

Herbie 'Bett' Wheeler lived at a cottage close to the school. He was a very nervous person and he and some schoolfriends were playing cards at the bridge in Porchfield (known locally as 'Slinks') when Constable Gamble (the Gurnard policeman who also served the area) arrived on his bicycle. The young Wheeler hurdled the brook as though it was not there and took off up the lane. In later life he took over the carrier service from Edwin Holbrook and Ted Huggins, and by the time of his marriage to Vi Whittington in 1936 he was an 'omnibus driver'.

Reg 'Sim' Hayward, from Little Thorness Farm later married Sally Lock from Elmsworth Farm. He took over the farm from his father [and the family still farm there in 2004].

It was not all work at school. There were several 'occasional-day' holidays each year to mark, for instance, the monarch's birthday (when the National Anthem was sung and the Union Jack was flown from the school pole), military victories across the Empire, the horse parade, or the village sports day. But at home, children were expected to make a useful contribution to the family from a very early age, dusting and cleaning, shelling peas and running errands. Often, before coming to school, a child would have helped milk the cows, or served breakfast as maid at a large house nearby, or delivered the bread. Herbert Foss occasionally helped his father empty the lobster-pots as early as four in the morning, and he collected milk in a jug from London Farm each afternoon after school, and once each week collected the family's pound of butter from Clamerkin Farm.

As a result, there was not a lot of time for more leisurely pursuits. At school, a favourite playground game was marbles (bottle-stoppers), and cigarette cards made their first appearance around 1890. Apart from collecting them, flicking them the furthest caused great entertainment. Most of the girls had skipping-ropes, and whipping-tops and hoops were very popular. Hoops and their long-handled steering hooks were made at the Locks Green smithy. Throw ha'penny was also popular. There were also seasonal games such as conkers, and 'winter warmers' were made by filling a tin with smouldering rags and whirling it on a piece of string. The girls often had home-made rag dolls, and the more fortunate might have had an early copy of *The Magnet* (first published in 1908) or *The Boy's Own Paper.*

Most such play activities among children were home-grown and these, like other generations, had their playground chants and rhymes, some of which reflected the times they lived through:

Red, white and blue,
The cat's got flu
The baby has a whooping cough
And out goes you.

God made the bees
The bees make honey
We do the work
The teacher gets the money.

Around the period 1910–20, the older children were able to congregate in a tumbledown cottage (since demolished) along from Locks Farm. There, thanks to the generosity of Edwin Holbrook, who furnished wood fuel for the open fire, they played darts and cards in some comfort.

This was the heyday of Locks Green School, when its roll just topped 100. From around 1912 its pupil numbers gradually fell away. Younger families were tending to move from Newtown and Porchfield in search of better earnings, and in 1920 the coastguard station, source of many of the school's children, was closed and moved elsewhere. The school suffered from a rather rapid turnover of staff and, with Revd Henry Rice Venn's health failing badly, perhaps the school did

Locks Green School's gardening class in 1912. Left to right, back row: *Godfrey Buckett, Jack Arnold, Jim Angell, Herbie Wheeler, head teacher Frank Cooper, ? Pragnell, Reg Hayward, Hughie Wells, Joe Osbourn;* front row: *Allan Mew, Herbie Foss, Jerry Humber, ? Lathey.*

Locks Green School's junior class in 1936. Left to right, back row: *Ron Angell, Bert Buckett, ?, Stanley Cosh, ? Kerley;* middle row: *Frankie Downer, ?, Dorothy Hawkins, ? Thompson, John Sanders, ?, Gracie Stone, Amy Pragnell, John Hayward;* front row: *John Cosh, Margy Attrill, Walter Flux, Yvonne 'Bubble' Wells, ?, Enid Angell.*

Shalfleet School pupils in 1935. Left to right, back row: *Barbara Meaning, Josie Critchell, ?, Marjorie Flux, Lily Angell, ? Hedges, ?, ? French;* third row: *? Osmond, ? Critchell, ? Dowty, Arthur Angell, Jack Grimes, Arthur Jupe, John Gamble, Andrew Reynolds, John Pocock;* second row: *Walter Flux, ?, ? Boswell, Nigel Harris, ? Harris, Eric Sloper, ? Dowty, Peter Self, ? Pocock;* front row: *?, ? Hodges, ? Pocock, Gwen Brett, ? Pocock.*

not enjoy the leadership it needed. It might be significant that no minutes were entered in the managers' log-book between 1912 and 1921, and even more significant that Miss Whitehouse, by now in her mid-sixties, had been reappointed as an assistant teacher in the 1920s! Reportedly it was common knowledge that she rarely arrived for work on time and she received very public warnings from the head teacher, Mr Warner. Characteristically, the children also expressed a point of view. Eileen Fallick, a pupil at the time, remembered their rhyme: 'Old Mother Whitehouse, number ninety nine, Her hair hangs down like a ball of twine.'

By 1931 the school's roll had fallen to 27 children aged five to 11 (by then, children transferred at age 11 to Shalfleet School). The best efforts of the managers, led by Edwin Holbrook, could not produce enrolments from a district that was losing its children. Yet the teachers, then including long-serving Miss Terry with the infants, still received plaudits from the Diocesan Inspector, Revd C.W. Hampton-Weeks who, in 1928, declared himself 'much impressed by the splendid answering of the children.'

At the same time, Shalfleet 'National' School was flourishing, both in terms of its achievements under the headship of Harry Lock and his successor Mrs E.J. Taylor, but also in terms of its pupil numbers. Improvements in motorised transport made it easier for some parents to place their children in the school of their choice. It also made more feasible the rationalisation of school provision by the local education authority. The days of Locks Green School were numbered.

The last entry in the managers' log-book was made in 1942. Clearly, all was not well but it was a further five years before the school was closed in 1947 and the last teacher, Lily Pragnell, lost her job. Pupils were transferred, by parental choice, either to Gurnard or Shalfleet Schools. Poignantly, it was a former pupil, 'Bett' Wheeler, who obtained the omnibus contract to transport local children to their new school in Shalfleet. Less than five years later, the school at Calbourne was also closed, and its pupils transferred to Shalfleet where, as if in celebration, electric light was installed!

Locks Green School, c.1942, with teacher Dorothy Terry. Left to right, back row: *Fred Wells, Cecil Smith, Fred Smith, Alfred Osbourn, Roland Wells, Billy Mustchin, Edward Osbourn*; third row: *Hazel Thompson, Florrie Wells, Hilda ?, Dorothy Morris, Ewen Dixey, Win Angell, Rita Cosh*; second row: *Olive Smith, Joan Sanders, Lily Angell, Joan Wells;* front row: *Tommy Dixey, Arthur Angell, Lenny Budden, Dennis Holbrooke.*

Chapter 7

'Keeping the Banks': Land Reclamation at Newtown

All those years, all them old boys with a ruddy wheelbarrow and a spade... admitted, they had all the materials from the copse... but they kept that water out.

One of Newtown's own men, Billy Mustchin, commenting in 1993, had forthright views about the feeble attempts adopted since the 1940s to keep the tides off Newtown Marsh. 'All them old fellers... they're all gone... they used to say if it comes through it'll come through at Clamerkin end.' They were, indeed, to be proven right.

It had been a constant battle for some 300 years to prevent the ingress of the sea on to land reclaimed for Sir John Barrington towards the end of the seventeenth century, and now that battle has been lost, probably for ever. The mighty storm surge in early 1953 and those of November 1954 overwhelmed the defences, breaching the retaining wall in several places and setting in process the return of some 140 acres to mud-flat and salt marsh.

Sited on the clays of North Wight, Newtown's residents are no strangers to excess surface water. In 1540 there was a Grant of Sewers for Newtown Marsh, but there is little evidence that anything was done. The town's Court Leet records for 1637 show that the Mayor and burgesses 'present that Sir William Mewes shall sufficiently skower his ditch from Thomas Holbrook's street-bars down to the marsh against Green Close.' Clearly, Sir William had not been doing his bit to keep Newtown dry.

But there was a demand for the marshes so they presumably had some commercial value. In 1547 John Mewes was paying tithes to the manor for Bernard Marsh at Newtown, and in 1664 a 31-year lease was taken on 'salt marsh extending from the port of Newtown to Shalfleet' by Elizabeth Countess Dowager of Peterborough and others.

Increasingly, over a period of several hundred years, the sluggish waters in the Haven had led to the accretion of mud and marsh and by 1656 Sir John Barrington of Swainston had asked his representative, John Hall, to enter into negotiations with John Kendall, an entrepreneur from Essex, regarding the reclamation of the marshlands adjacent to Newtown. As early as the reign of Edward I (1272–1307) some land had been reclaimed within Brading Harbour, and further acreage was added in 1562 and 1594. But it was probably the initial success of the work of Sir Hugh Myddleton during the 1620s in shutting out the sea completely at Brading that inspired considerations at Newtown. In addition, Sir John might well have had experience of land reclamation near the family seat at Hatfield Broadoak in Essex, which would explain his awareness of Kendall's skills.

Kendall's first offer was to improve the value of acreage from 1s. to 10s. per annum, in return for ownership of half the land reclaimed and half 'the Mudd'. He then moved to an offer of a rent payment of £50 per annum in perpetuity, in return for all the land reclaimed. Quite possibly, a scheme similar to that at Brading with a wall across the entrance to Newtown River was mooted. These negotiations did not proceed but by 1662/3 Articles of Agreement had been drawn between Sir John Barrington and Richard Hutchinson, gentleman of the City of London, to:

> *... dreyne drie inclose fence and banck in from the sea All that haven or marsh ground called Newtowne Haven or Newtowne Marsh in the mannour of Swainston.*

Little evidence remains of any reclamation at this time. It seems more likely that the major work was completed, probably in more than one stage, in the early-eighteenth century. Early maps hint at an inner bank, and leases refer to 'old marsh' and 'new marsh'. An indenture, dated 1730, records that Nicholas Dobree, a merchant from Guernsey, let farm land and salt marsh to local yeoman Robert Rogers, for 14 years at an annual rent of £50. The major reclamation work had been completed and Mr Rogers was to maintain the banks on the eastern side of the Marsh as far north as the stone 'bunney', and Mr Dobree agreed to maintain the rest. The indenture refers to 'the new marsh', implying that reclamation of parts of it had been recent, although Marsh Saltern had been established already, and salt

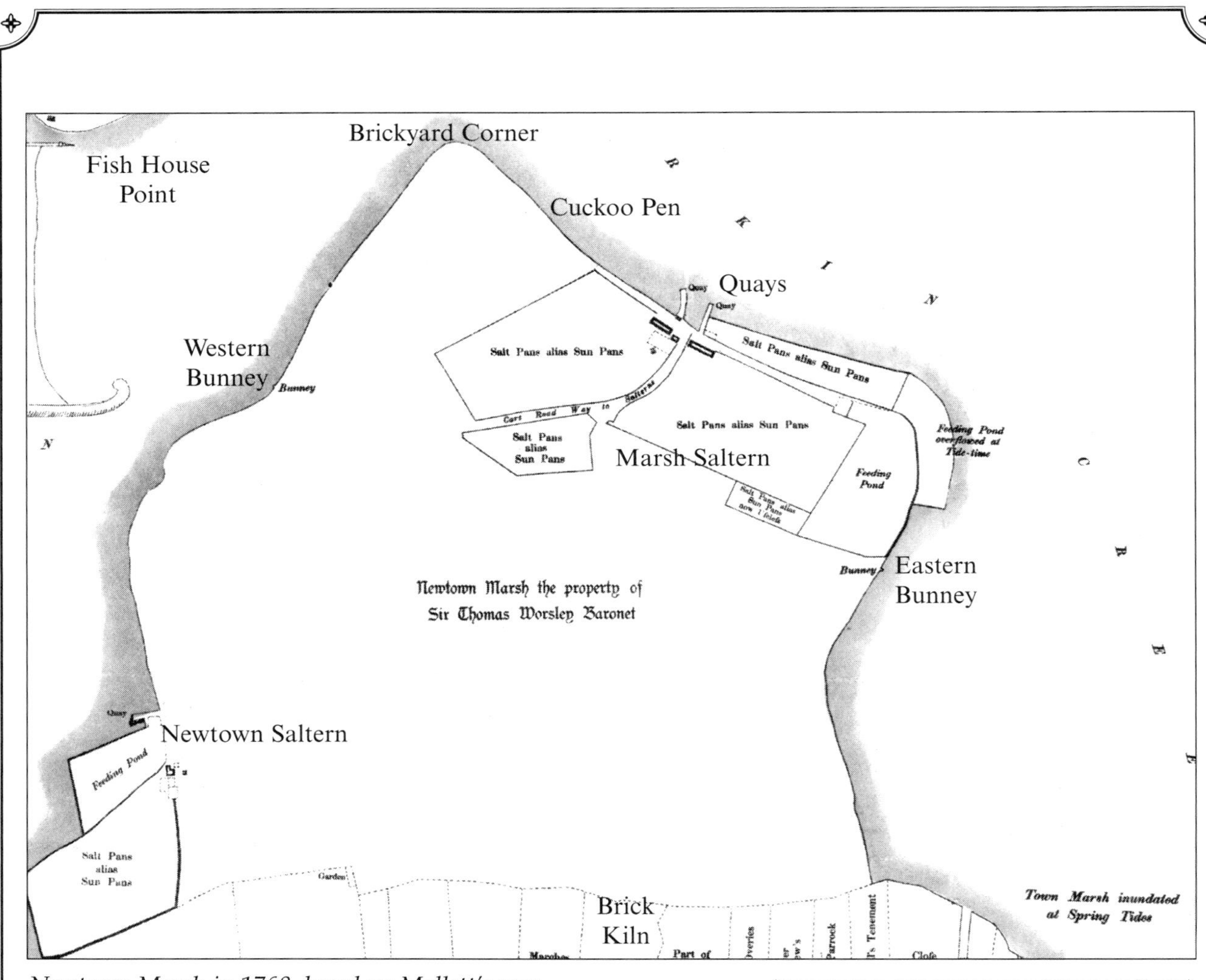

Newtown Marsh in 1768, based on Mallett's map. (REPRODUCED COURTESY OF THE NATIONAL TRUST)

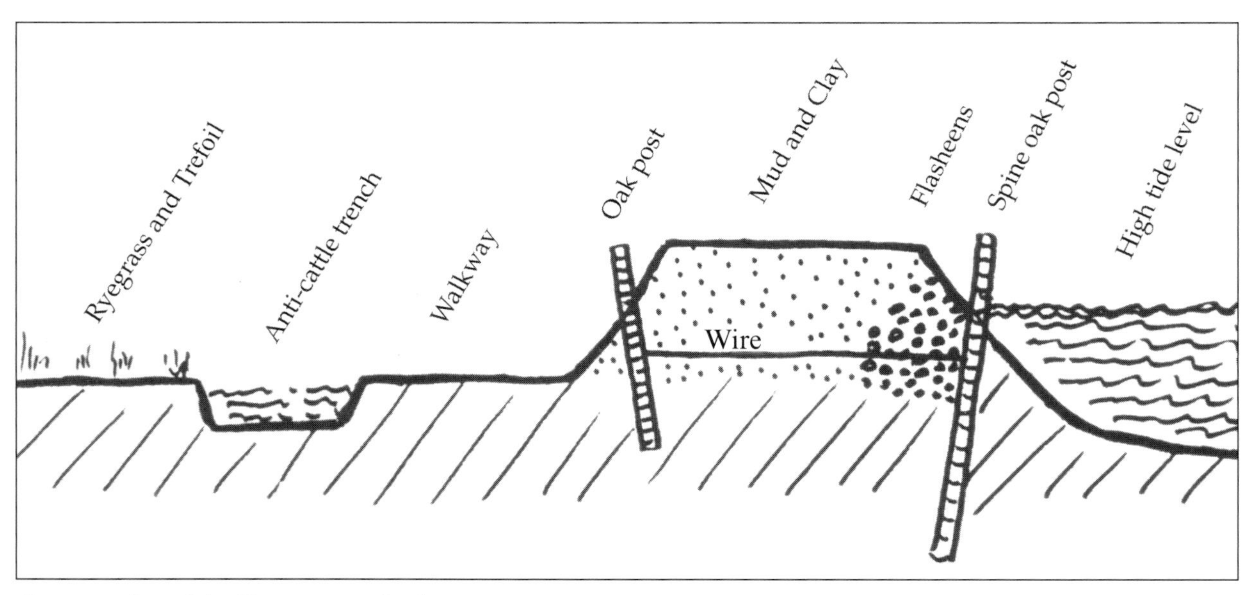

Cross-section of the Newtown embankment.

Looking south-east across Newtown Marsh in 2000 from the site of the former Newtown salt works.

officers occupied a tenement on the Marsh. It also referred to land that had been set aside 'outside the banks of the Old Marsh' for the construction of Newtown Saltern. More recent surveys showed signs of this inner bank, so it is likely that Newtown Marsh was reclaimed in stages.

By the time James Mallett produced his map of 1768 the Marsh was well established, enclosed by banks almost two miles long, and drained by two brick-built bunneys. It was now owned by Sir Thomas Worsley and contained two large salterns and their associated works. No doubt it was planted up with ryegrass and trefoil, which was to become its principal crop for around 200 years. Once established, the outline of the Marsh remained little changed throughout its existence, a tribute to the engineering skills of the men with wheelbarrows and spades. It was several feet below the level of high tides, thus it remained vital to maintain the banks. Equally, the removal of surplus water was a priority and the whole area became criss-crossed by major and minor drainage channels and ditches which fed water towards the two bunneys, which then opened to release it at each low tide. Without the assistance of pumps, drainage was sluggish and several large freshwater pools remained which attracted a great deal of wildlife, including wigeon, teal and duck, natural forerunners of the scrapes of today's bird sanctuary.

The traditional skills and materials, still being used by the Barton brothers of Harts Farm to maintain the banks during the 1930s, had remained largely unchanged for three centuries. Almost without exception local materials were used, mainly wood gathered from the woodlands and copses of the manor and clay dug from elsewhere in the Haven. The 1730 indenture of Nicholas Dobree provides a clue about one of the vital ingredients for a stable sea wall. Tenant Mr Rogers was given permission to take 200 'sticks of frith' from Locks Farm each year for repairing the banks. Blackthorn grows liberally on the clays of the area and is highly resistant to rot. Immersion in salt water further hardens and preserves the wood, so it made good sense to construct tightly-packed 'fascines' from it (the men called them 'flasheens'), to be used as a first line of defence against sea erosion.

That part of the embankment directly facing the entrance to the Haven had been built using a mixture of drystone-walling techniques (with Portland stone, and greenstone from the local outcrops at Salt Mead Ledge) topped off with mud and clay, but by far the longest stretch of the embankment was formed out of simple mud and clay, locally known as 'blue slipper'. Using spine oak cut from Calbourne Wood, which they split into four and cut into 10 feet lengths, estate workers would first drive a line of outer piles deep into the mud along the proposed line of the embankment. It was usually a two-man job (Henry Foss and Ernest Seagar often worked as a team during the period 1880–1920), using a double-handled 'bittle'. These, together with a parallel line of shorter oak posts on the inland side of the proposed bank, were driven in at an angle and tied with stout wire which passed through the bank. The outer 'fence' was then strengthened with horizontally fastened poles, and fascines were packed tightly behind the outer piles to break the force of the waves impacting on the bank. Hebberdens Roughs was a good place for cutting the blackthorn for the fascines, as was the scrub alongside the road from Locks Green smithy to the school. Henry and Ernest would then use the estate's lighter to collect mud and clay from across the Clamerkin River on Lambsleaze and Brickyard Marshes, and dump it behind the fascines to build the bank. It was a slow and arduous task done in tandem with the tides. The lighter was a heavy, flat-bottomed boat, with planks nailed to the ribs, leaving a front seat for rowing. Later, the estate replaced this vessel with a heavy galley, formerly used by the coastguards.

The manorial account books for the period 1868–80 reflect the rhythms of the seasonal work in relation to the banks. The greater threats to the bank came with the winter storms when regular work was

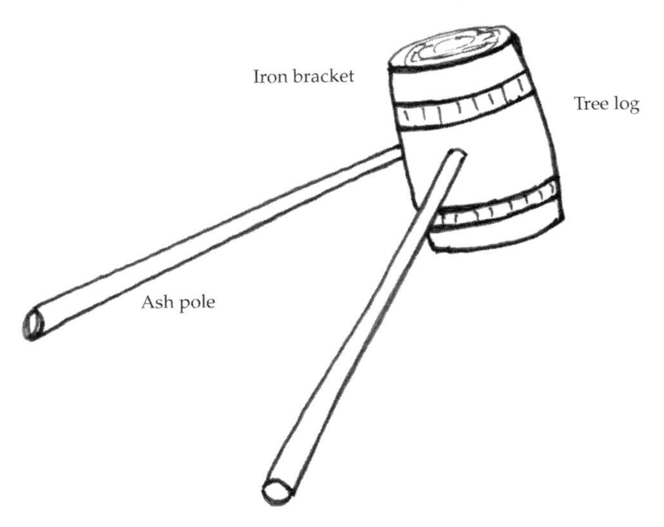

A traditional two-handled bittle.

Marsh Newtown
Men clearing out Water trench to
keep cattle from the Bank 212 roods at 9d = 7 19 "
Reuben Holbrook 24 2 6 3 " "
Jones Fox — 5½ 2 " " 11 "
Saml. Cotton 4½ 2 " 9
£ 11 19 "

Swainston account book extract for June 1869.
(Reproduced courtesy of the County Record Office, Newport)

Below: *Henry Foss, who worked on the banks almost all his working life, pictured in 1924.*

Remains of the western bunney with the flooded Marsh beyond, 1998.

Billy Prangnell with a young Richard Seabroke at Marsh Farm, c.1941.

available for several labourers and, in times of crisis when the bank was breached, for many more. In January 1868 Reuben Holbrook, Jonas Foss and Morris Rogers each earned 2s. a day on the banks, for six full days a week. The following summer Reuben was still employed full time, but Jonas was needed for only five-and-a-half days each month and Barnabus Cotton for even less.

The greatest potential damage to the banks during summer months came from the cattle which grazed the Marsh. In an attempt to keep them off the banks a gang of men was employed to excavate a deep trench along the length of the embankment on its landward side. In 1869 the gang had completed ditching for 212 roods (around 53 acres) and was paid 9d. a rood. It often became a task for Jonas Foss to keep the main trench flooded during the summer; for four months' employment he received payment of 15s. the following year! The men were often employed during the 1870s on a piece-work basis. The incentive clearly worked, for the weekly income of the labourers rose significantly. In 1871 three men were paid £6.13s.9d. for 'matting and claying twenty eight rods' (one rod being five metres), and later for 'mudding the bank one foot higher, thirty two rods at two shillings and sixpence, and re-building the wall near the saltern at ten shillings a rod.'

The two main bunneys were constructed from the characteristic yellow bricks of the area, probably from the long-established kilns that bordered the reclaimed area. At the seaward side the bunneys were fitted with a hinged 'gate' which was kept shut by the weight of sea water at high tides and pushed open by marsh drainage water as the tide dropped. In addition, several smaller bunneys were driven through the bank with which to flood the drainage channels each summer. These were simple constructions made from 5-inch boarding and were each fitted with a manual clapper.

The men earned a little extra for additional jobs on the banks. The account book records instances of 'looking to the bank on Sunday', 'mending the breach', and 'cleaning and tarring the lighter'. They kept their tools in a hut which stood atop the bank on the site of Marsh Saltern. Its low, west-facing door was not weather-proof, and when the rear wall collapsed, the path along the bank passed right through the building! In around 1900 a replacement hut was built inside the wall. Made of wood but with a brick chimney, it was thickly tarred against the weather. They stoked a log fire here from rotten piling and the tang of tar and smoke lingered into the 1940s. The old saltern quay, locally known as a 'hard', was used to moor the lighter, and the men kept a large patch of cultivated land nearby. The soil was a rich red from the cinder deposits of the saltern boiling pans, and they had all-weather access across the old saltern trackway from Newtown. It was rough work, often done in rough weather. Normal clothing for the job consisted of corduroy trousers, a heavy worsted jacket, leather boots and gaiters.

In 1932 large parts of the Swainston estate were sold off, including the 141 acres of Newtown Marsh which were bought by the Barton brothers of Harts Farm. At that time the tenant of Marsh Farm, Mr J. Warder, was paying an annual rent of £80 for the Marsh. The Bartons, together with Billy and Ted Prangnell from Lower Elmsworth brickyard, used some split oaks from Fuzzy Butt near Old Vicarage Lane to effectively repair some weak spots, and also used some ash posts driven straight into the mud, but the tasks of maintenance were onerous and costly.

From the late 1930s it had become increasingly common to use mud and clay taken from the trench inside the bank to raise the height of the bank. Descendants of the estate workers who knew the banks warned that this would weaken them, and the banks were, indeed, subjected to increased decay. The eventual demise of the banks was also hastened by the use of inappropriate materials in their repair. Around 1950, the Bartons included the Marsh in their sale of Oyster Cottage to a Mr Spearing, an antiques dealer. Regarded as being somewhat eccentric by many local residents, he put up a cowshed near the present scrape and managed to let some pastures. He repaired that section of the bank stretching from the boat-house towards the stone bank near Brickyard Corner with a layer of concrete sheeting (removing many of the oak posts in the process) which, when undermined by the tides, merely slipped seawards. He was not alone in underestimating the power of the elements. Sir Hansen Rowbotham, who had purchased some of the Marsh during the 1940s to accommodate his Suffolk Punch horses and Red Poll cattle, instructed one of his factory foremen from the Midlands to use corrugated sheeting to shore up the embankment!

Since they were first constructed the banks have been susceptible to storm surges. Several breaches are recorded in Swainston records, and 'Jumbo' Woolgar recollected a failure during the 1880s. A major break occurred in 1922 at Cuckoo Pen, just east of Brickyard Corner, when residents at London Heath, some two miles away, could hear the roar of the tide rushing through. At this time an inner bank in the shape of a half-moon was constructed to close the break. Eventually, this was the point of major failure in 1953, bearing out the predictions of earlier generations of Newtown men. A further major break came near Brickyard Corner in the storms of November 1954. Ron Burt took his horse and cart to mend the breach but lost both and had to swim for his life. Even Mrs Spearing, wife of the owner of the Marsh, was dragooned into wielding a spade, but to no avail! Despite a number of well-intentioned efforts to repair the damage, including the use of heavy machinery sent by the Government, little was achieved and the tide began its regular incursions,

The bank in 1985, looking south-west towards Newtown Quay, which was already badly damaged. This was one of the last accessible stretches of the embankment.

The spine oak posts, probably driven in during the nineteenth century, stand in tribute to a lost land in 1988.

working away from the inside in addition to its seaward attrition. Probably, any cost/benefit analysis would reveal the unlikelihood of it all.

Even so, at least one optimist purchased a part of the drowning pasture and came up with big ideas that amounted to nothing, before a keen yachtsman from Surrey, Mr Shortis (or Shorthouse), bought some banks and pasture along with Oyster Cottage, eventually bequeathing that part of the Marsh and its embankment to the National Trust in 1983.

But the area lost its grasses, marsh plants began to colonise it again, and millions of gallons of saline water returned large parts to its original ooze. Efforts to defend the land became concentrated on the two extremities of the embankment. Many of the concrete mooring blocks used by the Admiralty during the Second World War, each weighing two tons, were recovered and used to strengthen the banks east of Brickyard Corner, and several years later the National Trust, with help from the Manpower Services Commission, built a wall of vertical pine poles to protect the western salterns and quay. Desperate times call for desperate measures and in 1982 girls from Upper Chine School at Shanklin, who had joined the Young National Trust Movement, were drafted in to repair the banks! It had become an unequal struggle. The severe wastage of the eastern spit at the mouth of the Haven permitted more and more tidal ingress, and the wide expanse of water inside the Haven at high tides now encourages further storm damage in windy conditions. At the time of writing even the quay and the remains of Newtown Saltern are threatened, despite the use of traditional bundles of hazel and blackthorn to stem the tidal attack.

The two-mile walk around the banks is no more. Only at low tide can the remnants of the embankment be traced, the old spine oaks jutting skyward like broken teeth. Over 100 acres of prime pasture have been lost and the Marsh has become, once more, a haven for wildlife.

A school party just manages to navigate a muddy way around Newtown Marsh embankment at low tide, 1965.

Chapter 8

'Without Envy for What Others Enjoy': Brick Makers of the Haven

Throughout his adult life Ted Prangnell hid in the bushes surrounding Lower Elmsworth brickyard whenever strangers appeared in this remote part of Newtown. He had grown up here, knowing only his closest family, and he could never easily make new friends. Ted, who died in 1975, was the last surviving skilled brick maker of the Newtown area, one of the district's many industrial workers, a characteristic seemingly at odds with the rural tranquility of this corner of the Island.

Billy, Mary and Annie Prangnell outside their cottage in 1952. Ted was probably far too shy to be photographed.

It is difficult to imagine Newtown as a thriving industrial centre yet, until the nineteenth century, the estuary was home to no fewer than seven large salterns and their boiling houses. Locally registered trading vessels plied their trade, carrying salt, coal, stone and bricks. Two large brickyards throbbed with activity, and the fishing industry flourished. Most of these activities were associated with particular families who handed their business acumen from one generation to the next – Holbrook and Munt, the salt boilers; Abrook and Paskins, the fishermen; and Lindsay and Prangnell, the brick and tile makers. Assets, skills and experience were handed from fathers to sons, sometimes taking the family business to the very edge of commercial disaster.

The growth and the decline of Newtown's 'golden industrial age' is nowhere better illustrated than by the enterprising Prangnell family. It seems that they could have arrived in England as seventeenth-century Flemish immigrants. Their name can be traced on the Isle of Wight from the early-eighteenth century, and certainly by the early-nineteenth century they were heavily engaged in brick, tile and pipe manufacture at Shide (where Emanuel Prangnell, born 1772, was a brick burner) and Carisbrooke, where Emanuel's brother Edward

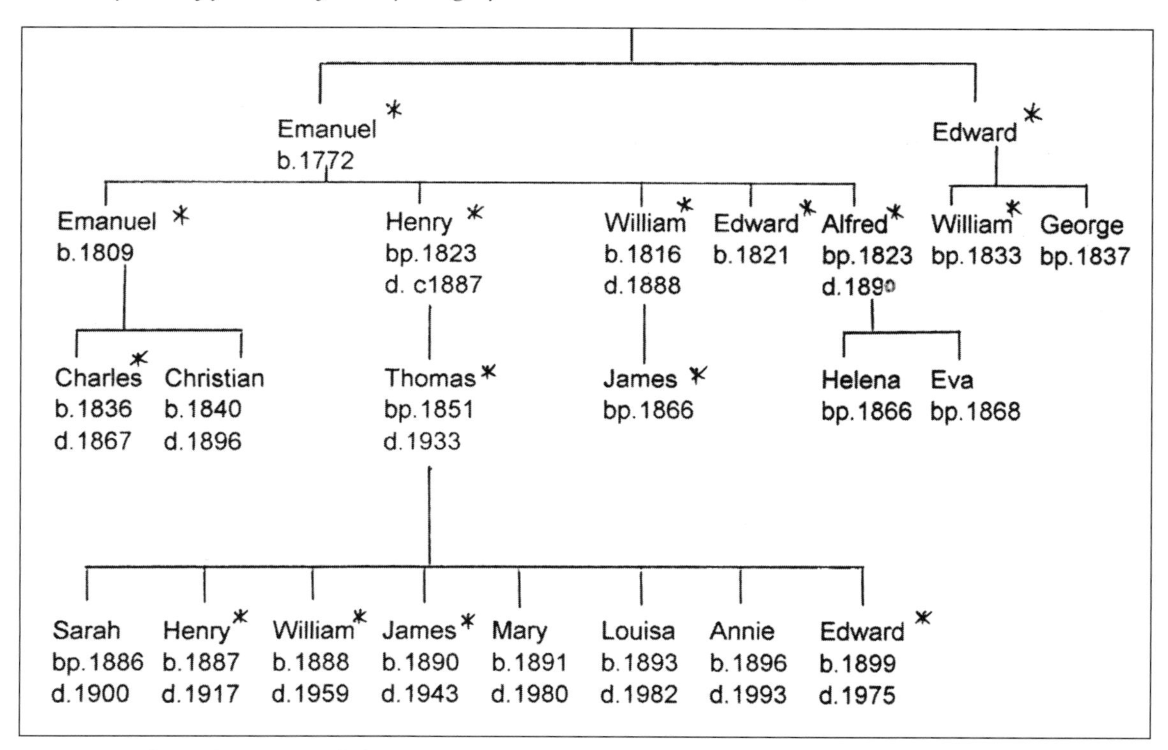

*An extract from the Prangnell family tree. (Known brick makers are marked *)*

But the family relied heavily on water transport. They built their own platform at the quay at the head of Causeway Creek and in the 1890s delivered their produce by carvel-built lighter to be collected by the carrier. Later on, they kept two heavily tarred clinker-built rowing boats for the same purpose. Sadly, but inevitably, for it was the tradition of such folk, Billy Prangnell broke up and burned the boats on the foreshore when the family left Brickfields Farm.

Naturally, the commercial brickyard was almost entirely dependent on water-borne transport. A horse could carry 60 bricks at most, or haul perhaps 350 in a wagon. (Sadly, one of Thomas' daughters, Sarah Maria, died at the age of 12, having fallen from just such a wagon. Medical assistance was several hours away.) The siting of the yards at Lower Hamstead and Lower Elmsworth was no accident. Over the years, thousands of tons of coal were delivered by boat, and many more thousands of tons of bricks, tiles and pipes were taken away from the purpose-built quays. In the 1830s the sloop *Wellington* was wholly engaged at Lower Hamstead, together with the *Weevil* and the *Houghton*. And in the 1870s and '80s the Holbrooks' boats *Dove* and *Wellington* were used mainly to convey bricks from Lower Elmsworth to the River Medina and as far as Littlehampton and Shoreham in Sussex, along with Harry Hollins' SS *Arrow* and Mr Rickman's sailing barges from Cowes.

Bernie Hayward's grandfather, a Shalfleet miller, was one of the 'mud pilots' employed to guide the barges moving bricks through the narrow, forever-shifting channels of the Haven, where movements were restricted to higher tides.

Thomas Prangnell always took charge of the loading operations at Lower Elmsworth, forbidding any visiting seaman to speak to his family, lest he revealed what day of the week it was. Rumour had it that Tom paid his workforce once a week – every ten days or so!

The rigours of such an isolated existence were bound to produce some colourful personalities, none more so than Alfred Prangnell. Somewhat self-opinionated, he was never long out of the news. In addition to his reputation for sailing, woodworking and brick making he also managed to make headlines when it came to his fondness for liquor. When boasting about his brick-making records he claimed that 'brandy did the work'. This prompted a member of the Salvation Army to make a poorly disguised attack on him during a meeting at Locks Green School in 1888, imploring the congregation 'not to drink any more of that damnable drink.' Alfred was furious and wrote a stinging letter to the Army captain at West Cowes, quoting liberally from the Bible to justify his views: 'It is not what goes into a man's mouth that defileth him, but what comes out.'

Paradoxically, every member of his nephew Thomas Prangnell's family was a lifelong teetotaler, a fact which is all the more surprising bearing in mind the family's long association with the Noah's Ark, although there is some suggestion that Tom was in fact a Quaker.

Ted Prangnell was the complete opposite of his great-uncle Alfred. Painfully shy and hiding his face behind a large moustache, he mixed only with his closest relatives. Even later in life, after the four siblings had moved to a small cottage in Carisbrooke, Ted remained unseen in another room when visitors were around. His sister Mary was similarly afflicted. She suffered a very severe speech impediment and, reportedly, also had learning disabilities. After a short and predictably unsuccessful spell as a barmaid at the Noah's Ark local lore maintained the claim that she never once left Lower Elmsworth in over 40 years until the family moved out in 1954.

Billy was much more outgoing. A short, thick-set and immensely strong man, with sparkling blue eyes and shovel-like hands, Billy willingly turned to whatever paid work was available. (When work at the brickyard ceased, an alternative cash income was at a premium.) He became the classic odd-job man, maintaining several caches of tools around the district, including that in the ancient, tarred hut which stood behind the marsh embankment opposite Brickfields Farm which he and Henry Foss had shared whilst maintaining the banks for the estate. For many years he worked for the Paskins brothers aboard their smack *Fanny*, becoming an expert on the raising of oysters, and was always available to Andrew Barton or Fred Fallick as a beater. Fred wrote of the time when Billy, together with George Hayward and some dogs, beat Fleetlands Warren for three 'guns' and for the entertainment of the young Simeon children, 'Master John' and 'Miss Betty'. If there was a towing job to be done Billy was there with his hank of rope, and he often worked for Sir Hansen Rowbotham, who kept Suffolk Punch horses at Marsh Farm in the 1930s and '40s, mincing mangel-wurzels and moving hay. He also helped Captain Seabroke, the Newtown harbourmaster, to lay moorings, including those at Ducks' Cove in Causeway Creek, using two canvas-sided lifeboats from the German liner *Berrengeria*. He was an expert waterman and a great authority on the movements of wildfowl in the estuary. Many local men who sported guns sought his advice about the sightings of wild duck, only to be told: 'Nah, but there's plenny o' those ol' tweezers [teal] abate!' More often than not wearing an old worsted suit and waistcoat, Billy always sported a pair of sea boots, a habit that caused him great discomfort with swollen legs in later life.

Aubrey de Selincourt paid tribute to Billy in his book *The Channel Shore*, published by Hale in 1953:

That farmer is the most contented of men, without envy for what others enjoy. I hardly know why it is, but I find a sort of reassurance in the thought of a man who

Billy Prangnell with young guest Richard Seabroke, c.1940.

The Prangnell family's memorials in Newtown churchyard, overlooked by two of the houses they built.

Opposite: *Wedding photo of Emma Louise Prangnell of Brickfield House, Newtown and Joseph John Osbon-Sanders of Clamerkin Farm, c.1920.*

has failed to observe the necessity for being always in a hurry and too busy to breathe.

Only two of Thomas Prangnell's eight children ever got married and moved away from Lower Elmsworth. One of them, Henry George (always known as Harry), was killed as a war volunteer in France soon after his marriage in 1915. His older sister, Emma Louise, succeeded Adela Foss as a housekeeper at Hebberdens Farm for the brothers Joseph and Robert Osbon-Sanders, and eventually married Joseph. Some of their descendants still live at Shalfleet.

Thus, with Annie's death in 1993, this branch of the Prangnell family name came to an end. But the family left an enduring legacy. Their distinctive creamy bricks and decorative styles are instantly recognisable. A particularly good example can be found in a stretch of some 15 double-tenement properties in Oxford Street, Northwood, and they feature in several properties in Newtown itself, notably Myrtle Cottage, which was built by the Prangnells bit by bit between 1870 and 1890 when the adjoining property (Rose Cottage) was in the hands of Henry and Maria Prangnell.

At the time of writing, the site of Lower Elmsworth brickyard has become very overgrown, the kiln and the drying sheds area being almost hidden by a thicket of trees, bushes and creepers. Between 1954–56 Bernie Hayward dismantled the drying sheds and used the materials to strengthen the trackway towards Elmsworth, and used the tiles from the former dairy to waterproof the main house. It is said that the dairy was later demolished in the course of a military exercise! When Mr Hayward left, Elmsworth farmer George Abblitt took over the use of the fields, and the Isle of Wight County Council purchased the brickyard site, refurbishing the farm-house during the 1960s as a field-study centre for Island schoolchildren. Lou Cox (Cowes Secondary School) and Oliver Fraser (Priory Girls' School) were leading players in this activity. Already designated as a nature reserve by the Isle of Wight County Council (the predecessor of the Isle of Wight Council), and declared a Site of Special Scientific Interest (SSSI), the

area continues to attract the attention of the National Trust, which owns East Point. In January 2004 a firm proposal for the Trust to administer Brickfields is being considered. A more serene and peaceful spot than Lower Elmsworth would be difficult to find. A profusion of wild flowers, birds, small mammals and insects are its only residents. But its very isolation invites intrusion. Little has been done to strengthen its sea defences since the military authorities put in groynes in the 1920s, and the cliff line is receding rapidly, stranding the groynes incongruously 100 metres offshore, and beginning to threaten even the main cottage. The fabric of the building itself is all too obviously vulnerable to vandalism and theft, and internet sites boast of barbecues.

It is said that the onset of arthritis finally drove the Prangnell siblings unexpectedly from their home. In December 1953, only a few months before they left, Annie wrote to a recent visitor to the farm, Miss Vera Baker, a granddaughter of Christian Prangnell (1846–90) and Jacob Pritchett: 'We can only say how pleased we was to see you, and we shall be looking forward in seeing you again next year.'

Although they took some of their ways with them to Carisbrooke (a small enamel bowl continued to serve as their sink, and visitors had to tolerate their reluctance to switch on the electric lights, even after dusk), with their parting from Lower Elmsworth a simple lifestyle, never to be seen again on the Island, left with them.

The nature reserve in 1998.

The landing-stage and site of the former quay from which the Prangnells left Lower Elmsworth for the last time.

that it may have been used as a breeding ground for oysters following the death in 1912 of the owner of Hamstead estate, Miss Rose Pennythorne.

The Simeon family at Swainston also owned the large saltern at Shalfleet, and by 1844 were leasing it to Abraham Clark. Significant remains of the boiling house and salt store can still be seen at Shalfleet Quay. Families immersed in the salt-making industry tended to move around the Island's salterns to work, and also 'commuted' to those on the mainland opposite. John Foss (1763–1813) worked the Newtown salterns until 1806 before moving to Nettlestone where Newport banker James Kirkpatrick was developing the local salterns. Similarly, John Matthews moved from the Hamstead Saltern in 1790 to become saltern manager at Nettlestone.

Production at Shalfleet Saltern ceased around 1865, possibly when George Tatchell, its last salt boiler, retired. An oyster-fishing lease dated 1867 stipulated that the recently abandoned Shalfleet Saltern must be well stocked with oysters by 1870, and the associated map confirms that only the Hamstead and Newtown Salterns were then still active. However, at the time of writing the outline of the feeding ponds and salt-pans at Shalfleet are still discernable each day at low tides just to the north of the quay which formerly served them.

By far the best preserved salt-pans around the Newtown Haven are those of Newtown Saltern itself. These works were planned by Nicholas Dobree as early as 1730, and were probably built shortly afterwards. When he leased part of the Marsh to Robert Rogers he excluded the existing Marsh Salterns and likewise:

> *... all that piece of ground at the west end of a certain field or close called Green Close and now set apart... for the erecting and building a new saltern which said last mentioned piece of ground is situate outside the banks of the Old Marsh.*

Despite being relatively small at seven acres, it became a very successful enterprise, finally closing down some time around 1885; it was the last working saltern on the Island, the last at Nettlestone having ceased production in 1819. Some idea of the considerable scale of the operation can be gained from an indenture of 1820. The contemporary leaseholder, Joseph Munt, had somehow become indebted to an affluent yeoman farmer from Shalfleet, Richard Arnold, to the sum of £120. To cover the debt the salt boiler had made over to Richard Arnold the rights of possession of 100 tons of salt stored at Newtown. The farmer was to dispose of it 'by public auction or private contract', retain sufficient monies to cover the debt, and to pass the surplus ('if any') to the salt boiler. Clearly, the anticipated price was little more than £1 per ton, a ridiculously low figure for the day. The extent to which the unfortunate salt boiler understood either the legal jargon of the document or his position of vulnerability regarding prices obtained can only be imagined for, like the majority of saltern workers, he was illiterate and made his mark on the indenture with a shaky cross.

The Munts, the Holbrooks and other salt boilers also had another problem to contend with, that of the Salt Officer. An unpopular salt tax was first imposed in 1694, sometimes rising to a cost in excess of four times the value of the commodity itself, and apart from a couple of years (1730–32) was not abolished until 1825. (It took a revolution to remove the French equivalent – the hated 'Gabelle'!) Three or four officers, operating independently of the excise authorities, were responsible for the whole of the Solent area. The 1730 lease, quoted earlier, noted that at least one officer was based at Newtown, whose unpopular task it was to weigh and monitor all the production and transport of salt, and impose a spot tax. He probably occupied the Watchhouse which was located near the Marsh Saltern, paying rent to the leaseholders in 1732, Jacob Marks and Joseph Bailey, respectively victualler and blacksmith of Lymington, and later in 1769 to a Mr Clavell who, as lessee, was paying an annual rent of £3 to the manor.

To reduce the possibility of corruption (and maybe also to protect the well-being of the officer!) these tax collectors were relocated every four years. By the end of the eighteenth century Newtown had no resident Salt Officer, although a list of Calbourne parish residents, dated 1803, included mention of two, John Abrook and William Munt, each aged 50 years and described as 'superannuated'. It is possible that in 1796 Nicholas Cory, one of two officers located at Bucklers Hard, earned part of his annual salary of £40 by becoming unpopular around Newtown where, at that date, six salt boilers and two saltern proprietors were at work.

By 1841 Richard Holbrook was leasing the Newtown Saltern from the Earl of Yarborough, probably having taken it over from his father Thomas Holbrook, and for the next 25 years until his death he, together with his brother Reuben, kept the industry alive in Newtown. When Reuben retired around 1880 his nephew Thomas Holbrook, a ship's mate, took over the lease, but it is unlikely that production continued for long after that. Reuben Holbrook was the last to be listed in a directory as 'salt maker'. Perhaps it was a pride in the lengthy family tradition that caused him to describe himself thus, because for much of the 1860s and '70s he was also a foreman for the Swainston estate, with responsibility for the 'gang' who 'kept the banks' around the reclaimed marsh, working alongside Jonas and Henry Foss, Morris Rogers and Barnabus Cotton. By these later years, the saltern was probably in a state of decay and the demand for salt from this source was dwindling. A second income became a necessity or, maybe like others in the village, Reuben alternated between

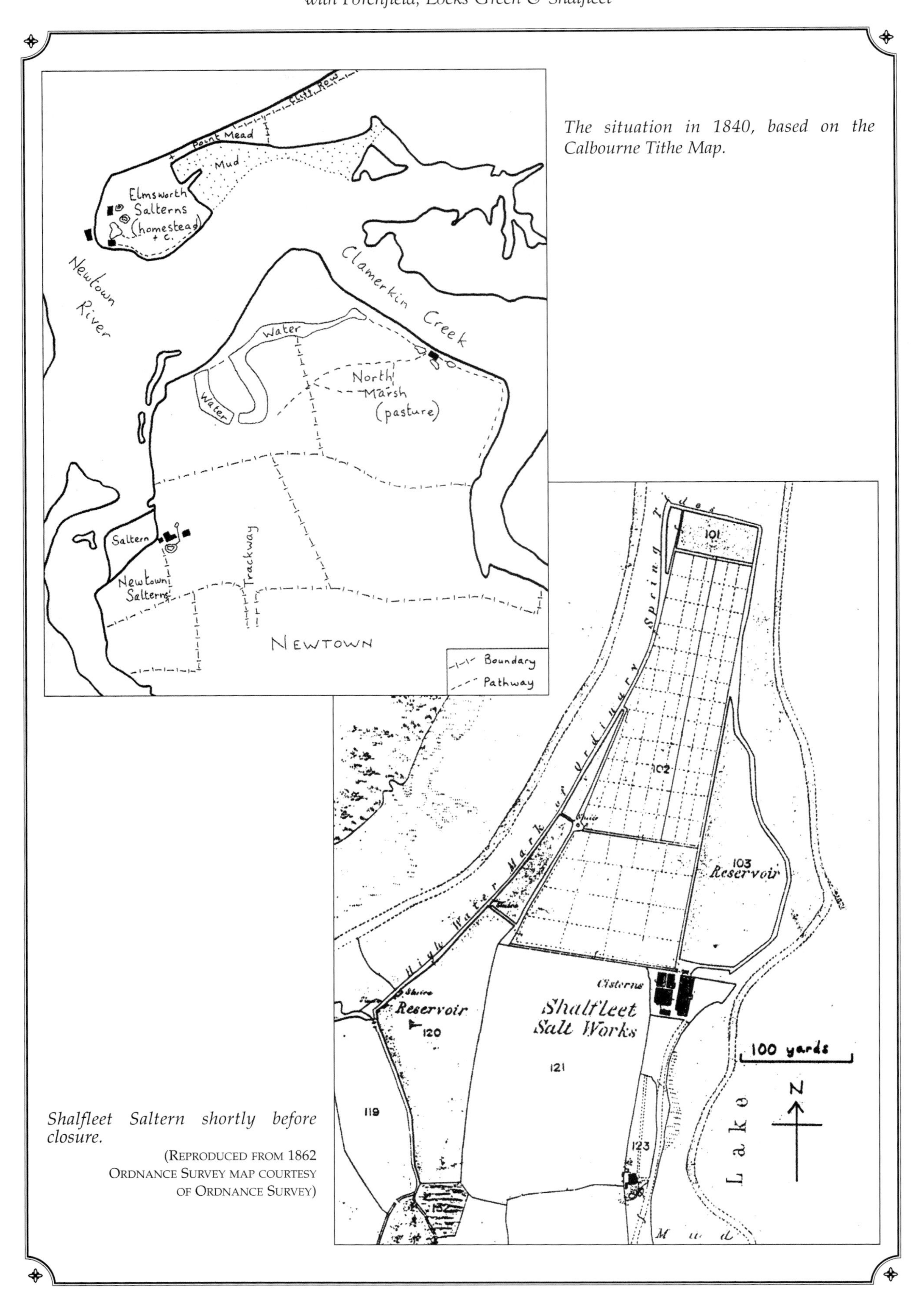

The situation in 1840, based on the Calbourne Tithe Map.

Shalfleet Saltern shortly before closure.

(Reproduced from 1862 Ordnance Survey map courtesy of Ordnance Survey)

Site of the former Shalfleet Saltern as it appeared in 1995.

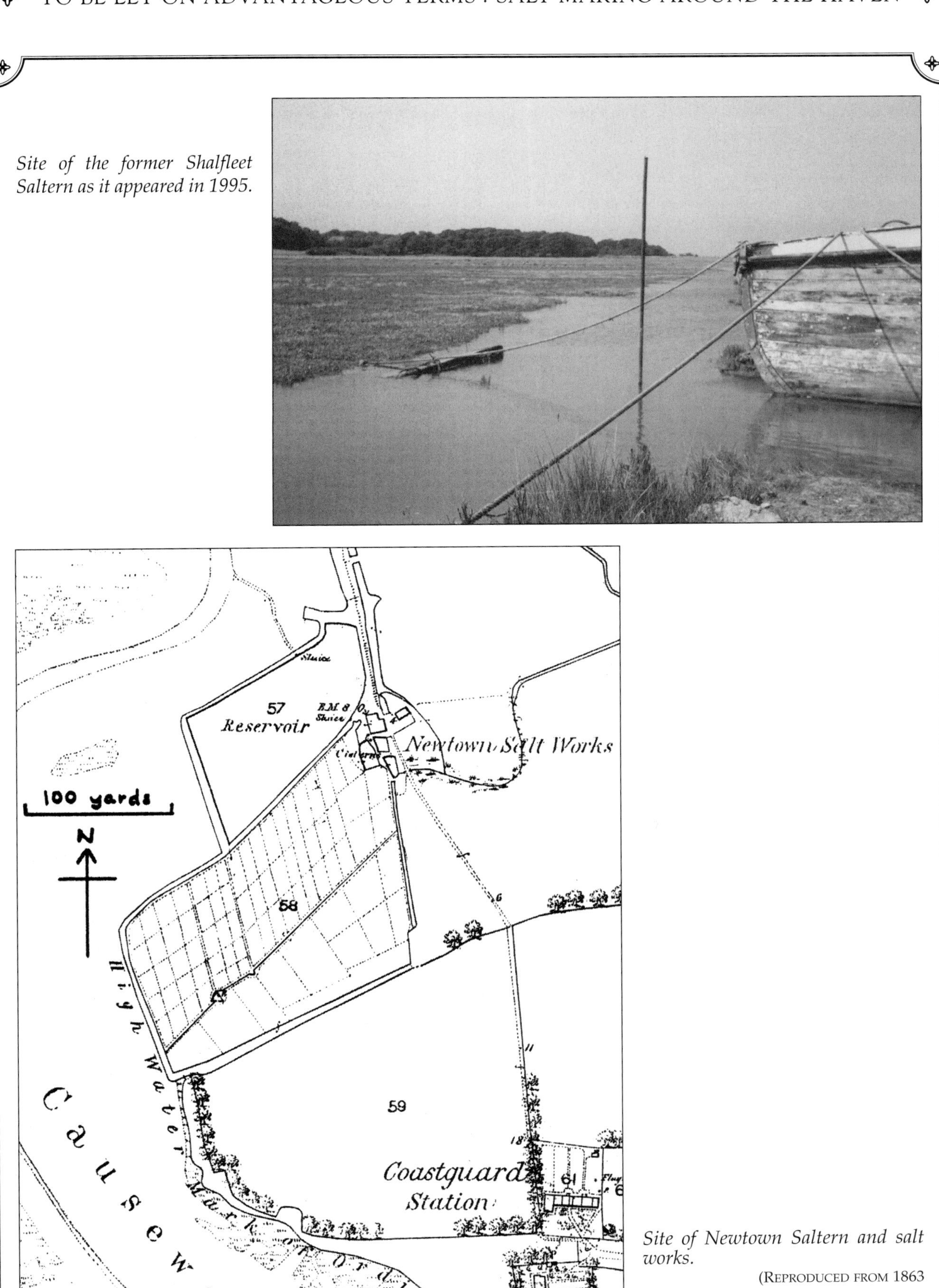

Site of Newtown Saltern and salt works.

(REPRODUCED FROM 1863 ORDNANCE SURVEY MAP COURTESY OF ORDNANCE SURVEY)

summer and winter jobs, salt boiling in the summer (the optimum months for evaporation) and working for the estate in winter. For at least 50 years from the late 1820s the Holbrook salt-boiling family had occupied Key Close Farm. The women, Thomas Holbrook's wife Ann and then their daughter Hannah, ran the nine-acre dairy, whilst two of their sons (Richard and Reuben) toiled at salt making. Reuben married and moved into nearby Rose Cottage where, many years later in the late 1870s, Hannah joined him in retirement.

Long after the saltern stopped production the red-brick salt house near the quay was used by local rivermen, the Paskins brothers, as a store for their nets and dredges. Abandoned by them around 1940, it fell into disrepair over many years, but its demolition around 1983 under the auspices of a national conservation group was, at best, irresponsible. Briefly, late in the nineteenth century, the salt-pans had been used for breeding oysters on a bed of tiles, but the spat sickened and died before reaching maturity. The salt industry, once the pride of Newtown, had faded into oblivion. The rising price of coal, the silting of the river, and the competition from the Cheshire and Worcestershire mines had all taken their toll.

Thomas Henry Foss died prematurely in 1870 and his widow, Emma Jane, then aged 41 and still with five young children to feed, soon married again, this time to a gamekeeper, Samuel Bourne, some 16 years her junior. According to her great-grandson, John Foss, they later acquired some lands at Newtown including some saltings, and when Emma was widowed again in 1908 she was persuaded to let them go very cheaply. Maybe Samuel and Emma had been seduced by the romance of that weather-beaten notice – 'To be let on advantageous terms'.

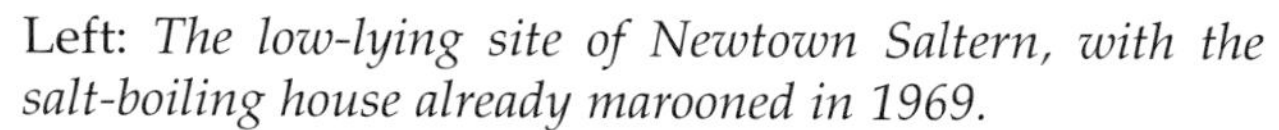

Left: *The low-lying site of Newtown Saltern, with the salt-boiling house already marooned in 1969.*

(REPRODUCED COURTESY OF *THE NEWS*, PORTSMOUTH)

Below: *A familiar view until 1983 towards the salt-boiling house and the boat-house at Newtown.*

(FROM A PAINTING BY PATRICK KENNETH TRUCKLE)

Chapter 10

'I Once Saw a Queer Bunched Figure': The Story of Shell-Fishing

Sitting on the shore and looking out over Saltmead Ledge and the Solent, near sunset, I once saw a queer bunched figure moving cautiously, thigh deep in the shallow water, a hundred yards from land: it was a man fishing for prawns, pushing his net in front of him.

Writing of the 1930s, but capturing 1,000 years of Newtown's history, Aubrey de Selincourt, in his book *Isle of Wight* (Elek, 1948), described a timeless harvest gathered laboriously around the Haven's shores.

In the twenty-first century the Haven provides opportunities mainly for leisure, but until the 1930s and beyond people made a living from its waters gathering shellfish of one kind or another, a tradition now limited to its oyster-farming activities. Newtown was full of mariners and fishermen in the mid-1800s, landing their catches at one of the 'hards' (shingle shores) scattered around the Haven at the head of Causeway Creek, Locks Hard, Newtown Quay, Quay (Key) Close and North Marsh Hard. Among them were Thomas and Henry Abrook, Oliver Wade, Henry Jacobs, Thomas Henry Foss, William Abrook and his sons George and William (already 'mariners' at the ages of 13 and 11), Alford Prince, and James and Jonas Foss – many of them with more than one form of employment, and most 'working around the edges' of the formal fishing lease, in order to earn a living from the sea. As late as the 1880s more than a dozen such folk worked the Haven. Commonly known as 'rivermen' until the 1900s, these were the men who gathered prawns, collected whelks and winkles, set pots for crabs and lobsters and, so it is said, more than occasionally took oysters illegally. When possible, they also took wet fish, and shot and trapped game to supplement their tables, all of it technically against the law. Even in 2004, the leaseholders hold not only the rights to fishing and fowling but also the authority to issue permits and collect royalties on such activities. Notionally, even simple rod and line could be used only at a leaseholder's discretion. However, apart from fiercely protecting their rights to oysters, and sometimes winkles, most leaseholders have been content to turn a blind eye to these rules.

Herbert Foss, aged 14, during his 'apprenticeship' into shell-fishing off North Marsh, 1916. It was the custom for rivermen to wear a full set of clothes for the business, including shirt and tie.

Some say the Romans marched on Newtown oysters, and the Domesday Survey (1086) refers to a 'Salt Fish House' in the area, possibly the origin of the name Fish House Point (now East Point) at the mouth of the estuary. Newtown borough's rent accounts record payments to the manor of 5s.0d. a year for fishing rights as early as 1303, a figure that remained unchanged certainly until at least 1655. When the borough was dissolved in 1835, one of the few borough incomes was the rent of £10 reserved on the lease of oyster fishing for a term of seven years.

For centuries, the lease for the fishery at Newtown carried an annual rent and an 'obligation to provide a good dish of fish, and a sufficient number of oysters for the mayor's feast.' Newtown oysters had become famous by the twelfth century and fishing rights are still jealously guarded to this day. The whole Haven was leased out by the borough 'for oyster fishing and fowling'. Seventeenth-century leases were available for only £1–2 per annum, when oysters constituted a 'poor man's diet' and fetched only £1 per 1,000. But by 1712 Thomas Smith, a Newport sword cutler, contracted with the borough for a complicated 21-year lease carrying the 'right to gather oysters with the royalties for other fishing.' He was required to pay £10 per annum for the first ten years, together with fish and oysters for each meeting of the Mayor and burgesses, thereafter 40s. for each remaining year.

In many instances leaseholders were not fishermen and probably employed local men to cultivate and harvest the shellfish. In 1720 the lease passed to Robert Harvey, a clerk from Shalfleet, moving successively to other Shalfleet residents – in 1751 to John Dore, a mariner; then to John Munt, a yeoman, in 1763; and in 1782 to a gentleman, John Miller, who renewed it in 1810. Oyster-fishing had become a thriving business and in 1752, for instance, many thousands were exported from Cowes to France.

Between 1840 and 1940 the industry became associated with two celebrated families who, for most of that time, were the leaseholders. By 1851 Henry Abrook, who occupied Nobby's Cottage and advertised himself as an oyster merchant and mariner, and his son Thomas, also a mariner of Newtown, were paying £20 per annum for the 'right of having, taking, dragging and gathering oysters in the Newtown Haven' on a 14-year lease which they renewed for £30 per annum in 1865, about the time they moved into Oyster Cottage, recently built by the manor in Newtown High Street, especially to house them. However, from 1866 ownership of the lease seems to have transferred from the manor to a syndicate of businessmen (including a Simeon, whose family was then resident at Swainston) which, the following year, established the Isle of Wight Oyster Fishery Company Limited and employed Thomas Abrook as foreman. He remained resident in Oyster Cottage.

A counterpart lease of 1867 – involving Spur Lake, nine acres of adjoining land, the salterns and lands with works, and a cottage and garden, together with the quay – extended the fishery's influence, carrying a rent of £42 per annum for 21 years plus a royalty for any oysters harvested.

In 1880 the Newtown and Beaulieu Oyster Fishery Company was established, which leased the beds and fisheries from the IOW Oyster Fishery, Sir John Simeon and Lord Henry Scott MP. The new company paid £600 to obtain the lease but throughout its six-year existence it ran into financial difficulties, raising only £400 in one season, having discovered that French oysters would not mature very well at Newtown. Thomas Abrook, by this time describing himself as a mariner, was able still to occupy Oyster Cottage because the new company's manager was Edwin Mursell who lived at Ben Farm, Shalfleet. By 1891 Thomas had retired from the sea and had moved out of Oyster Cottage back into Nobby's Cottage, next door, where he developed a dairy business. He died there, aged 90, in 1915.

By 1893, Thomas Paskins had obtained a 21-year lease at £50 per annum for the 'right of fishing and gathering oysters in part of Newtown Haven', and the following year obtained a lease for 19 years on a plot of land, probably that which contained the former salt-boiling house near Newtown Quay which they used for many years to store their fishing equipment. Already an established fishmonger at West Cowes, Thomas brought a fresh impetus to the industry, the lease remaining in the Paskins family until the mid-1940s.

After many years of declining fortunes the industry was revived by Thomas and, once again, Newtown became a social venue when Colonel Mew's Swainston shooting parties ended up at Noah's Ark for beer and oysters.

The Paskins family kept two fishing smacks, mooring them close to Oyster Pond which lies between Causeway Creek and Shalfleet Creek. Henry Paskins was based at Newtown, whilst his brothers, Charles, Edwin and George, and their father Thomas remained at West Cowes. Their main fishing business was oysters, trawling additionally for prawns and wet fish. They also laid over 50 prawn-pots, mainly offshore in the Solent. At the height of their activities in the 1920s lobsters were fetching 2s.6d. each and prawns were sold for 1s. a dozen.

None of the family took up residence in Oyster Cottage until many years later. Thomas had a home in West Cowes, and Henry quite possibly lived on one of the two fishing smacks they kept in the Haven. One of the last to call himself a 'riverman', Henry Paskins became a very successful businessman and a highly respected yacht-racing pilot serving on the famous *Creole* and the royal cutter *Britannia*. By 1919 Henry was living in Newtown and, by 1926, he had been joined by his fishmonger brother Charles. In the later years Henry employed an experienced oysterman from Essex, Robert Davy, a devout Wesleyan, who moved into Rose Cottage and organised most of the fishing business. Until Christmas 1934 Henry continued running his smack from Newtown to his own wharf at the rear of his High Street shop in Cowes (at the time of writing trading as Flowers) delivering fish and, especially during Cowes Week, prawns for the royal table on the *Victoria and Albert*, the royal yacht (for which he was granted a royal warrant). He was very well respected and quite affluent by the time of his death at Oyster Cottage (by then 'The Cottage') in 1935 at the age of 79, and all the local dignitaries were amongst the mourners at his funeral.

Left: *From the 1890s the Paskins family used the salt house to store their fishing gear.*
(FROM A PAINTING BY PATRICK KENNETH TRUCKLE)

Below: *The shop in High Street, Cowes, in the 1920s. On the left is Thomas Paskins with his brother Edwin.*

Remains of oyster-beds in the upper reaches of Clamerkin River, 1995.

Robert Davy went back to Essex following Henry Paskins' death and Henry's son, Norman Paskins, returned from Canada to take over the firm, initially moving into Rose Cottage, then into Oyster Cottage. A local resident described him as 'quite a dandy, cutting quite a bung at church, with spats and a bowler hat.' He had little experience of oyster farming and relied heavily on local men George Reynolds and Billy Prangnell. Expectations were unrealistic. Mr Reynolds was expected to row a boat from Cowes, dredge the oysters, and row back again to deliver them to the shop in time for the day's customers. The fishery declined and by 1950 meaningful production had ceased.

In 1953 the National Trust bought the fishing rights from the Swainston estate, licensing them the following year to the Newtown Oyster Fishery Company, a business established by Commander John Sherwood, a Ningwood man, who negotiated the lease through Stanley Ball, a trustee at Swainston. Commander Sherwood employed Robin Barton (simply because he could row an open boat!) to redevelop the Clamerkin oyster-beds which had been badly damaged during the storms of 1953, but they met with limited success. Most shell-fishing remained in Western Haven. In 1956 Commander Sherwood ordered a purpose-built, diesel-engined boat from Scotland, a small replica of a fishing smack and called *Zacky*. Two large wooden cages at Shalfleet Quay were used to purge the fish for several days, after which they were washed in a bushel-sized basket and bagged up to be sent to the next morning's Billingsgate Market, via Yarmouth. Traditionally, the seed oysters had come from Brittany but John Chalmers, who succeeded Andrew Barton as steward of Swainston, obtained seed from Cornwall. The business continued to struggle and after several years of decline another attempt was made to revive the industry when Cyril Lucas, who had his own open boat, purchased the company in 1960. He laid oyster 'seed' from France in Clamerkin River in 1961, but the severe winter of 1962/63 killed most of them. Despite local criticism that he had laid the oysters too far up the muddy banks of Clamerkin River rather than on the (frost-protected) deep-water shingle beds, Mr Lucas persevered and when he discovered that American clams, introduced into Southampton Water by chance, were breeding in the waters warmed by the outflow at Marchwood Power Station, he introduced them at Newtown. They thrived and were fattened, then purified for the markets in France and London, and the business returned to a sound footing. Pollution problems at the Whitstable oyster-beds opened the market opportunities again to Newtown, and oysters, brought from Beaulieu, once more successfully colonised the Haven. By 1970 the company was trading profitably in seeded oysters, mature oysters for markets mainly in London and France, and fattened clams, many of which went to America or to the ocean liners in Southampton.

In 1989 the fishery changed hands again and became known as Puffin Fisheries. This company sold the fish and shellfish rights back to the National Trust in 1996 and the area was declared a nature reserve. Despite this, poaching became a problem, some of the intruders claiming ancient rights of harvest. Claim and counter-claim continued for several years until, in January 2003, the National Trust once again leased out the Haven's fishing rights.

It is not known where 'seed' oysters were obtained for Newtown in earlier times, but in the nineteenth century, during the decline of the salt-making industry, abandoned salt-pans and feeding ponds were used for breeding, not always with much success. Broken tiles, laid in the feeding ponds at Hamstead, Shalfleet and Newtown, were seeded with the oyster 'spats' ('those tallow-drop scions' as 'Jumbo' Woolgar called them), but few survived.

The Paskins brothers imported spats from France, laying them on the river bed for two years and meeting with more success than their predecessors. They brought thousands of tons of hard clay and shingle from the seabed off Hamstead to make firm beddings for the shellfish along the Clamerkin River. An intimate knowledge of the sand, shingle and mud-banks of the Haven had been passed down the generations, so precise locations were chosen to obtain optimum conditions for the fish. Traditionally, the main oyster-beds have been just inside the Ningwood River towards the Hamstead side (a favourite site with the Paskins brothers that traditionally produced excellent fish), offshore near the Hamstead Ledge (although this site was later abandoned), and latterly in Clamerkin River. The imported seed oysters were already up to two years old and these were sowed over the stern of a boat at high tide, trickling them from the sacks over a shovel along the line of the oyster-bed. The beds were marked with long crooked sticks, until modern times a characteristic sight at Newtown. Sowing and harvesting was done from rowing boats, 14 feet long and fitted with workbenches at the stern. They were two-man boats, crewed during the 1920s and '30s by Robert Davy and George Reynolds. Traditional harvesting methods involved dropping anchor at the end of the oyster-bed facing the ebbing tide and allowing the craft to drift to the full extent of the anchor rope. The dredge was then dropped and the boat was hauled or rowed by both men back towards the anchor. The blades of the dredge had to be set at such an angle that oysters were scooped into the net without the dredge biting into the seabed. The dredge net was made from wire where it came into contact with the seabed, with hemp netting forming the top and the collecting bag at the end.

Harvesting was limited to the period from September until 1 April each year. The dredged fish were sorted for size and placed into containers, sometimes for a further period of fattening, but mostly to be cleaned and purified before being sent to market. Originally, simple bags were used and left on the mud to maximise the tidal flow of fresh sea water over them, but these were replaced by large wooden or wire cages fitted with floats in which the oysters could be constantly immersed so that purging was quicker and more effective. Because the cages could be moved quickly to deeper water their use lessened the risk of frost damage at low tides, and the method also facilitated the systematic sale of fish in the order in which they were dredged.

From the 1950s special washing sheds were established opposite the Town Hall at Newtown, where the shellfish were sorted, graded, bagged up and then immersed in large concrete tanks filled with fresh sea water pumped up from Causeway Creek whilst the molluscs purged their impurities. During the 1970s the fishery moved out of the village to a new site in Town Copse, still using two small boats to collect the oysters, one appropriately named *Sea Pie,* the local name for an oystercatcher. A small jetty was built into Clamerkin River and modern methods of purification using ultra-violet irradiation were adopted. Seed oysters are no longer scattered on the seabed but, like the clams which are brought to Newtown almost full-grown, are fattened in polythene net bags which, when ready, are hooked at low tide and lifted at high. Dredging has now become a distant memory.

The fishing rights of the leaseholders have always been jealously guarded, sometimes leading to litigation against poachers. Even the moribund borough authorities were alert to trespass on their rights shortly before their demise, threatening James Foss with legal action. The fact that he was never prosecuted might say more about the local constable John Holbrook's liking for oysters than James' probity.

A rather more celebrated case in the early 1900s involved the Paskins brothers prosecuting the Sheath family, fishmongers in Newport, for illegally collecting winkles at Newtown. For centuries, Swainston's river committee addressed such disputes. As late as the 1950s the committee deliberated, meeting in the railway carriage that sat in the gardens of Myrtle Cottage, chaired by the harbourmaster 'Pop' Meadows, and attended by Captain Seabroke and Dr Fairley among others. And half a century later, in 2001, the *Isle of Wight County Press* carried readers' letters threatening legal action over the ownership of oysters and clams laid in the Haven since the 1970s. Apparently, the arts and sciences of the longshoreman are still alive and well in the district!

Rivalry between rivermen was by no means unknown as each family vied for ascendancy. Some took direct action to dissuade competitors and in the 1920s Henry Foss often had his fishing nets cut or his lobster-pots raided and sunk. He, and men like Henry Jacobs, operated on a very modest scale compared to that of the holders of the official fishing and fowling lease. Henry Foss, and his father Jonas, often dredged for oysters in the open waters beyond the estuary (now the province of the Solent Oyster Fishery), or collected them during the very low September tides off the coast near Lower Elmsworth brickyard. They then carefully laid them where they hoped the oysters would not be found before sale the following winter. The Prangnell family at the brickyard were keen competitors for the oysters, and Henry always kept a sharp lookout before lowering his collection, perhaps a dozen or so on each visit, on that side of his dinghy facing away from the competition. He made his own storage cages with metal rings obtained from Gundry, a fishing-equipment

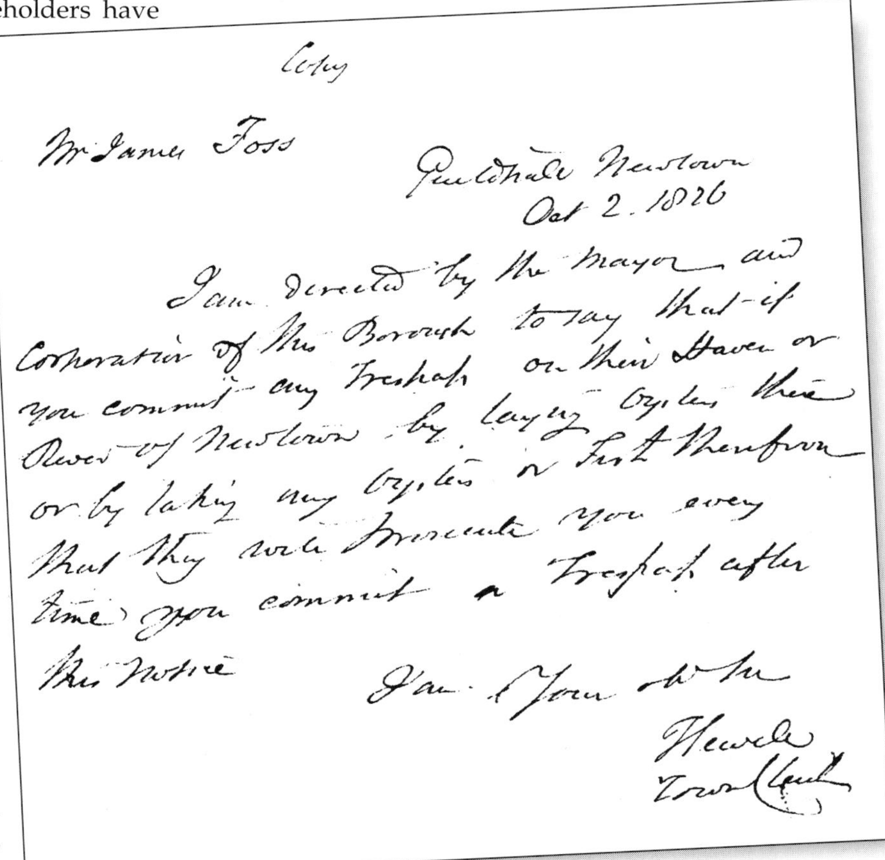
Copy

Mr James Foss

Guildhall Newtown
Oct 2. 1826

I am directed by the Mayor and Corporation of this Borough to say that if you commit any Trespass on their Haven or River of Newtown by laying Oysters there or by taking any Oysters or Fish therefrom that they will prosecute you every time you commit a Trespass after this Notice

I am Your ob[t] Ser[t]
Hewitt
Town Clerk

The borough letter to 'Captain' James Foss in 1826.
(REPRODUCED COURTESY OF THE COUNTY RECORD OFFICE, NEWPORT)

supplier in Bridport, and fashioned his small dredge with its two-foot beam and two-inch blade from the same source.

Another of Henry's incomes came from collecting gallons of mushrooms when in season from which his wife Adela made ketchup for sale in Cowes. The story persists to this day among farmers that to beat 'Hen' Foss to the mushrooms one had to rise before the cockerel. To maintain the good humour of Farmer Holden at Hamstead Farm in 1926 Henry 'paid' him 100 oysters.

Henry was employed by the estate during the winter months to 'keep the banks' but during summer such work was scarce. Then, like several generations of his family before him, Henry's income was gained from the sea, mainly from prawns and lobsters. Again, when compared with the scale of the Paskins' activities, whose boats had on-board cooking facilities, Henry's operation was modest. Occasionally he used a trawl-net from his larger carvel-built boat, but mostly he relied on home-made push-nets, a method which limited his activities each day to the period of low tide.

The frame of the net was made from locally cut ash and hazel, and fitted with quarter-inch mesh cotton netting from Gundry's store. This was pushed slowly through fields of sea grass, flag weed or bladderwrack trapping prawns, green crabs and small fish in the net which had to be sorted every 30 paces or so when the prawns were transferred to a wicker-made basket, known locally as a 'daucer', tied around the waist and capable of holding two gallons of prawns. It was a precarious journey over the treacherous 'blue slipper' clays, and the work was arduous, especially after winds had loosened the weed.

Whatever the time of low tide Henry had to be there. Sometimes he left home at London Heath at 2.30 in the morning, walked to his smaller, clinker-built boat which he kept on a stretch of marsh near the eastern bunney of North Marsh, where deeper water was available for most of the tide. He rowed out to Eastern Point to prawn for two hours at the lowest tide, and by the time he arrived home around 6.30 his wife, Adela, had the blackened pots of boiling water ready on the closed-hearth fires. She cooked the prawns, adding salt to taste, whilst Henry had his breakfast, then counted and graded them into hundreds and loaded them into baskets, each lot separated by starched white cloths or, preferably, muslin bags in which flour had been purchased, collected over a period and boiled pure white. Henry then cycled to Newport to sell his catch. Many of his customers lived along Carisbrooke Mall, and the Misses Shepherd, who owned stores and barges at Newport Quay, were always keen buyers. Returning in time for his main meal, he then repeated the whole process to catch the evening's low tide, even hauling his lobster-pots if there was time before prawning, finishing his working day around 8p.m. This catch was again cooked immediately and stored in the cool pantry ready for sale the next day. Henry also found time to bait his 50-yard-long 'trot' which he set on the sandbanks off East Point, hoping to catch mainly plaice and the occasional bass.

By late August the prawns had grown in size and in the early years of the twentieth century Henry could get 1s. for 100. Although they were more plentiful earlier in the summer they were small and the price was correspondingly lower. By the time the tiny 'hunters', next year's prawns, appeared in September the season was quickly slipping away.

Local knowledge was vital. Amongst his favourite prawning grounds were the sandbanks on the seaward side of the estuary, where long sea grasses grew. He fished these at the very low morning springs, working against the tide so that the prawns tipped into the net. A deeper pool off East Point was also favoured where, in the half-light, thousands of crustacean eyes shone like stars. Along the coast towards Brickyard House, passing beyond the hard clay banks and mussel beds, another sandy bank was covered with red sea grass which stained the prawns. Some customers preferred these to the colourless prawns caught from the Hamstead area.

He made himself unpopular with the Paskins brothers by prawning across their shingle banks in Clamerkin River, and he also prawned the deeper water opposite Walter's Copse at very low spring tides, pushing the net with one hand and steadying himself by pushing the smaller dinghy with the other. Like his forefathers, all of them fishermen, he could not swim!

To extend the prawning time each lunar month he rowed to the duver on the western side of the estuary and trudged along the beach to Cranmore and Bouldnor where good catches were available at neap tides. Also at neaps, but only when Herbert, his son, or Andrew Barton was available to assist, Henry used his larger boat to trawl for prawns in deeper water off Hamstead Ledge and up towards the brickyard.

The beam, six feet wide, was fixed to metal hoops which kept the top of the net a foot off the seabed, and lead weights on a rope loop dragged the lower side along the bottom. A good haul numbered over 1,000 prawns. The boat had no centreboard so only a small lugsail or spritsail could be used which was not large enough to tack against the tide; trawling could only be done, therefore, when a westerly was blowing, and the long haul back was always difficult. Either way, trawl or push-net, it was back-breaking work and if a north-easterly was blowing or a Union Castle liner passed through the Solent, the swell was such that two hours of hard labour might produce just 50 prawns.

In addition, from June until the end of August each year, Henry laid lobster-pots on the rocky ledges outside the estuary. Made from local withies by

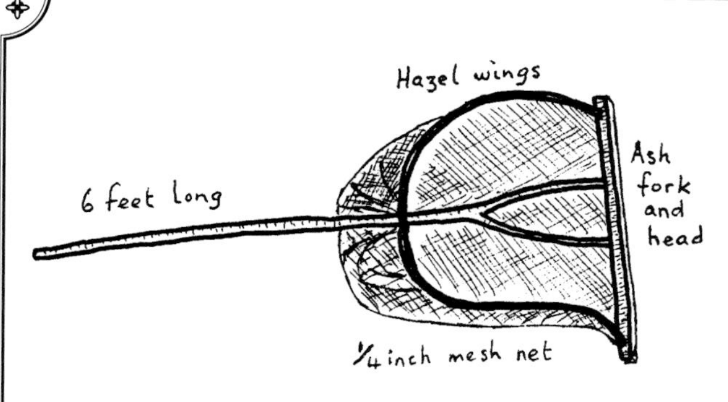

Above: *A riverman's traditional push-net for prawning.*

Right: *A traditional prawning net in use at Newtown.*

Below: *An impression of a traditional fishing trot.*

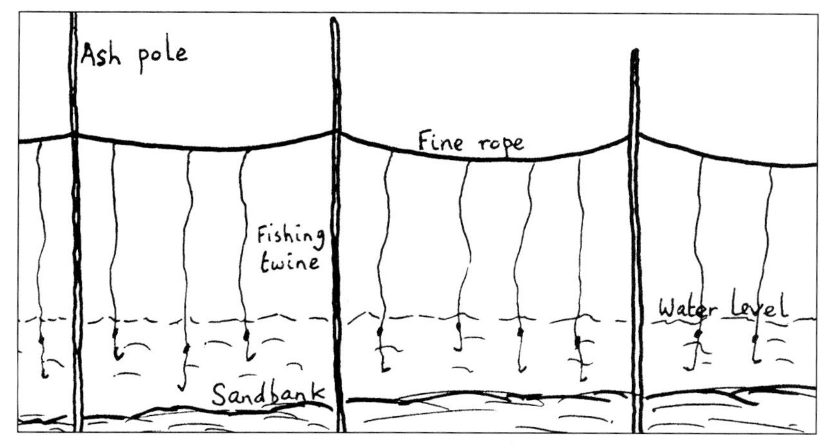

Henry Foss in his clinker-built dinghy, 1925.

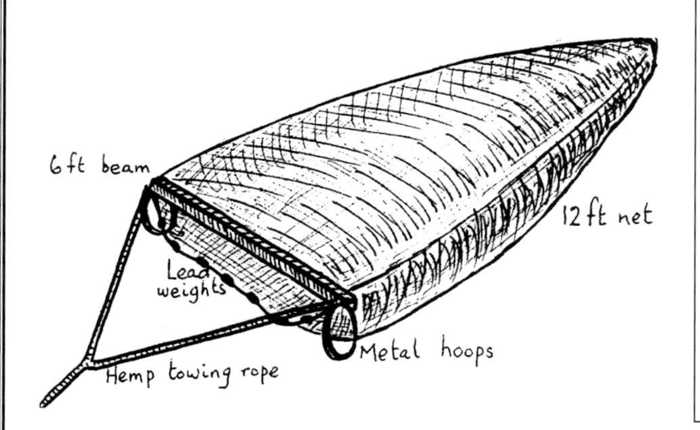

Above: *A home-made prawning trawl.*

Above right: *Henry's carvel-built boat at Newtown Quay, 1928.*

Right: *Herbert Foss prawning off the Haven mouth in 1957.*

Mr Cook, a resident of Brook whose black work shed overlooks The Green, or by Brook lifeboat man Alf Woodford, the pots cost 5s.0d. each in around 1920.

Henry's carvel-built boat, bought from Richards of Cowes in 1910 and usually moored on a whip near the eastern bunney of North Marsh, had been specially adapted with a workbench at the stern, and drainage holes cut in the gunwhales. A brass plate on the gunwhale allowed the rough hemp ropes, purchased from Whitehead's stores in Lugley Street, Newport, to slip easily over the stern as the pots were hauled. The boat was fitted with oars and a mast, set in the front seat, which carried a lugsail or spritsail according to weather and tide.

Again, keen local knowledge was required to make best use of the area. Only 15 minutes either side of the tide could be used at Hamstead Ledge before marker corks were pulled under by the strong currents, but there was a longer haul directly off the estuary mouth near the river buoy. The strong tides east of the river mouth made it very hard work to row up to the excellent Salt Mead Ledges off Burntwood Copse, where pots could be hauled at any tide.

The pots were inspected every day, weather permitting, to empty them of green crabs, whelks and hermit-crabs (known locally as 'gants'), to bait them with small fish (glennies, chubheads and gold-maids) caught earlier in the prawn nets or with scraps bought from the fishmonger, and on good days to collect up to eight lobsters. These were carried home in 'daucers' to be cooked immediately and sold privately for 1s. per pound weight. Lobsters are best if brought slowly to the boil, unlike prawns which are dropped into boiling water to make them curl for best presentation. A wood-fuelled fire was used to obtain sufficient heat for the cooking, the bundles of frith bought from the estate.

Stored carefully in the woodshed at London Heath each winter, the pots could last for several seasons, but many were lost in stormy weather and to poachers who dropped them in deep water, sinking the marker buoys.

Disputes arose frequently over winkle-picking 'rights'. In particular, the Prangnell family regarded those marshes bordering Spur Lake and Eastern Spit (Fish House Point) as their own and the Foss family ventured there at their peril. Henry Foss always believed that the net-slashing incidents were in revenge for his trespasses. But the risk was worth it. Winkles fetched 1s. a bushel in Newport, and many sacks were sent via the local carrier, Edwin Holbrook. Winkles can be collected when there is an 'r' in the month, and could be sold until 10 May each year. The best winkles were on the hard sand off East Point and on the mussel banks off Lower Elmsworth brick-yard where they were stained black. A two-gallon bucketful could be collected each low tide, purged and cooked at London Heath, then sent by carrier, or even taken to Newport slung on the handlebars of Henry's bicycle to be sold to private customers for 3d. per pint.

At particularly low tides colonies of whelks ('girt wilks' to Islanders) were exposed, clinging to the blue slipper clays. Amongst enthusiasts for this delicacy was local resident Gordon Rickman who, in the 1920s and '30s:

> *.. used to collect them in an old sack and take them home where Mother would deposit them into a large bucket, cover them with a liberal coating of salt or brine and leave them all night to spit their grit out... During the night you would hear much hissing and spluttering and in the morning they would be submerged under a blanket of slimy, frothy liquid. Then we would wash them thoroughly and cook them in a large iron pot of boiling water.*

Newtown's rivermen worked long, arduous hours for an uncertain income in the face of capricious weather, commercial competition, poaching and occasional vandalism. More than one lost his life to the sea, and the unwary could get into difficulties on the deep, glutinous mud-flats, even when wearing pattens. It was a lonely lifestyle, where a man had to be at ease with his own company, and confident in his own abilities. Quiet men, yet each greatly respected in the neighbourhood, Henry Paskins and Henry Foss could justifiably claim to be Newtown's last true rivermen. It was somehow fitting that they died within months of each other in the mid-1930s.

Henry Foss restoring a lobster-pot in 1932.

Chapter 11

'We Are Merely the Custodians': Farming & Farm Folk

Break up the fallow ground, the Prophet doth declare, Can there no rusty plough be found to make some furrows there? Root out the thorns and briar, that all too plainly show, Remove the tares that doth aspire so that the seed might grow.

From 'The Land' by Tom Essau Mussell (Shalfleet 1917).

At the beginning of the twentieth century most members of the Newtown community were touched in some way by the farming world, whether as employees, customers, tenants or suppliers. Alongside the former maritime role of Newtown, the land and its cultivation had been at the heart of local activities for many centuries. The basic patterns of land occupation, the administrative boundaries and the social hierarchies had all been established as long ago as Saxon and Norman times, and the local farmers of the late-nineteenth century – Kingswell, Sweet, Lock, Hawkins, Kemp, Sanders and Hayward – still lived and worked largely within these frameworks.

Out of the chaos of the Dark Ages the Saxon invaders eventually established order and peace and became kings of what is now called England. During the ninth century King Alfred and his predecessors gifted, by patronage, large manorial landholdings to barons and bishops alike, including Swainston, which was given to the Bishops of Winchester in 827.

Walter Rickman, still using a scythe in the 1940s.

Essentially, the Saxons were settlers and farmers, and the first patterns of tenanted holdings (farms) were carved out of these manorial estates. Already, in Saxon times, a pattern of relatively small farms (under 250 acres) was emerging in this part of the Island, and many of today's local place names originate from that period, for example:

'ton' (farm):	*Swainston (Sweyne's farm)*
'ing' (spring or well)	*Watchingwell, Ningwood, Fullholding*
'ham' (clearing in wood)	*Hamstead (homestead in the wood)*
'field' (open land shared in cultivation)	*Vittlesfield, Porchfield (Port's field)*

When the Normans surveyed their newly acquired lands in 1086 the Domesday Book showed that Swainston's 13 square miles made it the largest and most valuable of all 126 manors on the Island, maintaining 25 ploughs. King William purloined most of the manors for himself and his entourage and, having the power of life or death over all inhabitants, he had little difficulty imposing the feudal system on the populace, a system which lasted for 400 years and had a profound effect on the agricultural and social fabric.

The nobility rented out their manor lands in smaller plots to tenant farmers, known as 'bordars', who enjoyed greater freedom than other inhabitants and were permitted to trade any surplus production at local fairs and markets and thus accumulate their own chattels. However, they were still obliged to provide several days of service ('boon days') to the manor each year, particularly at harvest time.

Lower down the social scale were the 'villeins' who were born into a life of servitude and not permitted to leave the manor (unless they escaped undetected to a nearby town for a year and a day). Each villein was provided with a small plot of land (or several scattered plots) to cultivate, sufficient only to provide for his own family, any surplus becoming manor property.

At the bottom of the social order were the majority of the people, known as 'serfs', who were little more than beasts of burden, provided only with sufficient food and shelter to keep them fit for work.

The most common agricultural practice adopted was the 'open field' system. Usually, a farmholding had three such arable fields, each divided into furlong strips, known as 'landshares', separated by baulks of turf, and allocated to a villein for cultivation. Crops were rotated annually between the three fields – grains in one (wheat and barley or, on the poorer soils, oats), legumes and root crops in another (peas, beans, turnips and, much later, after their introduction from America, potatoes), the third being left fallow for pigs and fowl to scavenge. Pasture land was originally open ground, available to all inhabitants, as were the common lands, woodlands, roadsides and (in Newtown) the marshes, and many families kept a goat (rather than a cow), a pig and some fowl. Here, already, was the basis for patterns of landholding and social fabric that were to characterise agriculture until the twentieth century.

Many of the 77 burgage plots created in 1256 in the planned settlement of La Neuton can still be traced on modern maps and show the furlong divisions of the open fields and the subsequently enclosed pasture lands.

In order to attract a good quality of artisans, the burghers ('free men') were not obliged to plough or reap the manor lands in servitude, nor pay many of the common dues of the lord's demesne, and already by 1257 the reeve's accounts for the borough showed that all plots were taken at an annual rent of 1s. each. By 1297, 66 burghers occupied 70 plots, enjoying a privileged status compared with many of their rural contemporaries. At about the same time the manor had 42 free tenants and 81 customary tenants, almost as many as the whole of the remainder of the Calbourne sub-hundred.

Locks Farm, probably the oldest farm in the district. The origin of the farm has been traced back to 1378.

In 1318 the borough was granted the right to hold a weekly market and a three-day annual fair in July, 'unless such market and fair should be hurtful to neighbouring markets and fairs.' The prosperity of the manor (including the borough) was well established for the thirteenth and fourteenth centuries, and by 1377 196 local inhabitants were liable for the poll tax. Only a further 22 paid the tax in the whole of rural Calbourne parish. Clearly, both Swainston and Newtown were prospering.

But already the Black Death (1348) had taken a toll on the agricultural workforce and in 1377 the French invaders destroyed Newtown. Living conditions for the peasantry became intolerable. Nationally, the situation provoked the Peasants' Revolt in 1381. During the next 100 years landowners began the iniquitous practice of enclosing formerly open fields and common lands, thus depriving the poorest inhabitants of much of their livelihood. This was particularly widespread on the Island where much arable land was being converted to pasture as wool prices increased. Many of the surviving plot names in Newtown reflect the practice – Gore Close, Watch Close, North Close, Green Close – and it culminated in 1488 with the Island's parlous situation having the dubious distinction of being the cause of the first anti-enclosure Act of the English Parliament.

The divide between rich and poor in rural England was growing ever wider. Technically, the feudal system lasted on the Island until 1488, when the absolute powers of the Lord of the Island were removed, and the appointment's title became that of Captain of Wight. In 1513 Sir James Worsley of Appledurcombe became the first local resident to be appointed as Captain. His family was to exert great influence on the Island for the next 300 years, and by 1528 he was acquiring land in the Newtown area to add to his already considerable holdings. Soon, in 1553, Sir Thomas Barrington had acquired Swainston Manor.

By then, an agricultural wage was replacing obligation of servitude (although labourers were still tied to the land), the population was growing rapidly, and a new group of tenant-smallholders was emerging who often combined the cultivation of relatively small plots of land with another trade. An extract from the inventory of a local will, dated 1555, illustrates the nature and scale of such a smallholding:

In the stable

One olde harnes and roopes/a harrow/a rack and a stall
2 shillings & 8 pence
New boards and olde with plancks and a ladder
10 shillings & 6 pence
Cart rongs [rails or crossbars] *and lynes* [cords or ropes]
8 pence

In the barne

Five quarters of wheat and two quarters of barley
3 pounds 10 shillings
Three bushell of pease and fattches [vetches or beans]
3 shillings & 4 pence
A prong a flayl and two forkes
4 pence

The live cattell
Two mare coltts two kyne [cows] *and a bullock*
33 shillings
Five swyne hoggs [pigs] *and fifteen shepe*
32 shillings & 8 pence
Six ducks/three geyse and six pultrey
3 shillings & 3 pence

In the feylde corne
Nine akers of wheat sowen
45 shillings
In tymbre at the Wodende three lode
3 shillings

(Record 1555u/26 quoted courtesy of Hampshire Record Office. Translation by David Pedgley)

The inventory also lists amongst the smallholders' possessions a 'torne' (spinning-wheel), 'a payr of cards' (wool brushes), 'three pounds of yerne' (yarn), 'some keyres' (brewing vats) and 'a chesfatt' (cheese-making vat). This kind of smallholder-cum-artisan became a feature of the Newtown landscape until well into the twentieth century.

The farming industry in Newtown took a distinct turn for the worse in 1585 when the borough was granted the right to elect two MPs. Voting franchise was granted only to landholders and there followed some 200 years of unseemly land acquisition in the borough, principally by the Worsley and later by the Barrington families and their respective supporters, in order to gain a political advantage. Matters escalated even further in 1730 following a decision by the King's Bench that only landowners could be elected to become Chief Burgess of Newtown Borough. Highly inflated prices were paid for land-holdings that produced pitifully small rental incomes. 'Marches' sold for £679 with an annual rent of £1, and 'Slatfords' fetched £950 whilst its rental income was only just over £10. Holdings acquired in this way were often scattered, therefore difficult to farm, so they were almost always neglected commercially. To make matters worse, tenancies rarely lasted longer than 14 years and the requirements of many leases provided little incentive for investment by owner or tenant. For example, the 1730 lease of Marsh Farm to Robert Rogers, a local yeoman farmer, for 14 years at an annual rent of £50, forbade him to remove any produce of hay, straw, dung or fodder until the last year of the lease, and even then required him to leave the land fully planted with ryegrass or trefoil.

Tenants also faced petty restrictions from other quarters. The chief burgesses elected the Mayor, two constables, the sergeant-at-mace, and the haywarden, and appointed the steward who presided over the local Court Leet. Besides setting the local prices of beer and bread this court was also responsible for regulating the use of the common lands of the borough ('no steere bullocks above one year old, no horse-beasts, nor pigs unless yoked and rung'), the movement of cattle ('cattle driven for water shall be returned within an hour' and 'no cattle on the common after sun-sett'), and other potential nuisances ('no fuel to be deposited on common land to annoy the Highways'). The court also organised other communal duties and responsibilities such as cleaning out the clay pool, and hedging and ditching, and imposed appropriate fines for misdemeanors ('We present that William Woodkoke shall keep no goats within the liberty of this towne in payne of one shilling' (1637)).

In addition, the haywarden was responsible for enforcing the rules regarding stray animals, impounding them and imposing fines for their release. The town's assembly book records a meeting of all inhabitants in 1655 to raise a rate for the repair of the pound located near the chapel.

An air of agricultural neglect began to pervade Newtown. Most holdings were very small, absentee landlords took little interest, and occupiers worked within a very repressive environment, still embroiled in the constraints of the feudal system. In places, little more than subsistence agriculture was commonly practised.

In 1674 the Hearth Tax returns showed only 11 inhabitable buildings in the borough, and in 1768 only 12 of the burgage plots contained buildings. The last recorded fair took place in 1781 (although it was still advertised in some directories of the 1850s). At the time of the final Corporation Report of 1835, following its dissolution, no burgess lived in any of the town's 14 cottages. In earlier times, many of the burgesses had actually been resident in the borough, often giving their names to the plots they occupied. Descendants of some of them, the Holbrooks, Brewers and Harveys, were still resident locally in the late-nineteenth century, and leases still referred to past ways of life (an 1832 lease refers to 'a stich of land in common field' on the southern side of Gold Street).

The virtual absence of stone structures pre-dating 1800 further reflects Newtown's doldrums. The only known exceptions are the Town Hall (c.1699), the former Noah's Ark Inn, parts of Woolgar's Cottage, the former Church Cottage (on the site of Thistlefinches), some barns at Harts Farm and some walled foundations behind Rose Cottage from the former dairy belonging to Lord Heytesbury.

The great eighteenth-century changes in farming methods (with improved seeds, specialised animal breeds and the use of fertilisers and machinery) left the Newtown area virtually untouched. The emergence of the very wealthy landed gentry (or 'squirearchy') and the prosperous tenant farmer (the 'yeomanry') in the rest of the manor's lands went hand-in-hand with increasing poverty among the agricultural labouring classes, who turned to the 'free' churches for support. Widespread enclosures continued to be made, depriving the peasantry of its

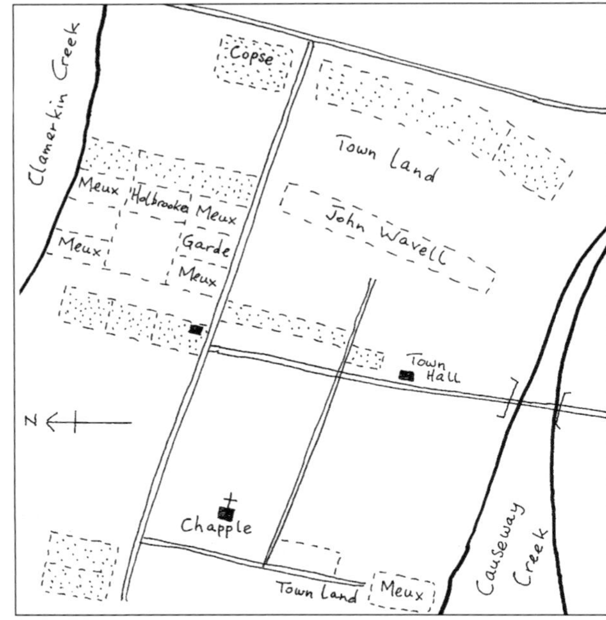

Above: *Early forms of mechanisation came late and stayed late. Baling straw in the 1930s.*

Left: *The scattered nature of Sir Thomas Barrington's holdings (shaded) in 1630.*

Above: *Marsh Farmhouse, Newtown 1996.*

Right: *The landholdings of Sir Richard Simeon (Harts Farm) and Lord Yarborough (Marsh Farm), based on the 1840 Tithe Map. The larger plots were tenanted by George Young (Marsh) and Robert Harvey (Harts). A variety of tenants occupied the smaller plots.*

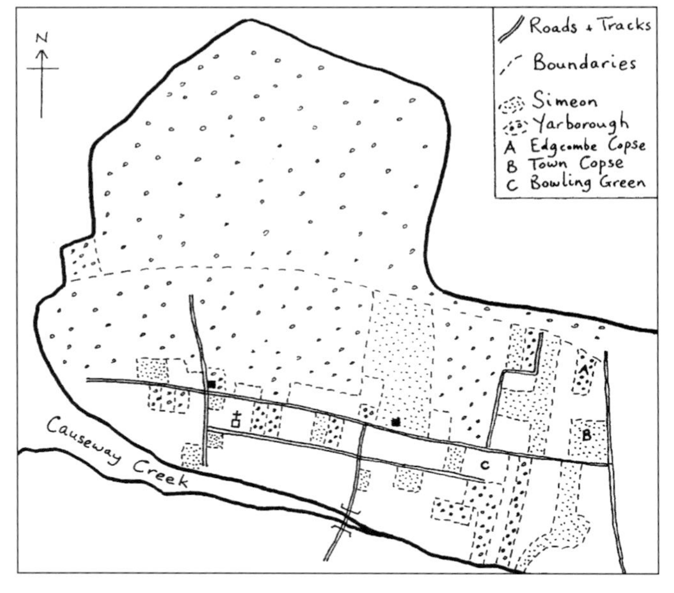

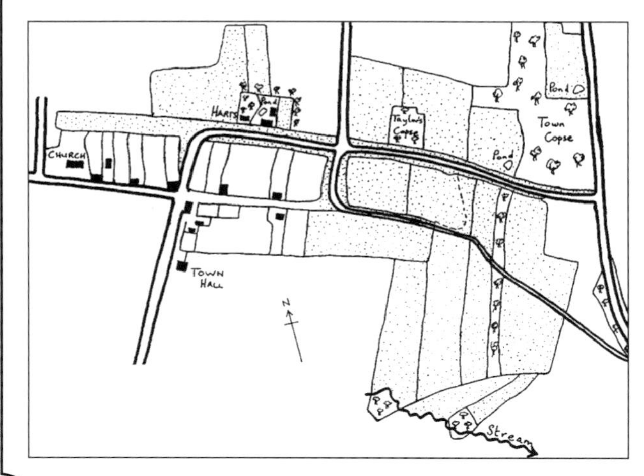

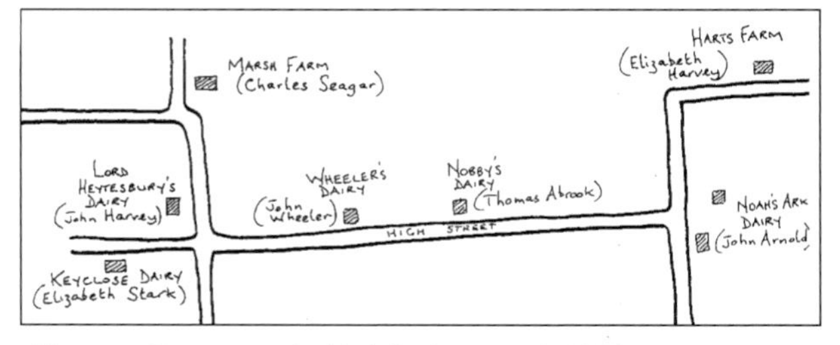

Above: *Newtown's 'dairies' around 1880.*

Left: *The holdings of Harts Farm in the 1860s when claim was made to some roadside verges.*

traditional rights of access to fuel, building materials and grazing for their animals.

Within the borough boundaries the piecemeal acquisition of holdings had left many tenancies small and scattered. Only two tenancies of any size emerged, each of them forming the basis of the borough's two farms, Newtown (Marsh) Farm and Harts Farm. The regular sale and purchase of plots of land over the centuries frequently changed the actual location and size of these farm holdings, although there is no record of how either tenement was acquired originally. But at least from the 1630s they dominated the borough in terms of acreage.

Marsh Farm, formerly known as Marches, might be a corruption of the name of Stephen March, who died in 1650 and had held this tenement at a rent of 6s.4d. He was succeeded as tenant by his son David March and his grandson Lewis March. The owner at the time was Sir William Meux of Kingston Manor, at one time the Mayor of Newtown and conspicuous in the political squabbles over borough lands. In 1658 he gave the land as part of a marriage settlement on his granddaughter. (At about the same date he also disposed of Harts Farm.)

Later occupiers of Marches included William Hatton and James Waivell (1705), and when the title was purchased by a merchant from Guernsey (Nicholas Dobree) Richard Radborne and Peter Cooke became tenants (1720). The rent of the holding went up rapidly from £10 in 1732 to £50 in 1741, probably due to the successful development of Newtown Salterns which formed part of the tenement. The occupier of the farm at the time was Richard Arnold, a yeoman farmer from Brighstone. The first use of the name Marsh Farm occurred in 1769 when James Worsley of Godshill purchased the title and sold the lease to his cousin Robert Worsley for £1,503. The title soon passed to Sir Richard Worsley, the last in line of the great Appledurcombe family, who purchased it in 1772, leasing it in 1789 for £50 a year to John Fry, a Newtown yeoman, and again in 1801 to another yeoman from Newtown, Robert Rogers.

Sir Richard and his adulterous wife produced no heirs and his great estates passed, by the marriage of his niece, to Charles Pelham who later became the first Lord Yarborough. When he died in 1846 and Marsh Farm was sold (1847) to Sir Richard Godin Simeon, the tenement once again became part of Swainston Manor. Sir Richard rebuilt the farmhouse almost immediately, using stone brought by horse and cart from Street Place Lane, Newbridge, and, as he did throughout the estate, improved the land drainage, introduced rotational cropping and grew root crops on which sheep could feed and manure the land.

The tenant until the time of the sale was 71-year-old Robert Harvey, who was also the tenant at Harts Farm. Robert was a direct descendant of the early tenants of Harts. It is not clear how Harts originally came into the possession of the Harvey family. In 1633 a 99-year lease 'for an old, decayed tenement, with lands and pasture for three kine (cows) and 20 sheep... in the occupation of Thomas Holbrooke' was granted by the ubiquitous Sir William Meux (Mewys) to John Granger of Watchingwell for £121 on the understanding that a new tenement would be built within two years. The lease was later (1656/7) assigned for £65 to John Harvey, a yeoman of Northwood, who was soon fined for failing to attend the local courts or council in his new capacity of burgess.

In 1660 John sublet the tenement holding (for 1,000 years) to his brother William Harvey who, in turn, passed the lease to his son, also William, in 1691. Circumstantial evidence suggests that the Harveys remained as occupiers of the farm throughout this time, but especially after 1768 the lease changed hands quite frequently, occasionally for large sums of money.

By the early 1800s the lease of the farm had passed to William Harvey who, in turn, passed it to his brother James in 1823, and in his will (dated 1834) James arranged for all property to be sold for cash at his death and distributed. Clearly this did not happen because when, by 1841, Sir Richard Godin Simeon had inherited Swainston Manor through his wife Louisa Edith, daughter and co-heiress of Sir Fitzwilliam Barrington, to become title-holder of Harts Farm, Robert Harvey was the tenant. Miss Elizabeth Harvey took over the tenancy from Robert around 1860, keeping it until her retirement about 1880, which brought to an end some 250 years of Harveys at Harts Farm.

John Sweet, a farmer from Somerset, took over the tenancies of both Harts Farm and Marsh Farm, becoming resident at Harts from 1888, in response to the wishes of his new housekeeper, Adela Hole. When he died in 1915 the tenancy passed to Charles Barton whose daughter-in-law is still in residence at the time of writing. Harts Farm and Marsh Farm were probably large enough, at between 70 and 100 acres, to produce a good living for the tenant and even some additional local employment. (As late as 1901 17-year-old Reginald Hardy was living-in at Harts Farm as a 'dairy lad'.) Rather more typical within the borough were much smaller tenancies which produced little if any surplus to the occupier's own requirements. These were not farms as such, but often claimed 'dairy' status. In the 1880s there were eight such dairies in a stretch of 600 metres within the village! In many cases, these smallholdings were run by the occupier (or his wife and older children) in addition to another form of employment.

Typical of these smallholdings was the area known as Lower Elmsworth, rented from the manor between 1840–63 by James Foss, until the sea overwhelmed his living quarters. Known locally as 'Captain' Faulse, James was really a fisherman who also did a bit of sea trading from a small boat, rather than a farmer. Originally the site of the Elmsworth Salterns, his 15-acre smallholding contained at least two cottages and some outbuildings. Over 11 acres of the plot were taken with the former salterns, which were probably unproductive, and the buildings. A little over one acre of pasture was just enough to support a couple of cows, and two acres of woodland provided building materials and fuel, and scavenging ground for his pig and fowl. He used various means to gather fresh rainwater and he also cultivated a large garden and was therefore self-sufficient for dairy produce, meat and vegetables. But the smallholding is unlikely to have produced much surplus for sale, and its remoteness militated against any sales process.

Several other con emporary residents of Newtown also held smallholdings alongside their regular employment, notably the Holbrooks at Key Close Dairy (whose main income came from salt making), James Taylor at the Noah's Ark Dairy (who was primarily the landlord of the inn), and Henry Abrook (oyster-fisherman) whose three-acre plot generated a 15s. tithe to the vicar each year, some five times more than that paid by James Foss for the poor ground at Lower Elmsworth.

Contrary to the worst expectations of the farming community the repeal of the Corn Laws in 1846, which had been in place to prohibit the import of cheap grains, did not bring ruin but heralded the 'Golden Age' of farming which lasted until around 1875. Farming had already become central to rural lifestyles, paying rents to landowners and tithes to the Church, employing much of the local workforce, and engaging many local support services, such as millers, smiths and saddlers. Nationally, major changes in farming practice were under way that were soon to change the pattern of farm working that had lasted 1,000 years.

Somewhat typically, many farmers in the Newtown area were slow to adopt these new ideas. As late as 1885, when Edwin Holbrook began work on a local farm, seed was still broadcast by hand and threshing was done with flails. Edwin later recalled his nervousness as an 18-year-old, trying to broadcast the seed evenly, and the agonising wait for the germination which would make public the level of his skill. Edwin wrote that a flail:

> *... was just two short rods, one about four feet in length, the other three, and fastened on* [the] *end with leather hoops... The man using it took the longest rod in his hands and swung the short one over his head and banged it down on the corn that had been spread thinly on the floor of the barn. It was a skillful job and young men would sometimes get a whack on the head if he wasn't very careful.*

Such methods were very labour-intensive, providing plenty of local employment, especially in the summer months. Hay and corn were still cut by hand. Edwin's father (William Holbrook, born 1828) was foreman of a typical gang which toured farms mowing the hay with scythes, being paid per acre according to the weight of the crop. Similar gangs cut the corn, using cradles to make and tie the 'stooks' which were stacked and later collected by the horse and wagon before being added to the rick.

In 1884, local youth Fred Fallick, aged 14, joined the gang led by his grandfather Philip Fallick to cut 30 acres of corn for Mr Hillier on his farms near Rowridge. Cradles were used for the wheat but not the oats. Fred found barley relatively easy to cut but the following year he joined a hay-cutting gang and discovered it to be more difficult than corn. Having walked from Locks Green to Cowes the gang of seven managed to cut seven acres in the day before plodding home again!

But machinery was making an appearance. In the 1890s Ernest Hawkins bought the first grass-mowing machine in the district for Lambsleaze Farm, despite dire warnings from other farmers that it would kill the grass! Mrs Anne Rice at Locks Farm, having taken over the tenancy in the 1860s from Robert Lock, seems to have been rather more forward-looking. By the 1870s a horse-driven threshing-machine was in use at the farm, probably rented from James Kingswell, the farmer at Fullingmills Farm. The horses were harnessed to four poles jutting like spokes from a central 'capstan'. A boy, perched precariously on the capstan, used a light whip to keep the beasts walking around at a steady pace. The turning capstan kept a large drum beater revolving which separated corn, straw and chaff. In addition to the boy, it still required a man on the rick to pass stooks to another who fed the drum, and a third who bagged the grain, but in both scale and speed it was a distinct improvement upon the flail.

Not many years later the same farm was using a steam engine to replace some of the work of the horses. Commonly, both the engine and the threshing-machine were drawn from farm to farm by a team of three or four horses to each, until soon the steam tractor (preceded by a man and a red flag!) replaced even these horses. The engine used in the Newtown area was owned by Mr J. Watts, an engineer of Lukeley Works at Carisbrooke, who followed it around the farms on his tricycle to make sure it was working properly. But it was many years later that horse power gave way completely to machines. Many of the early machines were pulled by horses and the early steam tractors were so heavy and cumbersome that they were of little use on the heavy local soils. (Ploughs were pulled back and forth across the fields by static machines using a system of ropes and pulleys.) The smithy at Locks Green continued to prosper until 1932 and several farriers survived for a further 20 years. Indeed, in times of trouble villagers were grateful for the existence of the

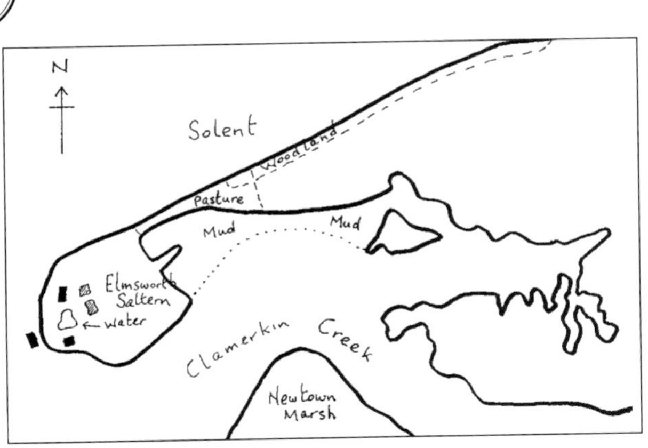

The smallholding at Lower Elmsworth, 1840.

Reginald, Oliver and Arthur Flux, c.1920, each born into farming. Oliver later bought London Farm.

Left: *The Mew family from Porchfield, haymaking c.1905. Lena is second from left, Edward is in the middle with a pitchfork.*

A threshing gang stand by their machine, c.1925. Left to right: *Arthur Flux, Reg Flux, Mr Pitman, Bill Small, Oliver Flux, ?, Billy Buckett, James Flux, Tim Attrill.*

farm's horses. Following the terrible storms of 1881 when two metres of snow fell, Edwin Holbrook and Barney Downer took a team of six heavy horses and a wagon to Newport for food supplies for Porchfield and Newtown which were completely cut off to normal traffic for two weeks.

Godfrey Buckett of Locks Green, c.1924.

Mechanisation at Wheatenbread Farm in 1921. The driver of the Case tractor is Oliver Flux, working with his brother Reg.

Fred Fallick's first job as an 11-year-old in 1881 was at Locks Farm where he had to 'drive plough'. This consisted of walking with the four horses (which were pulling in line) and turning each one at precisely the right moment at the end of each furrow. Fred's ears frequently took a pasting as the ploughman shouted 'Why didn yer come roun a bit quicker?!' or 'Yer too late! Yer too late!' Similar jobs were still relatively plentiful on local farms. Rather typically, in 1871 three young members of the same family were able to obtain such work. Thomas Foss (aged 17) and his sister Mary (15) became farm servants, still living at home at London Heath whilst their brother William (13) was a live-in farm servant at the nearby London Farm. A few years later, their younger sibling (Arthur) was a cowboy, living-in at Elmsworth Farm, sleeping in the apple store which was reached by an external stone stairway. Hedging, ditching, hoeing, weeding, stone-gathering and many other tasks kept men and women occupied on the farms, and there was often additional casual work to be had in season catching vermin, or picking beans and peas, or beating for the hounds, or for the 'guns' at pheasant shoots. A wide variety of more specialised skills were also in demand, offering rather more stable employment as carter, dairymaid or shepherd, for instance.

Until the middle of the nineteenth century hundreds of male and female farm servants flocked to Newport ('Nippert') from all over the Island, dressed in their best attire, on the three 'Bargan Zadderdays' immediately prior to Old Michaelmas Day (11 October). These were the fixed days when farmers hired their servants for the next 12 months. The first day was for hiring carters (who displayed a knot of whipcord on their headgear and carried a

St James Square, Newport, c.1907.

whip on their shoulder) and shepherds (sporting a bunch of wool and carrying a crook), each dressed in their best Sunday smock-frock. The middle Saturday was for carter's mates and teamsmen, together with shepherds' understudies, whilst the final gathering was for live-in farm boys and for dairymaids. The maids, in all their finery, gathered opposite the Vine Inn (popularly known as 'Gape Mouth Corner') and the men at the Beast Market (St James Square). After the hirings everyone adjourned to their favourite inns for a riotous evening of dancing, singing and drinking.

Although comparisons are difficult, the 1871–1901 census returns give some indication of the importance of employment on the land in the Newtown area. Including the farmers themselves, 27 of the 95 employed persons worked on the land in 1871, 30 out of 87 in 1881, 25 out of 56 in 1891, and 21 out of 54 in 1901. Clearly, the actual scale of farm employment remained far more buoyant than the regional trend and, with the demise of the local salt-making and sea-faring industries, agriculture became relatively more important within the local economy. The bald figures of employment disguise the fact that at one end of the earnings scale there were live-in farm servants as young as 11, who were paid around £2

Oliver Flux of London Farm (centre with moustache, and leg raised) *at Newport Market, 1930.*

per year, and labourers whose income was around 2s. a day, whilst at the other end were gentlemen farmers like Robert Lock who, in 1861, was employing five men and three boys on two farms (Newtown Farm and Locks Farm), and his son, also Robert, who employed a bailiff to run Elmsworth Farm in the 1890s whilst he kept a fine office and toured the area in a pony and trap collecting rates, or sat on the Highways Committee and the Management Committee of Locks Green School.

The wages for an agricultural labourer had always been poor. At the end of the nineteenth century farm labourers were getting 14s. per week, whilst skilled tradesmen received 25s. per week. Until 1914 many shops remained open until 10p.m. on Saturdays to catch the trade from agricultural workers who collected their weekly wage late that day. Sometimes, in addition to his wages, the labourer with a family was provided with a 'tied' cottage and was frequently permitted to sow one row of crops in a field as his own, a practice which was still taking place in the 1920s at Elmsworth Farm. Those without dependents were often permitted to bed down in a hayloft or a barn, or were provided with board and lodging at the farmhouse for which some of his wage was held back. In 1901, shepherd Mark Downer, aged 81, was bedding down in a barn at Fleetlands Farm, and in the 1940s Dickie Fallick and 'Nimble' Downer were still sleeping rough at local farms.

Carters and cowmen were usually supplied with a free cottage but worked very long hours with no holiday except Christmas Day and a few hours on Good Friday.

Women and children not only augmented the family income by gleaning ('leasing') the cornfields after they had been harvested, but they also obtained any menial paid work available on the farms. Local women planted ('set') beans with a dibber, earning a few pence a gallon, often in bitter winter weather wrapped in their husband's old clothes or perhaps an Army greatcoat. And in summer they went weeding in Swainston gardens, or haymaking. As late as the 1920s children picked stones from the fields to protect the blades of the scythes.

The Swainston account books record that in July 1876 Mrs Holbrook and Mrs Angell were each paid 1s. per day for working in the gardens, whilst Jane Whittington got 6d. an evening for 'cleaning young trees'. Earlier, in 1869, James Gosden got 2s.0d. per day and James Elderfield and Philip Munford each earned 1s.10d. for 'farm work', whilst Alfred Sanders was paid 3s.4d. a day in the dairy and David Butcher 1s.4d.

Life for many of the farmers themselves was often no less arduous, especially on holdings of under 100 acres, for they were also working men putting in long hours themselves and expecting the same from their wives and children. Few on this size of holding could afford to employ full-time labour. Even on the larger holdings many of those employed were teenagers, living-in, and receiving meagre wages. The 1871 census returns show the following pattern:

Farm	Farmer	Acres	Employed	Labourers living-in
London	*Frederick Saunders*	*170*	*3 men*	*George Meaning (18), Robert Kellaway (16), William Foss (13)*
Newtown (Marsh)	*Charles Seagar*	*60*	*1 man*	*Maurice Seagar (15)*
Newtown (Key Close)	*Hannah Holbrook*	*9*		
Dairy (back of Rose Cottage in Church Street, Newtown)	*John Harvey*	*20*		
Harts Dairy	*Elizabeth Harvey*	*70*	*1 man, 1 boy*	*George Hendy (13)*
Fleetlands	*Isaac Ridley*	*227*	*4 men, 3 boys*	
Elmsworth	*Morris Attrill*	*300*	*4 men, 2 boys*	*Frank Holbrook (30), Nicholas Rann (16)*
Lambsleaze	*James Hawkins*	*100*		
Clamerkin	*Osbon Sanders*	*92*		*John Sanders (18)*
Locks	*Anne Rice*	*172*	*3 men, 1 boy*	*Charles Rice (29)*

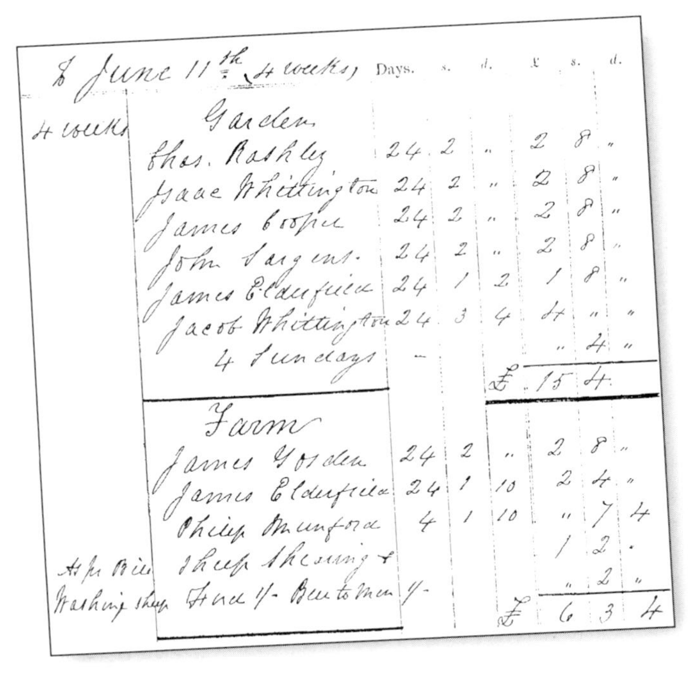

To June 11th (4 weeks)	Days.	s.	d.	£	s.	d.
4 weeks — Garden						
Thos. Rashley	24	2	"	2	8	"
Isaac Whittington	24	2	"	2	8	"
James Cooper	24	2	"	2	8	"
John Sargent	24	2	"	2	8	"
James Elderfield	24	1	2	1	8	"
Jacob Whittington	24	3	4	4	"	"
4 Sundays	–			"	4	"
				£ 15	4	
Farm						
James Gosden	24	2	"	2	8	"
James Elderfield	24	1	10	2	4	"
Philip Mumford	4	1	10	"	7	4
As per Bill — Sheep Shearing &				1	2	"
Washing sheep — Fare 1/- Beer to men 1/-				"	2	"
				£ 6	3	4

Part of the Swainston's Home Farm accounts for 1869.
(REPRODUCED COURTESY OF THE IOW COUNTY RECORD OFFICE)

In addition to the farmers themselves and their labourers and servants there were specialised jobs related to farming. In the Newtown district between 1860 and 1890 there were, at various times, Adam Hendy (cattle dealer), Thomas Westmore (drover), Henry Punch, John Hayward and Henry Calloway (carters), Charles Seagar (haycutter), Mark Downer (shepherd), Arthur Foss and William Abbott (cowboys), Charles Olden (domestic miller), William Smith (corn carrier), William Holbrook (carter's mate, aged 12) and Mary Seagar and Jane Davis (dairymaids).

Dairy farms tended to be small, family-scale affairs, sometimes run by a wife whose husband worked elsewhere. Some kept only a couple of cows. Mrs Ann Holbrook and Mrs Fanny Jacobs were just such 'cowkeepers' in Newtown (1850s), and Thomas Warne's two cows had only the verges to feed from in 1880s Porchfield.

Before the opening of the local railway in 1889 only a little of the fresh milk produce was sold locally, most 'dairies' using it to make butter, cream and (much less commonly) cheese. Isle of Wight cheese, known as 'Chock Dog' or 'Rock', was made from skimmed milk and was notoriously hard and dry. Revd Warner, writing in 1795, noted it 'can scarcely be cut by a hatchet or saw; is to be masticated only by the firmest teeth, and digested only by the strongest stomachs.' Rather more edible was 'Rammel' cheese made from fresh or unskimmed milk.

For those families on the larger 'mixed' holdings farming was not only a full-time occupation, it was also a way of life. Despite the fact that until 1875 there were few tenant rights (nationally, 90 per cent of farms were tenanted) and that many farmers faced insecure and short-term tenure, endured poor accommodation, and frequently suffered crop damage due to the landowner's hunting rights, there was usually a remarkable scale of mutual loyalty between the lord of the manor and the farmer. Some farms were tenanted by the same family for several generations, notably the Sanders at Clamerkin Farm (1850s to 1890s), the Hawkins at Lambsleaze Farm (1860s until January 2003), and the Locks at Elmsworth (1870s to 1930s). Alternatively, families immersed in farming simply moved between farms upon the expiry of a lease, rather than leave their lifestyle behind.

Most farmers and their families were 'born to the task'. Not only did the sons of farmers often inherit their fathers' tenancy agreements but, probably due to the business and social circles in which they moved, farmers often selected their wives from farming stock. Robert Lock of Elmsworth Farm married Sarah Ann Hillier from Compton Farm; his son Walter Hillier Lock married Elizabeth Hayward from Locks Farm; and two of Walter's children married into farming families – Sarah 'Sally' Lock to Reginald Hayward (her second cousin) of Little Thorness Farm, and Walter John Lock to Alice D'Ath from Mottistone Farm. The intermarriage between farming families meant that it came as no surprise to the wives to find they were not only responsible for the usual household chores but also for running the dairy, feeding the poultry, and attending the market with dairy produce, poultry, honey, jams and flowers! She turned the fruit into jams, pickles and wines; she cured the bacon and hams after the pig was slaughtered, usually in November (after lengthy drying and salting, the 'flitches' were smoked in the chimney or hung from the kitchen ceiling); and until late in the nineteenth century she also baked a great deal of bread.

Until the 1850s farms baked most of the local bread and supplied most beer and/or cider, each of which was paid 'in kind' to farm workers. (Traditionally, farm beer was served to the men in the fields at 'lebben o'clock' and again in the afternoon when they ate their 'nammet' – usually bread and cheese.) It remained common for the men to produce the beverages but it fell to the farmer's wife to bake the bread in a brick oven stoked with wood faggots, using a long-handled 'peel' to put in the dough and remove the loaves. An earlier brick-built bakehouse with parts of its oven still preserved stands against the stone-built Marsh Farmhouse, and remains of large ovens have also been found at the former Noah's Ark Inn and at Nobby's Cottage in Newtown High Street.

Mid-nineteenth-century prosperity on the larger farms encouraged the employment of domestic servants, enabling the farmer's wife and daughters to enjoy a little more leisure time. Family and work even became physically more separate as the parlour was turned into the 'withdrawing-room' and furnished to more sophisticated tastes, and farmers' daughters aspired to the position of governess. Thus, in 1871, Annie Long (aged 19) was resident as domestic servant at London Farm, Edith Barton (16) was at Fleetlands Farm, Fanny Harden (14) at Elmsworth Farm and Sarah Ford (15) at Locks Farm.

If a farmer was single or became a widower he often employed a housekeeper. Adela Hole worked for widower John Sweet from 1888 until she got married in 1901. Given the choice by her employer she opted to work at Harts Farm rather than his other holding, Marsh Farm, 'because there is more traffic passing Harts'! Adela was paid 20 gold sovereigns ('yallow-bwoys') once each year in addition to her keep, and her varied duties ranged from scrubbing the flagstone floors to acting as hostess at the frequent social gatherings at the farm. John Sweet, whose only child had died aged six, died himself in 1915 and Charles Barton (formerly the head game-keeper at Swainston) was offered the tenancy by his cousin Andrew Barton, steward of the estate.

The 'golden age' of farming came to an abrupt end in the late 1870s. Several poor harvests culminated in the dreadful summer of 1879. Farm income dropped dramatically. Many farmers had over-invested, especially in machinery, and cheap foreign imports flooded the market leading to a number of bankruptcies. Railway development led to keener competition, and smallholders found it difficult to reduce costs. Nationally, this combination of circumstances led to widespread shedding of labour, and between 1871 and 1911, half of those working on the land lost their jobs. The social order that had lasted over 1,000 years was breaking up. Whilst larger holdings cut costs by shedding labour to survive, the tenancies of smallholdings began to change hands more frequently as farmers struggled. The drift of labour towards the towns had begun in earnest and many sought a fresh start in the New World. Among the 'local' emigrants were Henry Angell (who stood in at the last minute for William Abrook), Arthur Foss, and siblings James, Jane and Frank Fallick. The appeal of the New World continued, especially in the difficult years of the 1920s and '30s, and Charlie Pocock of London Heath with his friend Robbie Lock tried their luck overseas, although Hilton Cousins of Porchfield declined their invitation to join them in Canada. Others who wished to remain in farming had to be prepared to relocate at frequent intervals. Sam Wells, son of Charles Wells of Locks Farm, occupied Whitehouse Farm and Thorness Farm in rapid succession.

Some dairy farms did benefit from the coming of the railway which enabled them to get their milk to the towns more quickly and therefore be less reliant on butter or cream processing. The Freshwater–Newport line had been completed in 1889 and Watchingwell Station had been built largely to service the farms on the Swainston estate. This might have contributed to the late survival of so many small 'dairies' in Newtown until the turn of the century. Mrs Kingswell's small dairy at Noah's Ark was still active in 1927, Key Close dairy was being advertised in the 1930s and the Bartons were still working the Harts Farm dairy until well into the 1970s. (When she married Ted Barton in the 1950s and moved to live at Harts Farm, Pat Rice found that the milking of the 30 Ayreshire cattle was still being done by hand.) But the more remote holdings, such as North Close Farm and Brickfields Farm, still faced the same problems and turned their milk into butter, cream and cheese.

To some extent farmers' failures to adopt new methods contributed to the problems they faced. Even some of the larger holdings were still using the most basic farming methods until the mid-twentieth century. (Whilst this held back the levels of production, it preserved, in a way rarely found elsewhere, the richness of Newtown's flora and fauna.)

Haymaking near London Heath, c.1920.

Elsie Lock was sent to Elmsworth Farm in 1920, at the age of 13, to learn how to farm. She learned to milk the cows by hand, seated on a three-legged stool with a pail between her knees. All the milk at Elmsworth was still made into butter. In the absence of a separator, it was put into large flat pans to settle and the cream was then scooped off with a 'skimmer' (an implement like a large fish-slice) and placed in large stoneware jars for three or four days before going into the hand-driven butter churn. The butter gradually formed in big lumps and was transferred to a ridged 'worker' for rolling to squeeze out the whey (buttermilk). Salt was added during the process and the butter was cut into half-pound blocks using wooden 'butter pats' (first scalded and then dipped in cold water to prevent the butter sticking). Finally, pats or rollers were used (Elmsworth did not have its own moulds) to put the farm's own mark on each half pound, and the butter was then stored in a cool wooden box with slate shelves ready to be taken to the shops – Hilliers at Cowes, the Cooperative in Newport and Mr Wise at Hunnyhill.

A farmer's wedding in January 1926. Left to right, back row: *Walter Hillier Lock (of Elmsworth Farm), Elsie Lock (of Forest Farm), groom Reginald Hayward (of Little Thorness Farm), Jack Arnold (of Bunts Hill Farm), Simeon Hayward (of Little Thorness Farm);* front row: *Lizzie Lock, Sally Lock, Mrs Hayward, ?, ?.*

John Sweet at Harts Farm, c.1888.

The Hayward sisters c.1875 at Locks Farm. Left to right: *Eliza, Caroline, Annie and Bessie.*

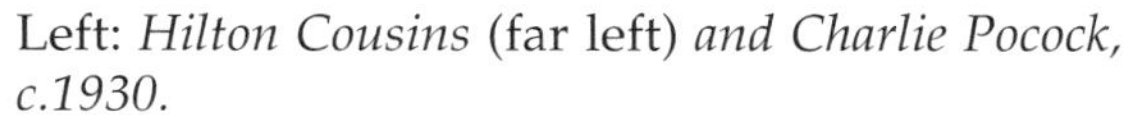

Left: *Hilton Cousins* (far left) *and Charlie Pocock, c.1930.*

Right: *The Wells family, c.1928.* Left to right: *Joan, Sam, Roland, baby Patricia, Gertrude.*

Elsie learned to wean the calves with primitive weaning boxes fitted with teats and known as 'little mothers', and she did all the free-range poultry work, supplementing the birds' feed with corn and boiled peelings, collecting the eggs, and making use of 'setty' hens to hatch clutches of eggs, whether they were chicken, geese or duck eggs. She was often amused by the bewilderment and concern of the hen when her brood sometimes took to the water!

Carrie Mew at Porchfield Farm, c.1915.

Despite the general decline in farming and the sharp drop in employment opportunities on the farm, Newtown was still steeped in the farming culture from the turn of the century to the 1930s. A child could still be sent along to the local farm to collect the family's daily milk or the weekly butter. London Farm was an 'all-dairy' farm and Enos Whatley and his son Alec insisted on keeping only Jersey cattle whose milk is rich in cream. (In 2004, dairy herds consist mainly of Friesian cattle which produce much more milk per cow, yet with much less cream.) It was a typical family-run farm, employing extra labour only in summer to assist with the hay harvest (cutting, turning and stacking the hay in 'pooks' to await loading onto the wagon with 'pitchen prongs' – long-handled pitch-forks). With the break-up of the estate, London Farm was sold in 1932 for just £1,000.

Along the road was Clamerkin Farm, another 'all-dairy' enterprise, which turned most of its milk into butter. By 1910 James (Jim) Arnold had the tenancy, having learned farming from his father at the Noah's Ark dairy. Jim was rather more interested in guns than in farming. Never without a weapon, he was a marvellous shot and built several hides along the nearby creek. The rather poor, bush-strewn land suffered some neglect during these years, as did the stables where only a gangway for the cows was kept open through the stacked droppings!

The Noah's Ark dairy had been taken over from her parents by Mrs Mary Kingswell (Jim Arnold's sister), who had married into the farming family from Fleetlands Farm. It was a typical smallholding with a few scattered fields near the Town Hall and London Heath. Her son, Joliffe, was used as cowboy to move the cattle to and from the fields on his way to school at Locks Green.

A similar dairy smallholding was run by Elizabeth Stark at Key Close. Her rented lands bounded much of the Causeway Creek around to the quay. She married near neighbour, Herbert Wheeler, who had worked for her for some years. Run for much of the nineteenth century by the Holbrook family, the holding was never very large, and when it was sold by the Swainston estate in 1932 it had stabling for only eight cows.

At the mainly dairy Harts Farm only a little land was under the plough for wheat and turnips ('turmets'), except during wartime. Yet it was here that an ancient ploughshare was recently discovered, and that Dickie Fallick, the district's excellent ploughman, always found work using a horse and single-blade plough until well into the twentieth century. Earlier, farmer John Sweet concentrated on dairy production, but also planted a sizeable orchard, mainly of Blenheim apples. The owner of Harts Farm at the time of writing, Mrs Pat Barton, still retains some of the farm accounts from the 1920s which illustrate the seasonal fluctuations of dairy and fruit production, and confirm that most milk was still turned into butter. For example, the week ending 26 May 1926 sees the following entry:

56 and a half lbs butter at one and fivepence	*£3.19s.10d.*
27 dozen eggs at one and tuppence	*£1.11s.6d.*
seven and a half lbs butter at one and sixpence	*11s.3d.*
3 doz. eggs at one and tuppence	*3s.6d.*
milk	*6s.8d.*
three sittings duck	*7s.6d.*
Total	*£7.0s.3d.*

The 1922 apple account includes the sale of 17½ bushels of Blenheims for up to 10s. a bushel. Fallers, 'reds', cookers and Russetts were also sold, together with two gallons of 'cridlens' (misshapen apples) – altogether a total of £16.13s.6d. income from apples that year.

By 1932 Marsh Farm had been reduced to 28 acres, almost exclusively grazing. When the farm was sold that year (for £1,150) its farmhouse still contained a dairy and brewhouse. Associated buildings, including stabling for over 30 cows and three horses, together with four piggeries, were sold separately for £135. Since the late 1880s the farmhouse had been let as residential accommodation to a wide variety of tenants, whilst the farm lands had been rented by, among others, George Abblitt (1920s) and James

Warder (1930s), but when Captain and Mrs Seabroke moved into the farmhouse in 1936 the building had been empty for some five years.

Marsh Farm had traditionally been mainly dairy but with rather more under the plough than other nearby holdings, especially the fields known as Promised Land and Upper and Lower Matthews, before these were bought by the Barton brothers for Harts Farm. Both this farm and Harts Farm incorporated parts of the reclaimed Newtown Marsh, the salt-laden grass of which was good for fattening stock. At various times horses and cows were kept on the Marsh (Maurice Rice from Elm Farm wintered his horses there), and in the 1940s Sir Hansen Rowbotham of Brook House rented parts of the Marsh, Curlew Field and Home Ground for his Suffolk Punch horses and Red Poll cattle. Much of the Marsh was put under the plough during each of the world wars.

Fleetlands Farm in 1996.

Neither of the two remote holdings survived at Lower Elmsworth. Each farm had been wholly dairy and had produced mainly butter and cream. In 1901 William Smith had taken over North Close Farm from Henry Calloway, whose family had been long-term tenants, but the farm buildings had to be abandoned from around 1911 when the Newtown Rifle Ranges were developed. By 1900 the cottage at the farm was uninhabitable, used only for storage, and the buildings eventually collapsed altogether. The farm land was absorbed, partly into the holdings of Brickfield Farm where the Prangnell family was in the process of abandoning brick making in favour of farming, and partly into Harts Farm. The Prangnells struggled on producing butter and cream until family illness caused them to leave the farm in 1953. Shortly afterwards some of the land at Lower Elmsworth became part of the Elmsworth Farm holdings, but the Ministry of Defence still retains ownership of over 800 acres at the time of writing.

Gerry Humber's parents, at Fleetlands Farm, insisted on sending him to Locks Green School in the early 1900s to avoid him mixing with the children of the farm's carter (Charles Whittington) who, living at Whiteoak Cottages, sent his children to Shalfleet School. This was a large 'mixed' farm with a very impressive group of farm buildings. The former tenant had been George Alford Kingswell, and as late as 1901 Mr Kingswell's cowman (Samuel Rashley, aged 51) and shepherd (Mark Downer, aged 81) boarded at the farm, sleeping in a barn. Before 1915 the tenancy had again changed hands as the Strickland family moved in. When it was sold in 1932 for £1,350 the whole comprised the farmhouse (with dairy), van house, cart shed, granary, cattle shed, barn, stabling for 18 cows and four horses, and five piggeries, together with Whiteoak Cottages and 152 acres. A descendant of the Stricklands is still in residence at the time of writing, but part of the farm land has been sold and the remainder is let out for grazing.

'Dark, damp and dilapidated' was how one contemporary described the typical nineteenth-century farm-labourer's cottage. This group has always been at the bottom of the earnings league and as late as 1940, even with the assistance of national bargaining, the farm labourer earned only £2.8s.3d. each week. Deprived, by repeated land enclosures, of his right of access to grazing and fuel, and faced with falling opportunities for full-time employment as mechanisation and farming depression became more common, many labourers still lived in the most humble of circumstances.

Edwin Holbrook's maternal grandparents, Mark Denness and his wife, were typical. From around 1825 they occupied a basic cottage, described by Edwin as follows:

The house... was built with mud walls and thatched roof, with very small lead-framed windows glazed with small diamond shaped panes of glass... In the living room by the side of grandfather's very high-backed arm chair there was a very old oak chest in which he kept his own personal belongings... There was only one fireplace in the house, and that was on the hearth, so all the cooking was done by boiling everything in a large oval iron pot hung on the crook over the fire. Meat (if any), potatoes in a net, and cabbage were boiled all together. The only pictures on the walls were large photographs of the Revd C.H. Spurgeon, Joseph Arch, William E. Gladstone, John Bright and the Carisbrooke Parish Church almanac. On the dresser two very old sets of jugs were hanging, the dinner plates were standing on edge on the shelves at the back, and the vegetable dishes in front of them. There was a very old Dutch striking clock.

Edwin described his grandparents' 'great horror of the workhouse' and how his grandfather hobbled miles with the aid of two sticks to break stones at the roadside in order to earn the few pence which would enable them to pay the rent.

A little higher up the social order was the artisan smallholder who had both a skilled trade and rented

The former blacksmith's cottage at Locks Green with its lean-to stable alongside, 1996.

a little land on which to keep some animals and cultivate some garden produce. In the 1890s, Fred Heal, the blacksmith at Locks Green, had married Louisa Arnold, and their grandson, Don Chessell, often spent his school holidays there in the 1920s in the cottage alongside the blacksmith's shop. In the 1970s he recollected that:

> *The two storey house was built around 1700 with lumps of Bembridge limestone, combined with bricks at the four corners, the whole capped with a roof of thatch. These bricks were typical of the 18th century being smaller than modern ones. The windows, too, were smaller than modern ones, with wide window sills revealing the thickness of the stone walls... At the back were two large stone-floored rooms. One was the 'Dairy' (grandfather kept a small herd of cows) where the cream separator was kept and where grandma made her butter... The other room with the back door was... the kitchen. It had a huge open fireplace reeking of wood smoke where hung a large blackened kettle and other 'witch's cauldrons'... From the beams hung hams, and there was always a packet of Robin's Starch on the dresser... Up one step and you were in the living room... The other front room, the 'best room' as it was called...* [contained] *...the large harmonium around which... the company draped themselves to sing heartily from the Wesleyan Hymn Book... Above the mantelpiece (loaded to capacity) was a large ornate mirror, as befitted the best room... and on the left (just inside the low door) was the grandfather clock with its beautifully ornamented face, high pitched chime, and sonorous tick.*

The stables were built onto the side of the cottage and across the yard were the pigsties behind the blacksmith's shop. In those days the holding consisted of four scattered fields, three off the lane from the Three Cocked Hat towards Coleman's Farm, and one at London Heath. The narrow, gorse-strewn field opposite London Heath Cottages was a favoured rabbit shoot for Charlie Heal, the blacksmith's son. The smithy closed in the early 1930s when Fred Heal retired, and ownership passed to a branch of the Pragnell family. Their only daughter, Mrs Amy Cosh, stubbornly survived the enormous changes in farming practice to tend her small dairy herd (of best Guernseys) from the same stables (which incorporated the former smithy) until her semi-retirement in 1997. Amy became a herdswoman at the age of 14 and always retained her hand-milking methods. In over 50 years of dairying she took only ten days' holiday.

Amy Cosh with one of her beloved cows, 1997.
(REPRODUCED COURTESY OF THE *IOW COUNTY PRESS* LTD)

Apart from Amy's activities, there had not been a great deal of conventional farming in the Newtown area for some years. In times of cheap imports (especially of dairy products) and large-scale, mechanised and often specialised cultivation, there was little call for the traditional smallholdings associated with Newtown's past, and many people formerly occupied on the land have found easier ways of making a living. Most of the dairies have long gone, many finding it impossibly expensive to reach the high standards of hygiene demanded by the public and later required by the Milk Marketing Board. (Before the pasteurisation of milk tuberculosis was all too common, hitting hard the Kingswell family at Fleetlands Farm and the Fallick family of Porchfield, among others.)

From 1932 until the 1960s, the Swainston estate was broken up and sold off, some of it at very modest prices. The National Trust bought 36 acres of Harts Farm land in 1982 and has other holdings in the district that were once farmed. Parts of Marsh Farm are rented out to Barry Angell of Locks Farm. Similarly, George Abblitt of Elmsworth Farm rents part of Harts Farm for his beef cattle and the Downer family rent part of Fleetlands Farm for sheep and cattle pasture. Most of the farming implements and machinery from Harts are now on display at an equestrian centre and tourist attraction at Binstead.

The National Insurance Act of 1911 had made payments towards pension and sickness benefits by all those in work compulsory for the first time, but once again excluded those on lower pay, thus disentitling them also to any benefits. As a result, doctors' bills became an increasing problem for Adela Foss in her later years. During the 1930s and '40s a prolapsed womb required regular visits from Dr Bruce, Dr Low, or Dr Stead, and from Nurses Bower, Cherity, Davies or Bowler. Charges as high as £1.10s.0d. for each visit consumed far more than her weekly income. But traditional remedies die hard. One of the nurses refused to visit again unless Adela desisted from applying pig's lard to the area of her discomfort! Country folk had a tradition of using herbal remedies and superstitions, passed down through the generations or sought from soothsayers and travellers. Curatives ranged from two black spiders in a little cotton bag, to incantations beneath the oldest oak tree, to the carrying of a rabbit's foot! 'Vargis' (or verjuice) was a concoction made from fermented crab apples and popularly used locally to cure sprains and rheumatic ailments. Village lore also attributed special skills to particular residents, thus Fred Fallick the gamekeeper was a regular recipient of requests to remove warts, and 'Posky' Saunders at Porchfield was said to be able to cure rheumatism.

Every winter, each of the Lock siblings at Elmsworth was given a small square of camphor sewn into a bag to hang around the neck in order to ward off infections. Any chest ailment was treated with a generous application of goose grease and a sheet of brown paper worn under the vest. Onion juice was used to treat earache, and the tips of brambles were boiled in sugar to ease a cough. A 'blue-bag' from the laundry was applied to wasp stings, and a lemon rubbed onto the forehead worked wonders for a headache.

Rural areas like Newtown tended to have a disproportionately high number of poor families. Though it was expected that every family member should make a contribution to that family's income (and most people did find some kind of work) wages for farm work, domestic service, or labouring on the highways were desperately low, and employment was often temporary.

Consequently, most families sought supplementary incomes. Many turned to some form of self-employment and, until the 1870s, very large numbers were also involved to some extent in smuggling or poaching with the attendant risks of being shot by the customs officer or the gamekeeper or, if caught, being imprisoned or even transported to the colonies. Others supplemented their income by keeping bees, a pig and some poultry, cultivating their gardens and keeping a small orchard, and by collecting from field, hedgerow and copse things such as mushrooms, nuts, blackberries, hips, haws and sloes. Few could contemplate retirement. 'Ready Money Charlie' Osbourn of Porchfield, a rag-and-bone man still working at the age of 76 in 1891, earned a few extra pennies in his younger days delivering the local post, having collected it from the mail coach on the Newport road. James Jupe, resident in a remote cottage near Porchfield, prepared and sold 'nicky faggots' (bundles of kindling wood) from his donkey and cart as far away as Niton. And there was Luke Saunders ('Posky' to the Porchfield children), 'a shrivelled little man, of peculiar looks and habits', turnip hoer in the summer and highways worker each winter who, each week, replenished his wife's little shop by driving his donkey and cart to Newport and back.

'Scrimping' became a way of life. Hand-me-downs and jumble-sale bargains filled the wardrobe, and the sewing-box and the darning needles rarely gathered dust. Threadbare sheets were turned into dusters and odd wool was knitted into children's toys.

Since the early 1800s national governments have sought ways to help a greater number of people to make their own provision for that 'rainy day' and for retirement, sometimes by persuasion, sometimes by force, but almost always without much success. Since the Middle Ages there had been Craft Guilds which, through subscription, accumulated funds with which to assist members in distress. From the mid-1700s many of these were replaced by a proliferation of Friendly Societies, each designed to insure members against hard times. But even these modest savings and insurance plans were beyond the reach of poorer members of the community. In the 1830s, the ironically named Isle of Wight Brotherly Society deliberately excluded anyone earning less than 18s. a week, and from 1843 actually banned all labourers from membership. Even as late as 1888, when Revd John Vicars, Rector at Calbourne, was honorary secretary of the local branch of the Hampshire Friendly Society, few labourers could afford to save more than their penny a week with the Prudential, which was done in order to avoid a pauper's grave.

Yet, as part of their drive towards greater self-reliance, the Government of 1817 passed the Savings Bank Act from which sprang, with the help of the Guardians, the Isle of Wight Trustee Savings Bank. Accounts could be opened with deposits as small as 1s., and the bank became very popular, opening a number of branches, including that at Calbourne in 1834. By 1823 the bank held 17,000 accounts, appealing to labourers and journeymen (6,547 accounts), servants (2,817), children and apprentices (2,824).

Before the twentieth century few occupations generated a pension. Few people lived long enough to draw them, anyway! Out of a total population of 880 in Calbourne parish in 1803 there were only 11 men over the age of 70, and six of those were still working. Later census returns (1841–1901) also reflect how few elderly residents there were (perhaps they were already at Forest House), and suggest that those who did still reside in the Newtown area either continued to work until they dropped, or moved into the homes of their offspring, as shown in Table A (below). A few were listed by the census as unemployed or receiving alms, and it is striking how rare it was to find elderly people receiving a private income or pension (Table B, opposite).

Older residents still working or dependent on their children

	Name	Age	Residence	Occupation
1841	William Wiseman	70	London Heath	Agric. Lab
	John Ridett	79	Lambsleaze	Yeoman
	John Saunders	70	Clamerkin	Farmer
	James Hollis	75	Elm Cottage	Agric. Lab
	Thomas Holbrook	84	Newtown	Lab.
	Alice Abrook	85	Newtown	Living with son
	John Holbrook	74	Newtown	Carpenter
	John Edwards	78	Newtown	Agric. Lab.
	John Whittington	73	Newtown	Agric. Lab.
	Richard Holbrook	73	Newtown	Salt manufacturer
1851	Fanny Jacobs	67	Newtown	Living with son-in-law
	Ann Holbrook	84	Newtown	Living with son
	John Holbrook	84	Newtown	Living with son
	Henry Abrook	67	Newtown	Mariner
	Robert Harvey	75	Newtown	Farmer
	Martha Harvey	76	Newtown	Farm servant
	James Foss	63	North Close	Living with son
1861	Alice Day	76	Newtown Town Hall	Midwife
	Henry Abrook	77	Newtown	Fisherman
	Richard Holbrook	66	Newtown	Salt merchant
1871	Alice Day	86	Newtown Town Hall	Farmer
	James Taylor	68	Noah's Ark	Innkeeper & dairyman
	Hannah Holbrook	70	Newtown	Dairy farmer
	John Harvey	67	Newtown	Dairyman
1881	William Prangnell	66	North Close	Brick maker
	Jane Skeats	86	Newtown	Living with daughter
	Ann Wheeler	79	Newtown	Living with son
	Hannah Woolgar	73	Newtown	Grocer
	James Holbrook	84	Lamb Cottage	Mariner
1891	Reuben Young	76	London Heath	Gardener
	Jonas Foss	65	London Heath	Gen. Lab.
	Thomas Abrook	66	Nobby's Cottage	Dairyman
	Mark Downer	74	Fleetlands Farm	Shepherd
	Maria Prangnell	75	Noah's Ark	Living with son-in-law
	Luke Barton	66	St Hubert's Lodge	Gamekeeper
	Isaac Arnold	69	The Retreat, Newtown	Bricklayer
1901	Mark Downer	81	Fleetland Farm	Shepherd
	John Ford	67	London Heath	Woodcutter
	Henry Ford	70	London Heath	Woodcutter
	Margaret Foss	72	London Heath	Living with son
	Jane Coleman	68	Vicarage	Domestic servant
	John Sweet	68	Harts Farm	Farmer
	Mary Skeats	66	Town Hall	Domestic cook
	Thomas Abrook	75	Nobby's Cottage	Dairyman
	Thomas Brett	68	Church Cottage	General Labourer

Older residents with private incomes, or dependent upon alms

	Name	Age	Residence	Source of income
1841	Sir Richard Simeon	55	Swainston	Independent
	Alice Day	55	Newtown	Independent
	John Harvey	60	Newtown	Independent
1851	William Wright	27	Lower Hamstead	Pauper (with parents)
1861	Jane Skeats	66	Newtown	Almswoman
1871	James Ford	75	London Heath	Annuitant (military)
	Jane Ford	70	London Heath	Annuitant's wife
	Jane Skeats	77	Coastguard cottages	Unemployed
	Mary Whittington	82	Coastguard cottages	Unemployed
	Henry Jacobs	59	Hollis Cottage	Unemployed mariner
	Joseph Westmore	78	Whiteoak	Retired farmer
1881	Reuben Holbrook	70	Key Close	Private income
	Hannah Holbrook	80	Key Close	Private income
1891	Roland Baxter	40	Marsh Farm	Living on own means
	William Abrook	75	London Heath	Living on own means
	James Henry Woolgar	55	Newtown	Naval pensioner
1901	Jane Lock	66	Marsh Farm	Living on own means
	Ellen Woolgar	63	Woolgar's Cottage	Own means supplemented by selling small groceries

Before the later twentieth century, very few Newtown residents could be described as wealthy. The values of individual estates upon death remained modest, even for seemingly successful tradesmen. Salt boiler Richard Holbrook (died 1867) left an estate valued at under £300, and the estates of his relations were of a similar order. Thomas (1871) left £165, Hannah (1883) £392, Captain James (1884) £413 and another Thomas (1886) less than £300. Similarly, former coastguard and shopkeeper James Woolgar (1899) left £230, farmer John Sweet (1915) £431, and the last licensee of Noah's Ark Sarah Maria Arnold (1922) left £597. Most labourers left just a few pounds, in sharp contrast to the likes of Revd Henry Rice Venn (died 1925), farmer Charles Barton (1926) and oyster fisherman Henry Paskins (1935), each of whom left well over £1,000. But even the most wealthy residents such as farmer George Alford Kingswell, formerly at Fleetlands Farm, who died in 1910, and retired doctor Howard Hawkins (1919) of Lamb Cottage, left estates of little more than £5,000.

The vast majority accumulated very little wealth. They could not, or would not, save for their retirement, and when they did it sometimes proved to be to their own disadvantage. The estate of shell fisherman Henry Foss amounted to £748 when he died in 1936. In 1915, Henry had been persuaded to invest his late mother's legacy in Government stock and had never quite recovered from the subsequent loss of its capital value. He resolved never to invest again, and saved from his modest earnings into the Post Office. His widow's Post Office account contained £273 in 1939, producing an annual interest of some £7 to go with her £2.11s.0d. from Government consols and annuities of £2.17s.6d. These modest incomes supplemented her State pension of 10s. per week. But the State pension was means-tested, and Henry's savings led directly to a reduction of 20 per cent in his widow's pension, following visits from agency officials. Savings, for this family as for so many others, had turned into a Catch-22 situation.

However, more people started saving 'rainy-day' monies mainly in very modest amounts. In January 1927, the first annual report of the newly established Calbourne, Newtown and Porchfield Penny Bank revealed that 90 accounts had been opened with a total of £76.6s.2d. deposited. And in 1926 the Calbourne, Newtown and Porchfield National Savings Association (with a minimum subscription of 6d. per week) had sold 215 certificates to a total value of £172.

Throughout the nineteenth century prospects for the rural poor had stayed grim. Many remained dependent on charity, which varied in scale from the large endowments and legacies of wealthy benefactors to modest church collections for waifs and

Above: *A romanticised view of nineteenth-century Christmas charity.*

Left: *Isaac Whittington in 1900, aged 92. Isaac worked for the Swainston estate until he was 88 years old before retiring to Stone Steps.*

This photograph of Dr Cottle hung in each almshouse in Shalfleet.

Two of the substantial Wyndham Cottle almshouses at Shalfleet in 1999.

strays. Although access to charity was somewhat random, targeting by some charities was almost zealously defined.

The Drake Charity for the village of Wellow and the parishes of Shalfleet and Thorley (1901) stipulated that:

> *... poor persons of not less than 60 years of age, and of good character, who have been resident* [in the area] *for not less than two years preceding the time of their appointment, who are not at the time of their appointment in receipt of Poor Law relief other than medical relief, and who, from age, ill-health, accident or infirmity, are unable to maintain themselves by their own exertions, are eligible for appointment.*

Preference was given to those longest resident, and the trustees had some discretion. Occasionally, endowments and legacies were very substantial. David Urry's Charity trustees were authorised in 1858 to sell a house, barn and 24 acres at Overton Farm, Calbourne, for not less than £1,200 for the benefit of the poor in Shalfleet parish. And in 1918 Ellen Woolgar, the Newtown shopkeeper, left her complete estate to charity, asking her executors, Henry Paskins and Frank King, to distribute half to the county hospital (around £219), a quarter to Dr Barnado's Homes, an eighth to the Frank James Hospital, and the remainder between the local Preventative and Rescue Society and the Newtown Church Fund.

Charitable cash awards to the poor tended to be uncommon and by 1900 most such relief was granted in the form of coal or clothing allowances, often at Christmas. The Farnall Charity was created towards the end of the nineteenth century under the will of Mrs Marianna Fletcher Farnall. In 1896, the *Shalfleet Church Monthly* magazine reported that the trustees had stipulated that 'by paying a penny per week into either a clothing, boot and shoe, or coal club, the following [were] entitled to their share of the Farnall legacy.' Clearly, the charitable awards had to be 'earned' by a demonstration of willingness to be partially self-reliant.

In 1903, trustees of the Farnall Charity invested £900 at three per cent annuity, and the same year the charity granted eight hundredweight of coal each to Mrs Mussell, Charles Barton and Thomas Hollis, all Shalfleet residents, and to Amelia Skeats of Newbridge, plus eight other widows from Shalfleet, Wellow, Newbridge and Ningwood. By 1924 there were 28 recipients of coal (costing the charity £18), one person received clothing (valued at 10s.), and further donations from the fund were made to the Royal County Hospital (£1.1s.0d.) and the Shalfleet Clothing Club. This club had a long history. In 1896 it had received payments from 57 members, plus other donations, and had distributed coal, clothing and boots to the local needy.

The Farnall Charity grants continue to the time of writing, but beneficiaries are now more likely to receive a frozen chicken each Christmas. A rather unusual charitable fund was established in 1837 at Newtown Church by the Simeon family, soon after the completion of its rebuilding. This still produces a small annual sum specifically targeted at paying the insurance premium of the church. Originally, it was designed to improve the vicar's stipend!

Local parish magazines of the late-nineteenth century often published the names of subscribers to a given charity. There was a certain social credit gained from having one's name published in this context, although some of the beneficiaries ('choir treat' or 'Sunday School tea') hardly qualified as the most deserving.

Almost as a matter of course, church congregations have raised modest sums to assist parishioners in need. Offertories for the Poor Fund were noted in 1885 as being £1.3s.0d. (Shalfleet), 3s.9d. (Newtown) and 3s.7d. (Locks Green), and in 1895 the Shalfleet offertories included the sum of £1.5s.3d. for the 'Waifs and Strays' fund, the charity through which, on a national scale, the Church of England Society provided homes for child paupers.

By 1926, the Newtown area was reeling from the effects of the agricultural recession and this, coupled with a severe winter, led Revd Glover at Newtown to appeal in the *Shalfleet, Calbourne and Thorley Church Messenger:* 'Owing to special demands this winter on the Sick and Poor Fund it is overdrawn, and I should be glad to receive donations for the same.' Local resident Captain Pirie responded, among others, with a donation of 10s.

At the same time the Newtown Sewing Party was meeting each week at the vicarage to make garments for charity. Also in 1926, Mrs Osment of Locks Farm held a sale and fête in aid of the Royal County Hospital, and another fête took place at Green Close, Newtown, by kind permission of Herbert Wheeler, in aid of the church's Poor Fund.

Retired Harley Street specialist, Dr Wyndham Cottle, left several charitable legacies in 1919, including one for the construction of four very substantial almshouses at Lower Dodpits, Shalfleet, and these were completed in 1922. He specified in his will that they were to be used for deserving married couples over the age of 65, but not for single women, Roman Catholics or Jews. Any balance from the legacy, plus interest generated, was to be used for the maintenance of the buildings and the support of their occupiers, initially Mr and Mrs Meaning, Mr and Mrs Grist, Mr and Mrs Armstrong and Mr L.J. Austin. During his working life, Dr Cottle's housekeeper, Mary Mew of Porchfield House, accompanied him on trips to London for periods of a month or more at a time. His wife was of independent means and preferred to remain on the Island improving her *haute couture.* Dr Cottle bequeathed his wife the family parrot and an annuity of £20.

Despite the compassionate actions of men like Dr Cottle, the feeling of 'them and us' ran deep in the area. It had a long history. For some 600 years the lives of so many in the district had been lived in the shadow of 'The Big House'. For many, this was the accepted way of things. One Newtown resident was frequently heard to remark 'What would become of the rest of us if the bettermost folk lost their money?' But a contemporary, invited in 1890 to Newtown's vicarage to air a grievance, wrote acerbically in the *Isle of Wight County Press*, commenting: 'there is too much of the 'touch your cap' element about this arrangement.'

When faced with the choice of the workhouse or nothing, earlier local generations had taken direct action, rioting, burning hayricks, physically abusing Overseers and smashing machinery. A national police force had been formed in the late 1830s, partly in response to similar unrest, and local parishes swore in teams of special constables. In 1854, Isaac Arnold (a mason at Porchfield), Edward Buckler (the baker at Shalfleet), Jacob Dore (a yeoman from Porchfield), and David Saunders (a timber merchant at Porchfield) became special constables.

Generally, communities have shown sensitivity and generosity towards the needs of their sick, infirm and elderly. There has been much less sympathy for those whose poverty stemmed from low pay or from unemployment and it took the tragedy of the Great Depression of the late 1920s and '30s for the public to accept that such poverty was not necessarily self-inflicted. The scale of suffering was a blast from the past and it brought about a sea change in public attitudes. In 1929, the Local Government Act replaced the Guardians with Public Assistance Committees and led to the phasing out of workhouses which became Public Assistance Institutions. Demand for such places was still buoyant. Despite the National Strike by agricultural labourers in 1923 their pay continued to fall towards an average of £1.10s.0d. per week during the 1930s, too low to pay National Insurance contributions which meant that, until 1936, farm labourers received no unemployment benefits. Many of them finished up 'on the National'. Many others had good reason to be grateful to Sir John Simeon who, when selling off parts of his estate, protected his workers by giving them lifetime tenancies. Henry and Adela Foss, together with Ernest and Celia Seagar and others, needed to reconsider their views about their lord of the manor.

Depression in farming even led to the farmers themselves, formerly among the squirearchy of the neighbourhood, refusing to pay church tithes and being forced from their homes by the bailiffs. Conditions were ripe for the development of a comprehensive public welfare system and the establishment, from 1948, of the Welfare State.

As recently as the early 1900s, one of the main measures of success for many poor rural families was their ability to afford a new pair of boots each year. These cumbersome 'clinkers' were built to order by the local cobbler, then handed over to the village blacksmith where tips, cues and massive hobnails were added. Few agricultural labourers wore socks, so Dickie Fallick, Reg Downer, Ned Scott and the others used a pad of soft hay as a shock-absorbing buffer between their feet and the inner soles of their boots. In the 1880s Jonathan Punch was the local boot- and shoemaker, working from his stone cottage in Dirty Lane at Porchfield under the beady eye of his mother who, in her nineties, occupied the high chair by the fire, where she sat taking her snuff. Few ready-made boots were available in those days and Jonathan used a contraption fixed to the floor to measure feet for his products which were usually of the sturdy variety. Lighter Sunday boots could be purchased from W. Cooke & Sons in St Thomas Square at Newport, or from Joseph Mitchell who had been trading in Holyrood Street, Newport, since 1830 and whose daughter married a Newtown fisherman and brought up her large family at the remote Fish House Point. The boots were essential, but expensive, and during the summer months many folk went barefoot as much as possible to extend the life of their footwear; and, to protect their Sunday boots from the mud many people wore pattens which were hung in the church porch during service.

In 2004, such levels of poverty are rare in the Newtown, Porchfield and Shalfleet area, not least because many from that section of society have left the area in search of work or an affordable home. Conversations now reflect changing priorities and residents tend to discuss the market value of their property rather than fret about the age of their boots.

Chapter 13

Laundress, Washerwoman or Char?: Some Nineteenth-Century Prospects for Women

There is no record of what the family pig thought about the indignity of being hoisted upstairs at each high spring tide to save it from drowning! But for 'Captain' James Faulse (Foss) and his family this was just one of the burdens of living in a former saltern cottage on the extremity of the eastern spit (Fish House Point) at the mouth of Newtown River.

Margaret Foss aged 83 in 1912 at London Heath.

As the relentless tides encroached further and further into their lifestyle (until finally, in 1863, driving them from their home) the Fosses were virtually surrounded by water yet faced the greatest difficulty in obtaining a domestic supply. All sorts of containers were used to collect rainwater, but most of their supply was carried from the nearest pond on the higher ground towards Elmsworth, that same pond which conferred so many health problems upon the brick-making Prangnell family and which was condemned by the Milk Marketing Board in 1953.

In 2004, the average consumption of domestic water is over 140 litres per person per day. In the 1850s, when James' brother Thomas Foss and his family also lived on the sand spit, there were 15 people there needing fresh water for washing, cooking and laundry. And 140 litres was probably more than the lot of them used in a week!

James' wife Mary had died in 1852, the same year that his eldest son, Jonas, had married Margaret Mitchell, a shoemaker's daughter from Newport. To Margaret fell the domestic chores. Could she have known before her marriage what life in this remote place was like?

It is difficult to imagine the privations of such a dwelling. Jonas, a fisherman, was away working most days and Margaret was left with four young children and the housework to cope with. Not least of her domestic chores was the laundry. How much water did she dare use? Where did she obtain the fuel to heat the water? How did she get laundry to stay dry in such a salt-encrusted outpost? How could she aspire to the Victorian adage that 'cleanliness is next to Godliness'?

Despite the upheaval of having to abandon their home in 1863, Margaret probably welcomed the relative comforts provided by the newly-constructed cottage they rented from the Swainston estate at London Heath. This sturdy semi-detached building possessed a kitchen-cum-dining-room with a built-in range, a pantry, an attached wash-house (shared with her neighbours William and Sarah Abrook) and its own, albeit shallow, well, although even this was not 'staned' (lined). A further plentiful supply of fresh water was available 'only' some 150 metres away across the road in Gravel Pit Pond, situated in Pickpocket's Field. (A nearby pond, however, was full of poisonous algae.) This was a major improvement in living conditions for her and, in the main, washdays became confined to a once-weekly event. Margaret raised a family of six children at London Heath and by the time she was widowed in 1893 only one son, Henry, was still living at home.

Henry was 42 when he married Adela Hole in 1901. She had been housekeeper at Harts Farm to John Sweet since 1888. She had probably been well schooled in domestic work because her mother regularly took in washing to augment the family income at West Pennard in Somerset.

Adela was a short, wiry person. With her background in domestic service she was a good 'catch' for Henry, and no doubt the continued presence of mother-in-law Margaret was a further spur to her high standards of cleanliness about the house at London Heath!

Herbert, grandson of Margaret Foss, at Gravel Pit Pond in 1983.

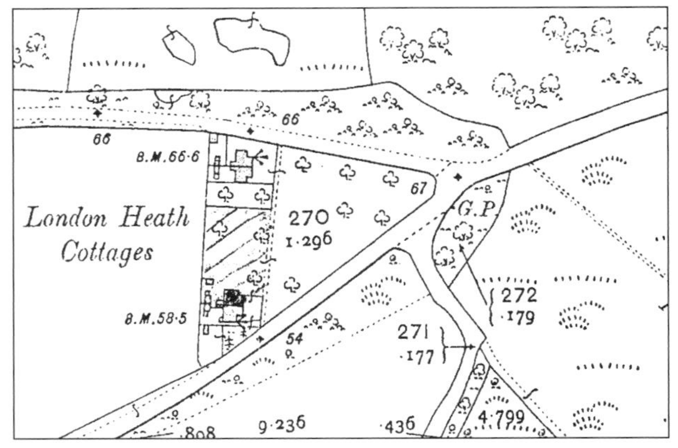

London Heath Cottages, showing the large Gravel Pit Pond in the field to the north.

(Reproduced from 1908 Ordnance Survey map courtesy of Ordnance Survey)

A challenge for any laundress. The 1896 wedding of Herbert Foster, former cowboy at Harts Farm, and Ruth Hole. Also pictured, left to right, back row: *Adela Hole, Bessie Foster, Mr Foster senr, Annie Foster.*

Adela Hole in 1893, aged 30.

The weekly washday, always on Monday, was characteristic of the drudgery and toil associated with housekeeping in those days. Girls were taught the skills of laundry at school, and many often missed school on Mondays to help out at home.

Adela chose to do her laundry in the pantry rather than in the shared wash-house, even though the communal facility was equipped with a brick-built fireplace (above which hung an iron cauldron) and a pump for the well water. She probably decided that the cost of heating the water for washing may as well also benefit the temperature inside the main house, especially in winter, although the fire in the out-house was sometimes used for summer cooking. The hand pump for the well needed priming with a jug of water, and the supply from this source was intermittent at best. Most of the water used was carried from the pond in pails slung across the shoulders on a yoke.

The whole of Monday was consumed with laundry work. Protected by a coarse sacking apron, Adela used two large iron-hooped wooden tubs set up on a sturdy table in the pantry. Water was boiled in heavy, twin-handled iron pots on the kitchen range, using faggots of wood to obtain a sufficiently fierce heat. (Although coal was bought in a ton at a time each August, the cheapest month, wood faggots had been a staple fuel for years. The Swainston estate account books of the 1870s regularly show that the household paid 8s.8d. for 50 bundles of wood, the product of regular coppicing.)

The clothes, often heavy and cumbersome, were washed in one tub using John Knight's Primrose soap which was bought in long yellow bars and cut into smaller blocks, to dry and preserve it. They were then placed in layers in the second tub with soda sprinkled between each layer. Boiling water was poured on and they were left to soak whilst Adela had her lunch. (Many people used only soda instead of the carbolic soap because it was cheaper, but its caustic nature wreaked havoc on the skin.)

After lunch, the clothes were rinsed in cold water in the first tub and then hung out to dry, a little Reckitt's Blue Bag having been squeezed into the last rinse of the whites. These whites were always done first, and contributed to the high regard her husband enjoyed in Newport and Carisbrooke for the attractive presentation of the shellfish which he sold from door to door. Adela wrung the whites by hand, there being no mangle. Her strong wrists twisted the cloth until the stitches crackled.

In wet weather the damp clothes were hung around the kitchen range to dry indoors. The extremely damp conditions led the whole family to suffer from chest ailments. Steam from the water pots condensed on the walls and flagstone floor (which themselves rested directly upon the earth), and damp clothes were hung around the room in a forlorn attempt to get them to dry.

Adela's hands were often red and raw from the soda and constant immersion in water. In districts with hard water, half a stone of soda and a bucket of wood ash was mixed with laundry water and left standing overnight before washday to partly neutralise the carbonate. Needless to say the murky water then needed plenty of Blue Bag treatment for the whites!

Once the clothes were dry they were damped down and rolled ready for ironing, which was done with a flat iron heated in front of the range. A little spittle on the iron was used to test the heat in an attempt to avoid scorching the clothes. Collars, tablecloths and aprons were starched before ironing. Lumpy starch was mixed with a little cold water before adding boiling water. Clothes were dipped or sprinkled, as appropriate, with Boot's Laundry (Maize) Starch or Robin's Refined Starch. Eventually, the clothes were aired on a fireguard in front of the range.

Around 1926, Adela was introduced to Hudson's Soap Powder – a giant leap forward in terms of laundry technology! The yellow packet contained standard powder, the silver one was 'de-luxe'. Cheaper powders could be obtained but these frequently caused dermatitis. Soon, Lever's 'Lux' soap flakes made an appearance and were used for woollens, and then Dreft became available.

It was many years before water was piped to London Heath. The first tap, at the top of the garden to serve all four houses, was installed in 1918, and some years later it was piped to a position alongside the shared wash-house. The work was carried out by estate labourers but paid for by the Council. The steward at Swainston, Andrew Barton, carefully recorded each charge in pounds, shillings and pence.

	£	s	d
Stone Steps Cottage			
Stone Steps		16	4
St Hubert Lodge	1	10	11½
Clamerkins Farm	1	14	11
Locks "	2	4	0½
Stand Pipe at Locks Green	2	11	11½
London Heath Cottages	1	1	7½
Harts Farm	1	5	0
~~[illegible] Inn~~		19	1
	1	19	3
Newtown Cottages	1	1	5
Marsh Farm	1	12	3

Swainston's record of the cost of laying on water in 1918, shown in pounds, shillings and pence.

It was not until 17 May 1936 that Mr Downer and Cecil Rann installed the first indoor supply into the pantry at London Heath, together with a shallow stone sink, at a total cost of £1.17s.0d.

Even in the summer months washday was arduous work in damp and cramped conditions. There were barely enough daylight hours in the winter, when washing was done by candlelight or that of an oil-lamp. In colder weather, chilblains and chaps were commonplace.

Slowly, improvements became available to ease this domestic burden. A brick-built 'copper', fired partly with domestic rubbish, replaced the pots on the Kitchener range. The butler sink replaced the galvanised bath. And a wooden mangle reduced the need for muscle-power. Some even bought an electric iron. But domestic chores remained a time-consuming, tiring, and somewhat demeaning activity. Those who could afford to farmed many of the chores out to others.

For many poorly educated women from the labouring classes, domestic service was one of the few means open to them of supplementing the family income. Some of them became laundresses, taking in the washing of the village, sometimes investing in a 'dolly', the first primitive washing machine which was a tub with a long handle in the lid that turned to stir the clothes. Others became 'domestics' or 'chars', involved not only with the laundry of their mistresses but also scrubbing floors, cleaning out grates, black-leading them, and laying in fires, sewing and darning clothes, preparing meals and seeing to the washing-up. Yet others, like Mrs Angell and Mrs Holbrook, did light work in Swainston's gardens during the 1870s, or picked stones and planted beans for local farmers.

Not only did the Barringtons and Simeons employ servants at the manor (17 of them in 1851), but farmers, tradesmen and artisans of all kinds made use of young girl servants who often lived-in and were paid very meagre wages. A survey of Calbourne parish in 1803 listed a total of 135 households. No fewer than 22 of these included one or more servants, the youngest of which was Ann Spanner, aged 11.

Later census returns (opposite) reveal just how common such employment of women was:

Washday at Pound Cottages for Louisa Rickman in 1922.

Laundry time at Porchfield House, 1920s. Ada Angell is on the right. Her colleague is possibly Caroline Mew.

Mary McIntosh (née Foss) in 1889 with her children, Jamie (left) who was disabled, and Arthur. Mary was a farm servant in Newtown during the 1870s.

	Name	Age	Position	Residence (relation to household)
1841	Hannah Jeanes	30	servant	Fleetlands Farm
	Fanny Woodford	16	farm servant	Lambsleaze Farm
	Eliza Moses	15	farm servant	Elmsworth Farm
	Edith White	14	farm servant	Locks Farm
	Ann Harwood	19	servant	Coastguard cottages
1851	Martha Keeping	14	servant	Noah's Ark Inn
	Jane Cheek	22	servant	Newtown High Street
	Ann Pierce	26	house servant	Fleetlands Farm
	Eliza Holbrook	10	nursemaid	Lower Hamstead (daughter)
1861	Ann Pierce	35	servant	Whiteoak Cottages
	Mary Whittington	72	housekeeper	Oyster Cottage
	Elizabeth Atkey	59	nurse	Newtown Farm (boarder)
	Jane Skeats	66	laundress/alms	Dirty Lane, Newtown (head)
	Emily Jolliffe	30	charwoman	Town Hall (boarder)
1871	Elizabeth Prangnell	20	domestic servant	Noah's Ark Inn (niece)
	Mary Foss	15	farm servant	London Heath (daughter)
	Annie Abrook	16	domestic servant	London Heath (daughter)
	Ann Elderfield	44	dressmaker	Locks Green (wife)
	Sarah Ford	15	domestic servant	Locks Farm (granddaughter)
	Fanny Harden	14	domestic servant	Elmsworth Farm
	Harriet Foss	12	general servant	Newtown High Street (daughter)
	Kate Abrook	21	dressmaker	Oyster Cottage (daughter)
	Charlotte Abrook	19	milliner	Oyster Cottage (daughter)
	Ann Pierce	46	domestic servant	Whiteoak Cottages
	Annie Long	19	general servant	London Farm
	Edith Barton	16	general servant	Fleetlands Farm
1881	Caroline Prangnell	18	domestic servant	Elmsworth Brickyard (daughter)
	Jane Elderfield	54	dressmaker	Locks Green (head)
	Louisa Downer	22	domestic servant	Locks Green (daughter)
	Sarah Barton	14	dressmaker	Keepers Lodge (daughter)
	Sarah White	21	domestic servant	Vicarage
	Kate Blow	15	housemaid	Vicarage
	Emily Morris	19	domestic servant	Noah's Ark Inn
	Maria Wickens	14	domestic servant	Noah's Ark Inn
	Sarah Seagar	16	housemaid	Newtown Farm (daughter)
1891	Frances Sturgeon	53	housekeeper	Marsh Farm (aunt)
	Ada Hole	27	housekeeper	Harts Farm
	Jane Coleman	58	housekeeper	Vicarage
	Mary Sanders	29	housekeeper	Clamerkin Farm (daughter)
	Ellen Woolgar	53	housekeeper	Woolgar's Cottage (sister)
	Frank Whittington	16	domestic servant	Key Close dairy
	Mary Skeats	58	housekeeper	Town Hall
	Elizabeth Draper	16	general servant	Noah's Ark Inn
	Kate Jacobs	21	housekeeper	Hollis Cottage (daughter)
	Annie Hayward	20	laundress	Locks Farm (daughter)
	Elizabeth Hayward	18	laundress	Locks Farm (daughter)
	Eliza Punch	72	laundress	Heath Cotts, Locks Green (mother)
	Caroline Holbrook	26	laundress	Porchfield (daughter)
	Fanny Holbrook	22	laundress	Porchfield (daughter)
1901	Ellen Woodford	14	domestic servant	Fleetlands Farm
	Elizabeth Whittington	16	housekeeper	Whiteoak (daughter)
	Fanny Merwood	50	laundress/seamstress	Whiteoak
	Jane Coleman	68	domestic servant	Vicarage
	Adela Hole	37	housekeeper	Harts Farm
	Mary Skeats	66	domestic cook	Town Hall
	Emily Brett	23	dressmaker	Church Cottage (daughter)
	Florence Griffiths	21	housemaid	Marsh Farm
	Elizabeth Eldridge	60	monthly nurse	Marsh Farm
	Caroline Hayward	36	laundress	Porchfield (daughter)
	Eliza Holbrook	23	domestic servant	Porchfield (granddaughter)

Jane Hayward was still advertising her laundry business at Homewood Cottage, Porchfield, in the 1912 edition of *Kelly's Directory*. Winnie Snow was born in 1914 and as a six-year-old was sent by her widowed mother, a laundress, from their home in Porchfield to Newtown's vicarage to collect the vicar's laundry. And in the 1920s Vi Cosh was employed at Forest Farm for a half crown a day to do the farm's laundry.

Adela Foss was an excellent needlewoman, making many of her own clothes and linen household items. She bought unbleached twill sheeting direct from Noble's factory in Lancashire to make bedlinen, hemming it herself. (It gradually became white with plenty of washing!) She often crocheted her underclothes or made them from red flannel. Harold Shepherd from Freshwater was the local tallyman and Adela bought blankets (for £1 each) and underblankets (5s. each) from him. Once or twice a year she shopped for clothes in Newport, usually at Dabell's for herself, and from Godwin's, Witcher's or Elderfield's for her husband's working clothes. His 'clinkers' (hobnail boots with steel toecaps) were purchased for 30s.0d. a pair from Hazard's (still in business until 1995). In the absence of wellingtons, Henry tied canvas leggings from boot to knee, not being able to afford 'strogs' (leather gaiters).

Adela also made use of the local seamstress and dressmaker, Emily Brett, who sometimes made clothes for her, especially her favourite high-collared blouses complete with mutton-chop sleeves. A number of women became dressmakers and milliners, usually working from home, and a few achieved the positions of governess, schoolmistress or nurse, although the latter was often a euphemism for the village woman who acted as a midwife and laid out those who had perished!

All these women contributed in their own way to the improvement of living standards, both in their own homes and those of their employers. But living conditions in the mid-nineteenth century remained stubbornly inadequate. Many homes were built of stone and thatch, with no damp-course, under-floor ventilation, or cavity walls. They were lit only by candles or oil-lamps, and heated solely by a kitchen range or paraffin stove. In these conditions illness was common, frequently caused by inadequate supplies of water, and by sanitation that left a lot to be desired. The general housing stock of the Newtown district was in poor condition, and towards the end of the century several wooden houses had collapsed.

Dampness was endemic in cottages like those at London Heath. Surface drains from all four houses flowed past the front doors until they were diverted towards the pigsties. Adela Foss, who lived at No. 2, stuffed newspaper between the flagstones to absorb some of the damp. The walls of the kitchen had to be distempered frequently; wallpaper simply peeled off! There was no damp-course and the lower reaches of plaster were always crumbling from the walls. Carpets rotted within a couple of years, so coconut matting was used in preference, this being brightened with home-made rag rugs. Adela dared not use curtains because they were blackened within days by smoke from the range, even after her son fitted the stove with a tin canopy. Nevertheless, every afternoon (excepting washdays) the kitchen was transformed into a living-room by the addition of a red tablecloth to the scrubbed wooden table.

In general, water-supplies were contaminated by farm animals, refuse tips attracted rats, and the cottagers' 'dunnekins' were little more than a hole in the ground next to the pigsty at the end of the garden.

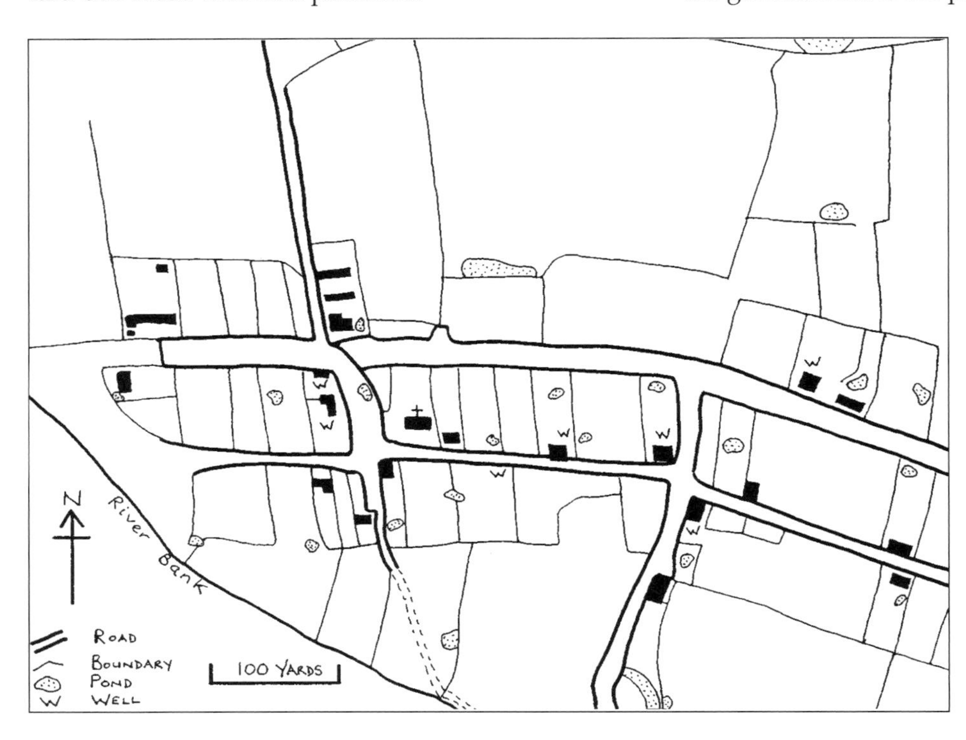

Newtown's ponds in 1862 with 1908 wells superimposed.
(INFORMATION EXTRACTED FROM ORDNANCE SURVEY MAPS)

Before the advent of piped water, country dwellers relied on ponds, streams, sunken wells and collected rainwater. In the early years there was communal responsibility for the village pond, with the Newtown Court Leet summoning residents 'to clean the clay pool' at regular intervals (probably the pond close to the Town Hall). Many householders dug their own wells, and several of them still survive providing water that is, however, unfit for human consumption, and a village pond existed on The Green beside the church until well into the 1920s.

The only general supply of water in Porchfield in the 1870s was from the stream, Rodge Brook, that flowed through the village. All water for domestic use had to be boiled, but there were still regular outbreaks of diphtheria which killed, among others, Walter Holbrook in 1875 at the age of 17. Around 1900, Dr Groves, the medical officer for the village who was based at Carisbrooke, ascertained that the illnesses stemmed from contaminated water, and the local government authority ordered that a rain-water tank should be dug for any house that did not have its own water-supply. Residents from that time recalled that the water, collected from roofs, tasted strongly of smoke, even after it had been allowed to settle for a few days.

From around 1880 several local farmers arranged to receive piped water from private suppliers and in 2004, by some quirk of administration, several farms and cottages in the Newtown and Locks Green areas still receive this supply free of water charges! Piped water eventually reached Porchfield in 1905 from springs at Calbourne.

Shalfleet's piped supply arrived in 1899, and by 1931 71 households in the village had been connected. (Some years earlier, the Parish Council had declined an invitation to purchase Mr Buckett's well at nearby Newbridge because it was too close to the Bible Christian burial-grounds!)

Newtown's residents had to wait a while longer! On 19 October 1893 the Parochial Committee met and resolved to obtain a water-supply for Newtown. With Revd John Vicars in the chair, George Weeks, Robert Morgan, Robert Lock and Henry Edward Mew asked for a report to be drawn up. (George Heal and Micah Morris could not attend that day.) Initially, the committee blanched at the proposed cost, and suggested that, instead, the parish should supply each household with a tank or reservoir for rainwater, but eventually agreed to seek a loan in order to sink a well 30 feet deep (about 10 metres), recommending to the Rural Sanitary Authority in February 1894 that the well be dug on land in the occupation of Thomas Abrook. A tender of £66 in May of that year was accepted for completing the well and fitting a pump.

Initially, the plan was to dig a 60-foot well, but at half that depth water analysis revealed mineral contamination so work stopped. Public subscription to fit the well with a pump fell short and Sir John Simeon provided the balance. The well was rarely used, the water being a little brackish and there being so many private wells and springs in the village anyway. Many wells, both in the village and at Lower Elmsworth, produced brackish water, but an inspection of the main village well in the 1980s proved it to be in a good state of repair, the lining brickwork having been strengthened with elm beams.

Newtown's restored village pump in 1999.

In 1904 Sir John Barrington Simeon paid £500 to the Isle of Wight Rural District Council for a 999-year agreement for the supply of water to Calbourne parish, though this included only a single standpipe for double tenements or terraced rows. The agreement included remote holdings such as Wheatenbread Farm and Brickfield Farm (although the latter was never supplied) and general water rates were set at 13s.0d. for a £10 rateable value and £2.8s.0d. for £40 rateable value. Extra payments were required for laundresses, cows, dairies, gardens, rick yards, piggeries, glasshouses, bakehouses, slaughterhouses, licensed houses and school offices. (A further agreement was signed in 1911 including arrangements to replace the windmill that 'lifted' the water from the chalk aquifers at Bowcombe with a diesel engine.)

But it was still to be many years before Newtown obtained its own piped water, and other services were also slow to arrive.

It was as late as 1919 that Calbourne Parish Council representatives (Maurice Rice and Edward Mew) signed a deed of arrangement with HM Paymaster General 'to open a Telephone Call Office at the Post Office for a term of seven years.' The parish had to guarantee at least £12 worth of business each year. This single telephone at Porchfield served the whole area for several years. A similar agreement was signed in 1928 by Maurice Rice (chair), Edwin Holbrook, F.D. Heal and E.A. Hawkins (clerk).

Apart from properties in Old Vicarage Lane, which have their own piped drainage and filter beds, Newtown is still without mains drainage, and there is also no mains gas supply in the village. Indeed, if it were not for the initiatives of the farmer at London Farm in 1960 Newtown might still be lit by oil lanterns. He funded a mains electricity supply to his own farm and the suppliers were then persuaded to connect the rest of Newtown to the system. Mr Spearing was able to sell his Lucas Freelight wind-driven generator which he had erected next to Marsh Farm, and the congregation at Newtown Church no longer had to memorise the hymns for evening services!

Perhaps the greatest benefit to the area has been the provision of piped water. Mechanisation has now taken over many household chores. Washing machines and dishwashers are plumbed in. Central heating has replaced the open fire in many homes. Modern fabrics, washing-powders and conditioners relieve inhabitants of some of the drudgery of their forbears. With tumble-dryers available it does not matter, now, if it rains on Mondays. Candles and oil-lamps are now in storage, and the galvanised tub and the bungalow bath have gone for good.

Adela Foss and her son Herbert, 1905. Despite the privations, Adela maintained the highest standards of family dignity.

Chapter 14

'Bowls, Quoits & Other Unthrifty Games': The Neighbourhood at Play

In the reign of Henry VIII there were complaints that archery was being neglected for such games as slidethrift, otherwise known as shove-groat! Several centuries later, around 1910, Newtown youngsters, Herbie Foss, Godfrey Buckett, 'Bett' Wheeler and Jack Arnold, could be found most Saturdays playing a similar game of throw-halfpenny halfway along Anley's Lane in Town Copse, using as their marker a line drawn in the mud between two saplings. In 2004 two handsome trees mark the spot and youngsters now have different interests, calling up the internet or chatting away on their mobile phones.

However tiring the work schedule or however brief the daylight hours, people have always found time for relaxation and leisure. In earlier times these pursuits often reflected the need for military prowess, or echoed the rhythms of the seasonal work on the land. Harvest celebrations and religious festivals were marked by communal activities which strengthened the social fabric, although particular activities reflected a person's social standing.

In those years before improved transport, paid holidays and shorter working hours villagers and country dwellers constructed their own enjoyment around such important focal points as the chapel, the smithy, the school and the local hostelry. Each venue had its own devotees, and supporters of one did not always approve of the activities of another!

Many a competitive sport or pastime can trace its origins to the time when men and boys could be called at the shortest notice to military combat. Almost 1,000 years ago Newtown's residents were involved in aggressive pursuits such as fencing and archery, and strategic activities like backgammon and tick-tack-toe (noughts and crosses) in part-preparation to repel the Danes, the French or the Spanish.

For several centuries their records of success against these invaders were, at best, patchy! Perhaps typical of the Island's state of unreadiness in the face of a Spanish takeover plan, was Sir Edward Horsey, Captain of the Island (1562–82), who was more interested in enjoying the favours of Mistress Dowsabel Milles at Haseley Manor than looking to his wife (who was in France) or to his militias. When Horsey died of plague he was succeeded as Captain by the strait-laced Sir George Carey who quickly issued instructions:

Every archer is to be furnished with a good bow of yew, fit of draught for his strength, a sheave of arrows, a braser and shooting glove, one spare string, a sword and dagger, and to be taught to shoot straight, strong and fair.

At this time even small hamlets sometimes had their own archery field. Two 'butts' were still shown at Newtown in 1768, although the smaller Well Butt, opposite the church and on the site of Rose Cottage at the time of writing, probably referred only to that patch of communal land alongside the well. The more impressive Daw's Butt occupied some furlong fields to the east of the village and its long, narrow shape suggests it was the local archery field, probably established several hundred years before. All able-bodied men were required by Carey's statute to attend archery practice 'utterly leaving the play at bowls, quoits or other unthrifty games.' He also replaced wrestling and throwing games with combat sports involving weapons. A variety of field sports still trace their origin to the martial requirements of these times, and even some children's games that were popular until recently – hide and seek or 'hoopie', piggy-back fights, conkers, leap-frog – have the flavour of combat.

The Maypole ceremony at Locks Green School, c.1905. Among the children shown are Winnie Mew (known as 'Cough Drop'), Mary Mew and Sally Lock.

No doubt there was much grumbling among the local men at being required to abandon their more leisurely pursuits at Newtown's Bowling Green, situated off Gold Street, opposite Marsh Lane, although elsewhere on the Island boisterous bowling meets continued to flourish until well into the seventeenth century. In later centuries archery became less practicable in warfare and by the 1800s its popularity among gentry as a leisure pursuit was growing rapidly and archery fêtes were organised at several local manors.

Rather more sedentary were the regular village gatherings, 'zet-outs', to mark feasts and festivals, a rich tradition of communal merrymaking that provided a comforting sense of anticipation and predictability each year. On 24 May 1910, the children at Locks Green School could be seen standing to attention, lined up smartly to face the fluttering Union flag and sing the National Anthem. It was Empire Day. Only three weeks earlier the children had celebrated May Day and Sally Lock from Elmsworth Farm had been crowned May Queen. In a week's time the boys would be expected to wear sprigs of oak in their caps to mark Oak Apple Day, and very soon after that everyone would hope to join the feasting at the hayricks to mark the first mowing of the new season. Set alongside the major Christian festivals were celebrations (often in the form of feasting or gift giving) related to the farming calendar. The completion of each annual task (ploughing in January, pruning in February, shearing in May, reaping in August, and so on) was marked by a coming together of those involved (the extended family, the farm workforce, or even the whole community) to enjoy a sense of communal achievement.

The church lent its blessing to many of these events, especially the harvest thanksgiving and supper which marked genuine relief at the safe gathering of another winter's food and fuel supply, and its influence could be found in other customs, some of which pre-dated Christianity itself. Wassailing in the orchards on the twelfth night after Christmas, singing around the houses for cakes on Shrove Tuesday in a frenzy of feasting before the onset of Lent's abstinence, and the benign approval implicit in the use of consecrated ground at Locks Green School for the earthy rituals of the Maypole, all mark the rich seam of influences upon village life. Virginal young girls dressed in white and carrying flowers rubbed shoulders with morris men, and hobby-horses mingled with Jacks-in-the-Green as the locals re-enacted a centuries-old tradition on hallowed soil. Professional storytellers had been around since Newtown's pre-Norman days and the rich family sagas and raunchy riddles so beloved by the Anglo-Saxons found later expression at the Newtown 'Randy', an annual fair granted from 1318 by Edward II on the feast of St Mary Magdalene in late July. Alongside the jugglers, tight-rope walkers, wrestlers and acrobats, the troubadours kept the crowds enthralled with stories of heroes and chivalry. For at least 450 years this annual feast of the performing arts continued but there is some dispute about the survival of the fair after 1781. It probably occurred sporadically and was certainly organised during the 1850s before it was revived in 1924 (at Green Close and on The Green near the church) at the suggestion of Laura, Lady Simeon. The revival was supported by most of the local residents, the *Isle of Wight County Press* reporting the involvement of Lady Simeon and Mrs Kindersley, Colonel Kindersley, Mrs Glover (the vicar's wife), the Misses and Captain Gibson, Geoff and Ted Barton, Messrs J. Long, E. Hawkins and Cassell, Captain Pirie, and Messrs W. Holden and E.S. Whatley. After another suspension, it was resurrected again in 1973 by the local Women's Institute. The British Trust for Conservation Volunteers became involved in its organisation during the 1980s, raising funds for disadvantaged young people, and the Randy, once more, became an almost annual event in the streets of the village until 1993 when, briefly, it was moved to Clamerkin Farm Park. Evocative of the occasion is the traditional verse reproduced from Percy Stone's collection, published in 1912:

I bunched a tutty, big ez a plate, and garbed me up a dandy O,
To meet my maade by her mammy's gate, and away to the Newtown Randy O.

Ef ar-a-one hed a vlouted zhe, reckon I'd hay tanned he O,
The volk they vairly ztared at we, a-walking to the Randy O.

I bought zhe a proper parazoll, happen her'll vind en handy O,
Chance zun do zhine or hrain do vall, gooin to Newtown Randy O.

Uz ztood to zee t' boxin' bout twixt Tinker Tim and Zandy O,
Zandy he knocked the Tinker out an tuk the prize at t' Randy O.

I bought zhe hribbons an' ginger cake, laces and zugar candy O,
Us danced away till our ligs did ache vor zure at Newtown Randy O.

I treated us both to the 'what is it'... an' a drop o' keeksy brandy O...
'Tired my maade?' 'Me! Not a bit, I'm just enjoyin' t' Randy O.'

Us zid the dwarf an' a proper play, an' a larned pig called Andy O,
Us zid most evrything thet day theer wuz at Newtown Randy O.

Last her gev in. 'Come, tek my arm wi' your pratty handy-pandy O.
Snoodle gen me an' I'll keep 'ee warm way back from t' Randy O'.

Us lingered most by ivery ztile, like lovin' goose an' gandy O.

I hugged zhe ivery quarter mile coming vrum Newtown Randy O.

... I'm a granfer nigh on vower score year, my back and ligs be bandy O.
Her's zetten theer i' the chimbley cheer...the maade I tuk to t' Randy O.

(tutty = nosegay, keeksy = sloe, snoodle = nestle)

Apart from the Randy, village 'fêtes' gradually replaced traditional events during the twentieth century. A fête could be a saints-day feast, a rural festival, or an outdoor entertainment, but at the time of writing usually involves some sort of fund-raising event. Thus it was that the youngest member of the Newtown and Porchfield Working Party, Rhoda Newberry, presented Lady Simeon with a small bouquet when she opened their Sale of Work and entertainment event at Locks Green School in February 1929. They had been working all winter at the home of the Misses Gibson at Newtown and at Mrs Clement's at Locks Green and the fête raised £12 for the church account. Similar nineteenth- and twentieth-century fêtes are recorded as having taken place on the village greens at Newtown (Bowling Green and Church Green) and Porchfield (Locks Green), or in nearby fields generously loaned by farmers such as Herbert Wheeler (Green Close in the 1920s) and Barry Angell (in the 1980s) for the revival of the Randy.

Thus, in many ways the social calendar of the Newtown area was a richer experience then than it is in the early-twenty-first century. From the sophisticated entertaining offered by the Barrington and Simeon families at 'The Big House', and those musical soirées favoured at Newtown's vicarage, through to the boisterous annual parties thrown by some of the local farmers (the Lock family at Elmsworth Farm was well regarded for its Guy Fawkes parties), to the good, clean fun of the chapel-room social (musical chairs and marmite sandwiches), the whole community had an opportunity to become involved.

Most of the village entertainments were home-grown, some more proficiently than others. Robert Woodman Lock had survived the Boer Wars virtually unscathed, but as a member of the Newtown and Porchfield Entertainments Committee during the 1920s he faced an altogether more daunting task. How could he persuade local singers Reg Hayward and Ivy Long that their enthusiasm and public spiritedness rather outweighed their talents? Reg's annual insistence upon rendering a woefully tuneless 'Abe, my boy' challenged even the modest requirements of this outpost of the performing arts, much to the mocking amusement of local youths, leering in at the schoolroom windows. In those days home-spun entertainment ranged from a singsong around the family's piano to a fund-raising concert or playlet at the schoolroom or chapel hall.

From the 1870s until its closure in the 1940s Locks Green School became the venue for many of the local performances, a tribute as much to the stoicism of those who turned up to be entertained as to the enthusiasm of the performers. An advertisement notice for a concert at the school in January 1886 was keen to provide every incentive possible for turning out: 'we would mention that there will be a very good moon that night, which is a great advantage.'

Neither the unlit, muddy lanes, nor the struggling efforts of the smoky old boiler to take the chill off the air in the schoolroom were great obstacles to the talents and enthusiasm of the likes of the Gibson sisters or Edwin Holbrook. Ida Gibson (1869–1954) was a gifted violinist and her vocalist sister Lisa had, on occasion, performed at Covent Garden. Whilst living at Porchfield, and later at the coastguard cottages at Newtown, the sisters organised many successful musical events at Locks Green, encouraging contributions from across the neighbourhood, and even organising a juvenile orchestra. Farmer's daughter Elsie Lock's vocal rendition of 'When you come to the end of a perfect day', accompanied on the piano by her cousin Sally Lock, was typical of such concerts.

Always fond of music, Elsie cycled each week with her childhood chum Aggie Mew from Porchfield to Beckford Road in Cowes for their piano lessons with Miss Cushion, returning to practice on the farm's old Broadwood piano with its blue silk front. In 2004, at the age of 97, she still recollects with pride singing duets with Edwin Holbrook at fund-raising concerts held at Porchfield Congregational Chapel.

Almost 90 children from the parish crowded into the spacious parish room over Revd Rice Venn's coach-house in December 1888. A Christmas tree with a girth of nine metres was centre stage, decorated with tree candles and Chinese lanterns by H. Punch and Mr Kissick, and surrounded by presents. Mr and Mrs Baxter gave each child an orange to go with the bun and bag of sweets everyone got from the Misses Scovell. The Misses Ridett and Miss Alice Kingswell organised games and many others contributed 'warm and useful articles for the young of both sexes.'

A similar communal event occurred at Locks Green School in 1925. About 100 parishioners responded to an invitation from the Church Council to attend an evening of recitations and music arranged by the Misses Gibson of the coastguard cottages. Contributions were included from Edwin Holbrook (song), Ida Gibson (violin), and Arthur Anderson (poetry), whilst piano accompaniment was provided by Mrs Heal and Miss Long. Edwin (1867–1963) epitomised the enthusiasm of the time for making music. As a teenager he was taught 'tonic solfa' by his cousin David Holbrook, a great aid to unaccompanied part-singing. With several Porchfield friends he joined the newly-formed

The 1924 Newtown Randy included this theme on food, presented in a marquee on The Green near the church. Left to right, back row: *Mr Wall, Herbie Wheeler;* standing: *?, ?, Master Wall, Aggie Mew as 'Nippy' at Lyons Corner Café, ?, ?, Elsie Lock as 'Café au lait',* seated: *?, Master Wall, Hope Vincent, ?, Mrs Wall, Mrs Glover the vicar's wife as Mazawati tea;* front: *?*

In the Grounds of
SWAINSTON
(by kind permission of Sir John Simeon, Bart.)

HISTORICAL
PAGEANT
AND FÊTE
Wednesday & Thursday, July 13th and 14th, 1927.

Organised by The I.W. County Federation of Women's Institutes.

President:
LAURA LADY SIMEON.

Programme
and
Synopsis of Pageant

PRICE THREEPENCE.

Programme cover for Historical Pageant at Swainston Manor, July 1927.

The Randy procession passes along Newtown High Street in 1991.

Above: *An historical pageant, part of a two-day event at Swainston in 1927, organised by the Isle of Wight Federation of Women's Institutes whose president was Laura, Lady Simeon. Mrs Mussell of Shalfleet is seated third from the left.*

Right: *Sally Lock* (standing) *and Margie Dale dressed as Pierrettes during rehearsals for a concert at Locks Green School, c.1925.*

Newport Choral Society, walking five miles there and back to choir practice after a long day's work in the fields! Writing in the 1950s, he recollected a time around 1888 when he was a member of a mowing team at Maurice Sanders' Clamerkin Farm. One wet afternoon Mr Sanders (who was organist at Porchfield Chapel) suggested they sing to pass the time, and to the accompaniment of a harmonica the walls of the barn echoed to their lusty harmony.

Singing groups proliferated. Towards the end of the 1800s the Newport Wesleyan Singing Society was formed and by the 1920s the Calbourne Glees Club was flourishing – each, in those days, within walking distance for the enthusiasts from Newtown!

But new technologies and improved means of transport widened everyone's access to entertainment from the beginning of the twentieth century. Recorded sound, projected pictures, the bicycle and the charabanc all played a part. From around 1900, the Porchfield branch of the Band of Hope Temperance Society employed the 'magic lantern' to get across its message, and in 1932 Newtown and Porchfield filled a charabanc for a showing of the missionary 'talkie' entitled *Through China and Japan* at Newport's Medina Picture House (admission 3d. or 6d.). An outing to one of Newport's cinemas or dance halls became increasingly accessible to village residents from around 1920 as motorised and timetabled buses replaced the carrier's van. But as late as the 1930s residents of Newtown and Porchfield were making their own way there and back, 'stabling' their bicycles and ponies and traps at the Charles I public house for a small fee.

Musical bands are always a major spectacle and from around 1912 residents in this area were entertained by the visiting military bands stationed at Locks Green Camp. Earlier still, the demanding beat of the Band of Hope's Tinkers' Lane (Pallance Road) Fife and Drum Band had stirred the area from its slumbers. But the gramophone (phonograph) and the crystal wireless set introduced people to the music of the dance band and they pursued the likes of Geraldo, Maurice Winnick, Ambrose, Harry Roy and their bands during the 1930s to summer venues at Sandown and winter programmes at Alexandra Palace and the Guildhall in Portsmouth.

Sir John Simeon's friend, Alfred Lord Tennyson, was a frequent visitor to the area, where he penned 'In the Garden of Swainston', but few local opportunities existed for the more studious working man to pursue his interests. He needed plenty of time and determination to make use of the opportunities opening up in Newport. The Mechanics' Institute had opened in around 1800, and the gentry had been meeting in Nash's Isle of Wight Institute building since the late-eighteenth century. The Assembly Rooms were available for meetings and, by 1813, a Philosophical Society had been established in the

Pallance Road (Tinkers' Lane) Band of Hope Fife and Drum Band, c.1895. Standing, left to right: *C. Early, Reg Vine, Fred Flux, ?, ?, Harold Vine, ?, Jim Griffin, ?, ?, ?, Ted Holbrook, ?, ?, ?, ?, ?, ?, ?, ?, George Early on the far right;* those seated include: *the Chessell brothers Fred* (left) *and Harry* (third from left).

town. In 1867, the Cowes Young Men's Improvement Society met in the Literary Institute, seeking a 7p.m. closure for all shops in the town, and in 1877 the Newport Young Men's Literary Society was founded, which flourished until 1955, and within a few years the Seely libraries were established.

By the mid-1880s a Reading and Recreation Room had been opened at the Ningwood schoolrooms, and this was soon followed by an opportunity to subscribe a penny a month to join the Lending Library, run by the parish at the same venue. A few years later Newtown Parochial Library was established with the support of the Seely family, precursor of the local travelling library run by Henry Angell. Few books were found in cottage homes. Books had been published for children since the early-eighteenth century and the offspring of the Barrington and Simeon families, and the likes of the Mews, the Woolgars and the Harveys could have afforded them. Children of cottagers might also come across them through dame-schools or Sunday Schools. Initially, the books were turgid and moralising, later becoming more appealing to children, but still with a strong instructional tone. The popular *Lilliputian Magazine* (1750s) claimed in its frontispiece to be 'an attempt to mend the world, to render the Society of Man more Amiable, and to Establish the Plainness, Simplicity, Virtue and Wisdom of the Golden Age.' Later, the 'Penny Books' series, the publication of stories drawn from folk-tales (*Tommy Thumb, Mother Goose,* and others), and the use of pictures, made books more attractive to children, and the availability of works such as Edward Lear's *A Book of Nonsense* (1846) and Beatrix Potter's *The Tales of Peter Rabbit* (1901) encouraged children and parents alike to use these new facilities.

Learning was becoming fashionable and during the 1880s a series of public lectures on the sciences and the arts took place at Locks Green School with admission to each lecture costing a penny. In 1894 Newtown's vicar, Revd Henry Rice Venn, delivered a series of five lectures at the Wellow Institute to enlighten the local community about the County Council's scheme for technical education.

Newport's Boy Scout troop was formed in 1907 and around 1930 Corfe became forever associated with the scouting movement when Lieutenant Colonel Archibald Ogilvie Lyttleton Kindersley CMG DL, by now resident as Hamstead and County Commissioner for Scouts, established the residential camp there (major new facilities were opened in 2002). Some years earlier, in 1926, he had also founded the Shalfleet Sea Scouts group. At around the same time a Girls' Club had been started, meeting in the Women's Institute premises on Ningwood Hill.

The Women's Institute Movement was founded in 1915 and a local branch soon flourished alongside the Calbourne and Shalfleet Mothers' Union and Women's Fellowship meeting which, in 1932, expanded its territory to include Porchfield.

Newport Literary Institute in Quay Street, c.1910.

For many years, a person's involvement in a particular leisure activity had reflected their social status. In 1538 Henry VIII departed the Island a disappointed man. His visit to Parkhurst Forest to hunt game birds with hawks had been a failure. Admonishing his erstwhile hosts for permitting poachers to get there first 'with nets and other engines', he wrote that game birds must be 'cherished within Our said Isle for Our disport and pleasure.' Almost 500 years had already elapsed since the Normans had removed the Anglo-Saxon rights of the common man to hunt the forest. Stag-hunting in Watchingwell Park was now a royal prerogative, and falconry was the sport of nobility in Parkhurst Forest. Thus, the distinction between hunter and poacher had been fostered, marked also by a social divide and a difference of purpose – the pursuit of pleasure or the relief of hunger.

When stags and boars had been hunted out of existence on the Island, fresh quarry was brought in. In the 1570s Sir Edward Horsey provided a reward of a lamb for each hare brought in to Wight, and in 1843 wild foxes were introduced to complement hare coursing, as hunting with dogs ('a frisk with the hounds') and on horseback became very popular. As the gun almost completely replaced the falcon, gamekeepers such as Luke Barton and Fred Fallick were employed on the estates of Hamstead, Shalfleet and Swainston to breed tens of thousands of game birds each season. Almost without exception, these were sports only for the landed gentry and their guests, on whose land they took place, although, by invitation, tenant farmers and others could join the annual culling of rabbits and pigeons.

In the 1890s James Woolgar reported that Newtown River was well stocked with trout, and already for several centuries the risk and excitement of sea fishing had appealed to some of the Island's gentry. A natural development for a maritime nation was the growing popularity of yacht racing. In 1815 Charles Pelham (later to become Lord Yarborough) formed the Yacht Club at Cowes which, by 1820, had attracted royal patronage and in 1833 was renamed the Royal Yacht Squadron. He acquired lands at Newtown including Marsh Farm and some salterns, and his yacht *Falcon* was a frequent visitor to Newtown Haven. The heyday of the large, privately-owned ocean racing yachts was during the period 1860–1914 and Newtown had many visiting craft. In 1883, Newtown's own 'Jumbo' Woolgar was bosun on the pleasure yacht *Gitana* (ON 8942) on her round trip from Cowes to Dublin. But by 1914 the river was silting and Mew and Langton's yacht could no longer be safely moored there and dropped anchor offshore.

By this time yachting was becoming the aspiration of professional people and smaller leisure craft were beginning to appear alongside the working boats of Newtown as more people sought to emulate the sporting tastes of the wealthy. Revd Rice Venn's yacht was moored alongside his private jetty in Clamerkin Creek, and local resident Ida Gibson (1871–1954) was a prominent member of the Royal Solent Yacht Club and was sailing competitively until the age of 80. Yachting was still an exclusive activity, but by the time keen sailor Captain George Seabroke moved his family into Marsh Farm in 1936 and, much later, became harbourmaster, a broader section of society could afford to participate.

The working man enjoyed less spectacular pursuits. The Locks Green smithy, worked by the Arnold family through four generations from around 1800, was a favourite gathering-place for 10 or 15 men of all ages every evening, especially in winter months. Towards the end of the nineteenth century there would be Henry Ford (a veteran of the Crimean War), Harry Punch (carter at Locks Farm), Philip Fallick (farm labourer) and others, each making an impression on the local youth, like 16-year-old Robert Lock from Elmsworth Farm whose father, a local dignitary, probably did not realise where he was! As soon as James Arnold finished work for the day (around 7.30p.m.) out would come the large piece of sheet iron to be placed on the anvil as a table-top for a game of 'Tip It', played between teams of five or six men.

The public house was also an exclusively male domain until the middle of the twentieth century, although women often worked behind the bar. Each village had at least one such hostelry, some with a particularly long history. The Horse and Groom at Ningwood was a staging inn from the early 1600s, although the popular belief that the Sportsman's Rest at Porchfield had once been an Elizabethan hunting lodge has little basis in fact. Shalfleet's New Inn remained part of the Swainston estate until sold in 1946 and is still trading strongly at the time of writing, but the Newtown Arms (sometimes called the Borough Arms or, as the locals knew it, Noah's Ark) surrendered its licence around 1916, having existed since at least 1700.

Traditionally acting as a social centre for the local community, the inns provided not only liquid refreshment and good company but also an opportunity to enjoy dominoes, dice, cribbage, darts or solitaire, long-time favourites of the working man. 'Mine host' tended to retain the licence for many years, thus providing another dimension of stability within the village. For much of the nineteenth century the Sergeant family ran the New Inn (Shalfleet), the Woodfords kept the Sun Inn (Calbourne) and members of the Taylor family (which included the Prangnells and Arnolds) were hosts at the Newtown Arms for almost 200 years.

More active sporting pursuits for the working man tended to be limited to occasional, even annual, communal events such as regattas or sports days, often providing him with an opportunity to test his everyday skills and equipment in a competitive environment. Thus, in early-twentieth-century Newtown Dickie Fallick almost always won the ploughing competition, Henry 'Japhet' Foss came last again, having once more joined the 'gobbies' in their rowing galley to race the local rivermen, and Jim Arnold and Ted Barton, 'loaders' at the game shoots on Swainston estate, usually took the prizes at the pigeon shoot.

Alcohol always provided some form of retreat from the stresses of everyday life, and by the early-nineteenth century excessive consumption of 'keeksy brandy' (sloe gin) had become a problem across all strata of society. From the days when mead and ale had enlivened the telling of bawdy Anglo-Saxon tales, to those more recent times around 1915 when the Newtown Arms sold beer at 1s. a gallon, Edwin Holbrook's observation that 'a few old topers got beastly drunk' held true, especially when there were no restrictions on opening hours. On one occasion, in pitch blackness, Edwin almost ran right over the prostrate figure of a drunk, his horse (Dolly) stopping just in time:

I waked him up and found he was quite helpless, and it was quite hopeless to try to get him into the van, so I got him on his feet and steered him round the back of the van, put his hands on the tailboard and told him to hang on like grim death while I drove on quietly. He hung on, his feet touching the road at short intervals, and I went some distance out of my way to take him home.

Above left: *The tranquility of Newtown Haven in 2001.*

Above : *The former Locks Green smithy in 1999.*

Left: *The main road at Porchfield, 1922. The Sportsman's Rest public house is on the right.*

Lads about town. Standing on the right is Herbert Foss, behind Bill Price who, with the Earl brothers, visited Newport in 1915.

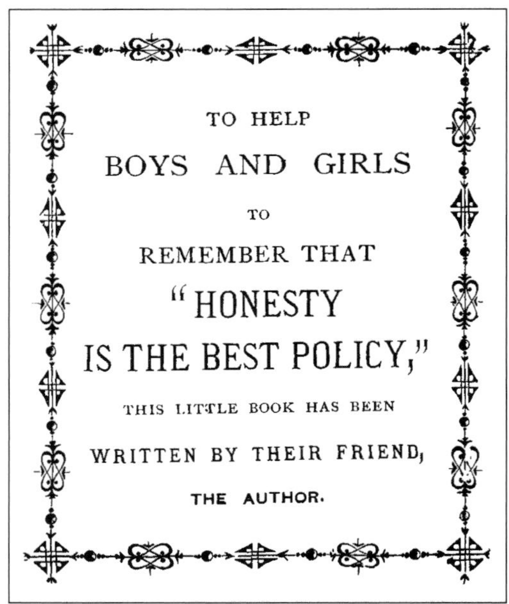

TO HELP
BOYS AND GIRLS
TO
REMEMBER THAT
"HONESTY
IS THE BEST POLICY,"
THIS LITTLE BOOK HAS BEEN
WRITTEN BY THEIR FRIEND,
THE AUTHOR.

First page of a book given to Adela Hole when she was 13 years old, in 1875, inscribed 'from a friend'.

Edwin's attitude to 'intoxicating liquor' had been conditioned when, as a youth, he had been witness to his elderly mother, of relatively slight build, grabbing a local man named Broomfield by his beard and berating him for molesting his wife whilst in a drunken stupor. The man reportedly gave up drinking and joined the local branch of the Band of Hope which had been formed in 1870. Another said to have foresaken alcohol was local personality Albie Jupe whose 'friends', unbeknown to Albie, had flavoured his drink with a dead mouse!

More often than not, the working man had a beer in one hand and tobacco in the other. Tobacco had been introduced into England in 1586 and enjoyment of 'the weed' had spread rapidly. Most nineteenth-century labourers smoked, even if this was sometimes a tobacco substitute such as dried moss. Very often, farm workers shared a plug of 'baccy' for chewing, each user carefully replacing the masticated lump into a recognised 'store' ready for the next man! For agricultural labourers, often leaving home before daybreak to walk several miles to work, the smoking habit was sometimes problematic and the shared plug often eased their craving.

Harry Pritchett, writing in the late-nineteenth century, observed that:

> *... a teamsman departing* [the stable] *with his glossy coated 'hosses' on an early jaunt called over his shoulder to a 'mayet' still rubbing down his own charges preparatory to a start... 'I zay you, th' kay o' th' wut bin's en the bottom uv th' lantern, an th' chow o' baccy es up en Norman's collar. Mind an putt un back when you'm cum'en away.'* [Norman was the horse.]

At the age of 14 in the 1880s, local boy Fred Fallick was working alongside his grandfather Philip Fallick (1829–1911) cutting wheat for Mr Hillier near Rowridge. After a break for midday 'nammet' Fred noticed him fiddling to remove some lining from his old coat. Philip had almost run out of matches to light his clay pipe, and it would be many hours before he set foot indoors again. Using his last match to partly burn the piece of rag, Philip made tinder with it and placed it in a tin. Later, at a break for tea, Fred watched him find a flint stone and take out his knife:

> *After filling his pipe he got out some tinder and placed it on the tobacco, and holding it close to his mouth he struck the flint sharply with his knife. The spark caught the tinder rag alright and having the pipe in his mouth he was able to draw and get the contents of the pipe to burn.*

Throughout the nineteenth century and beyond girls had much less freedom than boys, rarely being allowed out to play, more often being deployed to look after younger siblings, to assist with the laundry, even to milk the cow. Such was the life for Sally Lock and her cousin Elsie Lock in Porchfield until their teenage years when they escaped on their bicycles to Mrs Heal's tearooms at her cottage next to Locks Green smithy or to those of George Whittington at Stone Steps. Later still, with their friends Gertie and Minnie Cousins from Youngwoods Farm and Aggie Mew from Porchfield House, they even travelled as far as Newport to attend a social gathering.

In contrast, boys enjoyed more freedom, and at Locks Green School in the early 1900s were more likely than the girls to be involved in swimming lessons at Locks Hard, or ball games on the adjacent field, or skating on the frozen pond in Locks Farm yard. Many boys had home-made tops, kites, ninepins or a yo-yo, and most had access to an iron hoop, usually made by local blacksmith Fred Heal or his Arnold predecessors, to trundle along the road with a stick or special crook. (These were banned in Cowes from 1852.) There were also some quieter games for boys – bottle-top marbles were very popular, as was a game of cards down at 'Slinks', the stream banks in Lower Porchfield. Well into his nineties, Herbie Foss recollected with fondness and gratitude the district's unofficial youth club, based in an empty cottage situated near the Porchfield war memorial which had been the home of William Fallick in 1891 and then John Hayward. Here *(see page 27)* the boys of the district gathered to play darts, cards, skittles, conkers and table games, warmed in winter months by wood fuel kindly supplied by Edwin Holbrook.

Some 40 years earlier, during Edwin's own childhood in the 1860s and '70s, local boys gathered on Locks Green, opposite the school, to play games, many of which they invented themselves, like Duckstone and the even more boisterous game, Stag. The former involved a large, flat quarry stone being used as the 'duck' and each boy had his own, smaller stone called a 'taw', roughly twice the size of a cricket ball. One player's taw was placed on the duck stone and he would stand by whilst, 15 paces away, other players lobbed their taw to displace the one on the duck stone. Once successful, there followed an almighty scramble as the player by the duck attempted to replace his taw and then catch someone before they could recover their own taw.

Stag was a very rough game, but thoroughly enjoyed. It was a kind of tug-of-war, using bodies rather than rope! Two teams lined up facing each other across the road and linking hands. Taking it in turns, the aim for each team was to steal a member of the opposing team. Fingers were pointed at the chosen target boy and they all shouted 'Stag-a-rag-a-ree, the man I see, and the man I mean to have!' The ensuing struggle could last up to an hour, and the final state of the participants' clothing can only be imagined!

The adults also enjoyed games, a great favourite among local farm workers being Mariners (also known as Nine Men Morris), a fourteenth-century board-game, often played in the snug of the stables using the lid of an oat bin ('wut-bin') as the board. By the dim light of a candle set in its 'lanthorn' socket two players, each with nine pegs or stones, aimed to place straight rows of three pegs or stones at the intersections of lines drawn or drilled on the board, without intervention by the other player. The more complex game called 'Fox and Geese' was based on the same principles. The stake was more often a 'chow o' baccy' or a 'copious pinch o' snuff' than a coin.

Most such village activities have been overtaken by social and economic change, but the game of cricket survives. In the late-nineteenth century this game was a great unifying force in the countryside, bringing together the squire and the labourer who, together, engaged their mortal foe, the team from the neighbouring village. Thus began the keen, and generally good-natured, rivalry between Wellow Cricket Club (founded in 1880), Shalfleet United Cricket Club (formed in 1901), and their contemporary clubs at Westover and Porchfield, and a new breed of women emerged – the cricket widow.

Single families often produced several good players. One family named Lock founded the Wellow cricket team, and another branch of that family featured strongly in the fortunes of Shalfleet United Cricket Club during the 1930s on their delightful ground alongside the manor. Similarly, the Angell and Hayward families were stalwarts of the Porchfield Cricket Club from its nineteenth-century inception. Playing first in a field at The Homestead, Porchfield, the team later moved up Dirty Lane (New Road) to a field opposite the Bible Christian Chapel, and played their matches there for almost 100 years before occupying grounds off Coleman's Lane, where they play at the time of writing.

It is said that in the early days Porchfield's fast bowler, J. Hayward, kept a bottle of beer in the long grass at the start of his run-up in order to sustain his efforts! Maybe, in 1910 when the team played Rookwood, everyone had secreted bottles in the grass. In reply to their opponents' score of 82 runs, Porchfield managed to score only 28 in their first innings and, following on, had lost six wickets for ten runs when a storm brought an end to proceedings. (The team that day was W. Downer, H. Smith, A. Attrill, F. Ridett, F. Fallick, G. Attrill, G. Angell, F. Gray, H. Osbourne, H. Cooper and J. Hayward.) 'Farmer' Hawkins, who lived opposite the ground, offered £1 to any batsman who could break his windows with the ball. Philip Fallick and Jack Coombes came closest, but nobody got their pound! Family traditions are retained at the time of writing. John Hayward, of Little Thorness Farm, aged 76, played for Porchfield for 40 years and is still the club's president.

By 1910 more people had begun to look beyond their own village for their leisure pursuits. Bicycles of one sort or another had been around for some 50 years, the 'dandy horse' and the 'penny farthing' paving the way for the modern free-wheel cycles. Walter Holbrook owned one of the first 'bone-shakers' in the district. Its wooden wheels, bound with iron 'tyres', were not conducive to a comfortable journey on the unmade road surfaces. Neither were its fixed pedals at the front-wheel hubs designed for those of a less physically fit disposition. For some, the invention made their job easier. Newtown's vicar, Revd Henry Rice Venn, toured his parishioners on his tricycle, and his contemporary, Aaron Fallick, became a local celebrity, puffing and pushing his old-fashioned tricycle on delivery journeys to Cowes with several baskets tied precariously behind the saddle. For others, bicycles offered another form of sport, or a means of visiting family and friends, or simply a way of seeing the countryside. By the 1880s cycle races were being organised, and from 1900 touring by bicycle became increasingly popular, although it was not without its difficulties, given the dress of the period. By 1912, the Island's motorcycle club was also an attraction for a few.

By 1920, the motorised bus and open-topped charabanc were opening up fresh vistas for a larger section of the community. 'Combined Outings' were advertised during the 1930s, with residents from Calbourne, Newtown and Porchfield enjoying trips sponsored by the fund-raising activities of the Locks Green Social Committee, generously supported by Captain Pirie. Porchfield Chapel members enjoyed each other's company on the annual outing to Sandown. For others, league football at Portsmouth, dance bands at Sandown pavilion, and Cowes fireworks all became realistic aspirations.

Entrepreneurs learned to call the 'outing' a 'day-trip', and as paid holidays became more common the day-trip became a 'long weekend'. Since the early 1800s parts of the Island had attracted wealthy visitors seeking to exploit the 'curative sea water' and 'beneficial climate'. Poets, writers and artists gathered, and royal patronage grew. Then, 100 years later, railway mania helped to generate the growth of mass tourism.

George Whittington had turned Stone Steps Tea Gardens into a big attraction, popular with chapel and Band of Hope outings when up to ten horse-drawn carts would deposit over 100 excited guests, lighting up the countryside en route with their lusty singing. But the Newtown district stood aloof from all this. Local residents could journey out to Sandown or Ryde by bicycle or carriage to sample these new attractions, but experienced no fresh invasion at home by these new visitors at play, save for a few discerning sailors and naturalists. Even in the early twenty-first century the area still has to be sought out and found, and is popular mainly for those seeking a refuge from the modern pace of life.

A growing awareness of the fragility of the district's environment in the face of an invasion of

Shalfleet United Cricket Team, 1938. Left to right, back row: *scorer Jack Cheverton, Peter Self, Leslie Feaver, Bill Pomroy, guest player from St Helens Mr Miles who worked for 'Farmer's Trading', umpire Robert Lock;* middle row: *Freddie Smith, Bill Shiner, Frank Cowley, Dick Lock, Gordon Rickman;* front row: *Bob Cowley, John Paul.*

18. September 1902.

Mr Nunn.

TO G. WHITTINGTON,

STONE STEPS TEA GARDENS.

Cut Flowers supplied. Bouquets & Wreaths made to Order.

27.	Children at 5d per head	11	3
26.	Adults at 9d per head	19	6
2	Coachmen at 6d per head	1	0
6	Horses Stabling	2	6
		1.14	3

Received with thanks
18. September /02 A. M...

Above: *A receipt for the visit of Pallance Road Band of Hope in 1902.*

Left: *Adela Foss near London Heath, c.1920.*

visitors, or an exploitation of its land values, led to the creation of the Newtown Preservation Society which campaigned during the 1960s and '70s. The careful acquisition and management of land by the Newtown (Isle of Wight) Trust Company, formed in 1964, and the National Trust has, to the time of writing, been successful in protecting the area's special heritage through controls on car parking, moorings, public access and building regulations. In 1975 the Isle of Wight County Council declared part of the estuary a nature reserve, and this pioneering work has been extended by the National Trust which, in 1980, used a World Wildlife Fund grant to develop a 'scrape', containing a variety of nesting habitats for the visiting birds including tern, mallard, shellduck, redshank and ringed plover. Most of the Haven is now a National Nature Reserve. Other groups keen to protect local heritage, such as the British Trust for Conservation Volunteers, have also been active, and the National Trust has appointed a full-time warden.

Visitor numbers are growing. Around 5,000 people each year visit the Town Hall at Newtown, a National Trust monument, and a growing number of school groups and others use the local trails. A letter published (1988) in the *Isle of Wight County Press* commented upon the problems faced by the National Trust and local residents alike: 'Nature reserve and public access are really a contradiction in terms.' But brent-geese still far outnumber human visitors and the district is standing up well to the explosion in the leisure industry.

In 1580, Sir George Carey raged against 'unthrifty games'. In the seventeenth century, Oliver Cromwell fined parents for allowing their children to play on Sundays. Until 1870, there was no such thing as a public holiday in England. Before 1938, employers were under no legal obligation to provide paid holidays. There were longer working hours, fewer holidays and lower incomes. Yet, despite this, there was a rich tapestry of social and cultural activity pursued right across the social spectrum. The aspirations, even of humble folk, knew few boundaries. Porchfield's choir of farm labourers, laundresses, domestic servants and their like normally set off on its weekly perambulation around the village after chapel, but on that special day in 1880 when members posed for the camera they were about to journey to London's Crystal Palace to perform on the larger stage.

Porchfield's Dirty Lane Bible Christian Chapel choir by their original chapel, 1880. Left to right, back row: *Edwin Holbrook, Ellen Holbrook, James Angell, Rachel Holbrook, David Holbrook, Harry Holbrook, Henry Fallick, Carolyn Holbrook, Philip Fallick, William Smith;* sitting, middle row: *Elisa Holbrook, ?, Ann Holbrook (née Dennis), Lucy Ford, Fanny Louisa Holbrook, Bessie Hayward;* front row: *Fred Fallick, Alfred Holbrook, Annie Holbrook, Caroline Hayward.*

Chapter 15

'Up Goes a Pound, Pop Goes a Penny & Down Comes Half a Crown': Local Field Sports

Like many of his contemporaries, Henry Foss ('Japhet' to his friends) was an elusive poacher, and Fred Fallick, head gamekeeper for the Swainston estate, knew it. In 1910, determined to catch him returning from one of his nocturnal expeditions, Fred and his assistant keepers staked out London Heath cottages for a seemingly endless night. As dawn broke, the weary keepers were startled into wakefulness. 'Good morning, Mr Fallick!', called the beaming Henry from his bedroom window!

In the 1940s, the poaching skills of London Heath residents were sorely tested again, this time by Police Constable Trigg who, hiding in the bushes one late-October day, surprised two men landing in a rowing boat, complete with four freshly killed rabbits, a gun, some nets and a ferret. The culprits were each fined £1.

At the beginning of the twentieth century the estate teemed with pheasants and rabbits, fair game for a good many local residents looking to supplement their larder or their income. Bred and protected by the keepers to provide sport for the gentry the game reflected a thriving rural pursuit that had a history of more than 1,000 years.

In the early-twenty-first century, the whole issue of field sports has become contentious in the face of rapidly changing social values and the alienation of the urban community from things rural. Many country dwellers fear a total disintegration of the rural fabric, of which the hunting of game has been an important part. Hunting in the Newtown area can be traced back to the lifestyles of the Saxon and Norman kings of England who established Royal Forests and imposed strict forest laws to protect their own hunting enjoyment. Parkhurst Forest, once far more extensive and encroaching into the Swainston estate, contained the oldest Royal Park in England (Watching Park), its 350 acres already well established at the time of the Domesday Survey in 1086. Some of the names in the former Forest area reflect these origins – Great Park, Park Place, Greenpark, and Swainston's own sixteenth-century North Park.

Various Forest freedoms existed for Forest residents – freedom of pasture (to turn out cattle), of piscary (to fish) and of turbary (to dig turf and peat) – and there were also rights (or 'botes') granted to take wood for various purposes. In addition, the Lords of the Island were granted the royal privilege to take or drive stags (or harts – the name of Harts Farm in Newtown is probably significant).

On the other hand, Forest law was severe. Tenants were vetted and were permitted to enclose their holding only with banks or fences low enough to be hurdled 'beyond the pale' by a hind (deer) and her young. The king was permitted trespass, the tenants were not. Ferrets and nets were banned, and dogs were either contained or maimed to prevent them joining the chase. Until around the year 1230 the death penalty was automatic for anyone caught taking a falcon or disturbing its nest!

In the 1250s Henry III sent three huntsmen, 20 hounds and 12 greyhounds to catch, salt and store 100 deer from Parkhurst Forest, and around 100 years later John Matravers was charged to attend King Edward III for the buck-hunting season in Watching Wood. Many royal successors also enjoyed the sport in the area and as late as 1650 the Forest contained almost 200 deer. Over the years it was at times re-stocked with deer and with hares from the mainland until the woodland was plundered by George III for the Napoleonic Wars and clearance and enclosures restricted ancient privileges for rich and poor alike.

Prior to the invention of hunting guns in the sixteenth century, falconry was the means by which small game was hunted. Like stag hunting, it was restricted to royalty, nobility and gentry and it also reflected a scale of contemporary social values. Only royalty was permitted to use gyrfalcons, peregrines were for noblemen and merlins for noblewomen, whilst landed gentry and clergy had to make do with sparrowhawks and goshawks.

People lower down the social scale also had their field sports including cock-fighting (introduced to this country by the Romans and outlawed, but not stopped, in 1849) and bull baiting. (The last known bull baiting on the Island took place at West Cowes in 1815, for which George Beck was prosecuted.) Rather more common was the trapping of rabbits (although royal tithes were still raised on the catch), and the shooting of wildfowl, for which no permission was required. The culling of pigeons was actually encouraged and there were organised annual shoots.

By 1800 deer had almost disappeared from the Newtown area and field sports had become focused on the shooting of game birds on the manorial estates, and on hare coursing, a favourite of the squirearchy. Then the introduction of wild foxes to the Island in 1843 quickly led to hunting with hounds.

The landscape of the Swainston and Hamstead estates is ideally suited to the rearing and shooting of game birds, especially pheasants. Woods, copses and 'roughs' (furze, bracken and blackthorn thickets) interspersed with open fields provide plenty of ground cover for nesting and feeding, tree cover for roosting, and open ground for 'the guns'. Improved transport and increasing wealth during the nineteenth century led to a growing demand for access to 'shoots' and gamekeepers were kept busy extending the number of 'beats'. Shoots were leased by the manors to enthusiasts for large sums of money. By 1916 Francis Mew, the Island brewer, was paying £1,500 each year for the Swainston shoot alone. (He even enlarged the shoot from 6,000 to 7,000 acres in 1910 by purchasing the neighbouring farms of Colemans, Bunts Hill and Youngwoods, and rented further shoots at Northwood, all in addition to his associations with fox-hunting and beagling.)

Enormous numbers of birds were shot, the Official Game Record of Swainston during his 11-year lease (1907–18) showing 48,303 'kills':

Pheasants	*33,000*
Partridges	*3,630*
Hares	*81*
Rabbits	*9,850*
Woodcock	*387*
Snipe	*97*
Ducks	*359*
Various	*899*

Fred Fallick (1870–1957) and his dogs.

Swainston's main beats at the time were Home (centred on St Hubert's Lodge, home of the head gamekeeper), North Park, Highwood, Burnt Wood (developed 1887), Walter's Copse (developed 1910), and Three Gates at Heathfield. Norman laws and seasons still applied and a clear annual pattern of activity emerged, dominated by the shooting seasons (1 September until 1 February for partridge and woodcock, and 1 October until 1 February for pheasant), although sporting etiquette (and common sense) limited the later months to cock birds.

By late March and April the birds paired off and started nesting. These same months the keepers were busily preparing the nesting boxes and houses, noting the sites of nests in the wild, and reducing the level of vermin. May was the egg-gathering month when keepers and others collected 'wild' eggs and put them to fowls in the nesting houses, around 20 to each hen. Wild birds then laid a second clutch to be reared naturally. Keepers hunted the boundaries of the estate first where eggs were most vulnerable to predators and paid the traditional shilling to any local resident bringing them a clutch of eggs or identifying the site of an unknown nest. Three very busy months followed for the keepers. A good clutch numbered up to 20 eggs and by the late 1880s around 1,000 eggs were collected each year to be transferred to the 'sitting' houses and boxes supplied by Messrs Long of Five Houses. Some 20 years later, 'production' had risen to some 4,000 eggs a year, although by now mowing machines, which were replacing scythes, were proving to be a problem and many nests were lost. Frank Mew began paying mowers 5s. and shepherds 2s.6d. (12 new pence) to protect more nests.

In addition to collecting wild eggs, keepers captured and penned wild pheasant hens to lay in nesting boxes. These and the sitting boxes were bottomless, set down in neat rows on narrow-meshed wire to keep out rats and moles. The young chicks were hatched after 24 days, usually during June and July, and moved to coops. In 1888 keepers Fred Fallick and Charles Barton were handling 80 coops just at North Park, and by 1910 there were over 200, built to the Gilbertson and Page design. The coops had to be moved quite frequently to reduce the risk of disease and protect them from the prevailing weather. Food for the hens and the growing chicks was prepared in the 'pothouse' and as soon as they were large enough each coop full of birds had to be 'stretchered' to nearby 'roughs' of furze where they were released into good ground cover. Here they foraged for themselves and were fed barley rakings, and for several weeks, before they learned to roost in the trees, the birds were at their most vulnerable to predators.

Different fields, known as 'pheasantries', were used each season for this rapidly expanding operation of breeding in order to reduce the risk of diseases such as gapes, cramp and blindness, more common in wet seasons. In 1909 some of Ernest Heal's fields at Fullholding Farm were used. The whole process became increasingly refined and regimented,

London Heath Cottages in 1983.

St Hubert's Lodge in 1932.

Below: *Fred Fallick and an assistant keeper attend to the regimented rows of hatching boxes and feeding pens, c.1912.*

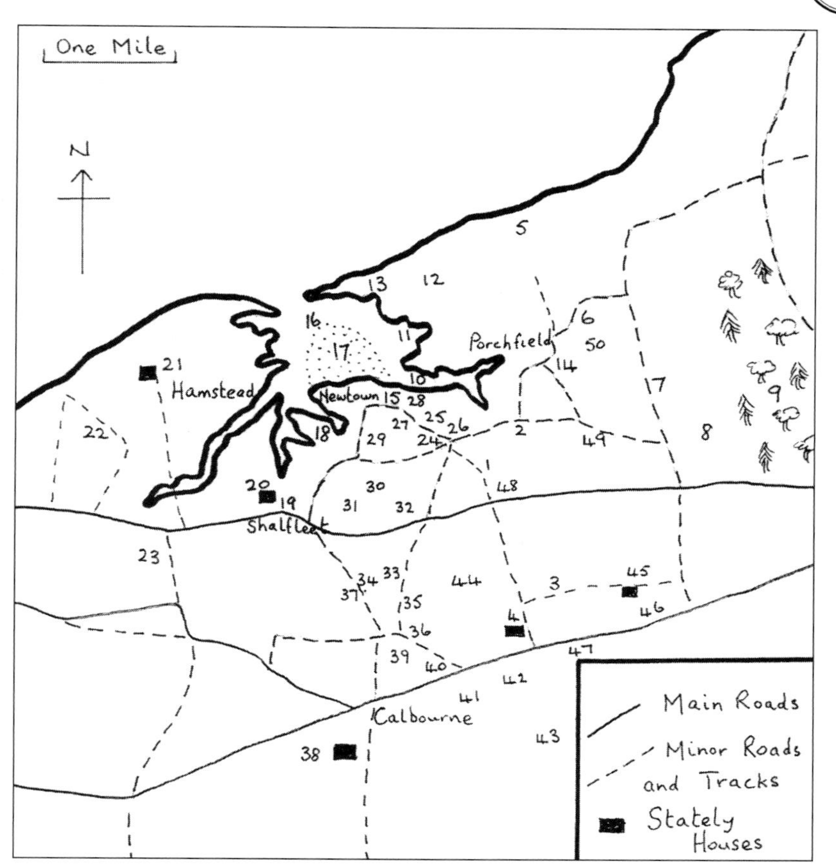

Above: *The field sports context around Newtown.* Indicated are: *1. St Hubert's Lodge, 2. Corfeheath Firs, 3. Watchingwell Station, 4. Swainston Manor, 5. Burnt Wood, 6. Bunts Hill Farm, 7. Sandhills, 8. Forest Farm, 9. Parkhurst Forest, 10. Clamerkin Lake, 11. Spur Lake, 12. Signal Hill, Porchfield, 13. North Close, 14. Sportsman's Rest, 15. Harts Farm, 16. Brickyard Corner, 17. Newtown Marsh, 18. Fleetlands Farm, 19. New Inn, Shalfleet, 20. Shalfleet Manor, 21. Hamstead Grange, 22. Cranmore, 23. Ningwood, 24. London Heath, 25. Walter's Copse, 26. Windgate Copse, 27. Old Vicarage Lane, 28. Town Copse, 29. Fleetlands Copse, 30. Woodwax Copse, 31. Yatlands Copse, 32. Hebberdens Farm, 33. Pound Copse, 34. Elm Farm, 35. Fullholding Farm, 36. Five Houses, 37. Calbourne Station, 38. Westover Manor, 39. Crainges Copse, 40. Pump Copse, 41. New Barn Clump, 42. The Temple, 43. Highwood, 44. North Park, 45. Great Park Manor, 46. Park Place, 47. Round Copse, 48. Three Gates, 49. Coleman's Farm, 50. Youngwoods Farm.*

Left: *Young pheasants on the 'roughs' near Hebberdens.*

reaching the stage where each nesting box and sitting house (set out in serried rows) had its own tethering stick where the fowls were tied whilst being fed. Thus, the estate always had a mix of tame and wild game birds, and when shoots took place the beaters sometimes had real difficulty persuading the 'tame' birds to take wing!

By each autumn the estate was home to perhaps 12,000 pheasants (many of them the product of the specially introduced Mongolian cocks from Liphook, and Japanese pheasants introduced in the 1920s when Commander Sauroun's syndicate took the shooting lease) and 5,000 other game birds, and the 'guns' then began to arrive. Keepers boasted about the size of the 'bags' – 450 pheasants (plus some rabbits) on one day in 1897, downed by 'four of the best shots in England', or the 76 pheasants shot at one rise alongside Little Windgate copse in 1911.

It was time for the keepers to engage the services of 'beaters', 'stops', 'loaders' and 'runners', and to contract farmer Bob Flux with his horse and van to take away the 'kills', most of which were sold.

Fred Fallick himself had started out at age 11 as a stop, armed with a stick, for head keeper Luke Barton in 1881 at a gateway near Round Copse, as beaters and 'guns' moved the game towards him. (Sticks beaten on hazel wood make the best noise to 'drive' the birds.) Friends Herbert Foss, Gus Stark and Ted Barton were regular beaters during their teens (1915–22) earning 2s.6d. for a day's work (whilst doing rather a lot of damage to their clothes!). The older men wore an ancient pair of corduroy trousers with sacking tied around, and a very old frayed jacket, with thick leather-palmed gloves and hobnail boots. Everyone had to gather at a pre-arranged time and place, firstly to drive the birds from the turnip fields into a nearby copse to await the arrival of the guns and then, at the sound of a horn or whistle, to flush them out and into flight. They often met at The Temple (Swainston's former summer-house) to join keepers Charlie Fallick and Dave Angell and drove into New Barn Clump or New Barn Hummit, or joined keeper Jim Barton at North Park near Watchingwell Station, or Fred Fallick at his own Home Beat, driving into Fleetlands copse. Meanwhile, the runners scampered to collect winged birds (sometimes with dogs) and load the kill onto the van, whilst loaders worked furiously to have the guns ready. A loader held a prestigious position and the experts – Andrew Fallick (1870s), Jim Arnold, Dick Hayward and William Smith (all early 1900s) – were allocated to the most important guests. One loader, a particularly good shot, merited the nickname 'Woodcock', a notoriously difficult bird to shoot in flight.

The shooting party occasionally retired to the Noah's Ark for beer and oysters but more often took lunch at the nearest keeper's cottage. The beaters' lunch consisted of sliced mutton, bread and cheese. There was usually hot tea and, especially when Frank Gray of the Sportsman's Rest was a beater, a jar of cool beer!

The Fallick family at St Hubert's Lodge, c.1912. Left to right: *Frederick James, Edith, Fanny, Fred, Harold, Charles and Lily.*

Fred Fallick's granddaughter, Eileen Fallick, was sometimes at St Hubert's Lodge as a child in the 1930s when the gentry took wine in the front room before eating a roast of beef or lamb with vegetables, whilst the keepers and loaders ate in the back room (with beer or tea rather than wine), and the beaters were placed in the pothouse with cold brisket, bread and cheese, with a bucket of tea! Even as a child she noticed how her grandfather 'looked up' to the guests and how her mother (who had spent time 'in service') 'felt inferior'. (Fred once wrote of the time in 1930 when he was invited to shoot with Sir John Simeon and was offered first shot: 'This was very fine of him as I was only a servant.')

At the end of the day the beaters were called together to be told where and when to report for the next shoot, then they were paid and, perhaps, offered a damaged bird or rabbit. Old stagers knew what was coming and, carefully eyeing up the choice, sidled towards the plumpest animal!

The 'guns' were usually gentry guests of the leaseholder of the shoot and often travelled from up-country to enjoy the sport. Following Major Hamilton, Mr Charles Seely of Brook House took a seven-year lease in 1887 and wanted 1,000 pheasants reared. The first day's shoot met near London Heath when 'a pair of fine horses, coachman in high top hat, with valet sitting close up and so very erect' delivered Mr Seely and his three sons, Charles, Jack and Frank. The popular Prince Henry of Battenberg, husband of Princess Beatrice and Governor of the Island, often joined the shoot, as did Lord Aberdair and Sir Barrington Simeon who, in 1895, took over the shoot himself until 1907, when, in failing health, he leased it to Francis Mew.

Except for a short break after 1918 (when Fred Fallick, Newtown's Dr Howard Hawkins, the steward of Swainston Andrew Barton, and a few farmers were the only guns trying to make the shoot 'break even' by selling all kills to Paskins' shop at Cowes, including fox pelts for 15s.), Frank Mew retained the lease until the early 1920s, by which time Sir John Barrington had settled into Shalfleet Manor and had taken the western half of the shoot himself, with Andrew Barton as head keeper. Shoots were becoming increasingly expensive to maintain and when Mr Mew retired Swainston reflected a national trend when the first of several syndicates took the lease, firstly Commander Sauroun's syndicate for five seasons, then Sir John Simeon's from 1928. (By 1915 the cost of rearing each game bird had risen to £1, each cartridge cost a penny, and a cleanly killed bird sold for 2s.6d. The financial implications were obvious!) At the time of writing, a season's lease costs anything up to £12,000, and guests pay £200 for a day's shooting.

Holders of the Lease to Swainston's Shoot & Some Principal Guests

	Leaseholder	*Guests*
1882–87	*Major Hamilton*	
1887–95	*Mr Charles Seely*	*Prince Henry of Battenberg, Sir Barrington Simeon*
1895–1907	*Sir Barrington Simeon*	*Lord Aberdair, Lord Kensington, Sir Pennistant Millbank, Col Campbell, Edmund Simeon*
1907–18	*Francis Mew*	*Mr E. Gunner (steward at Swainston), Col Howard Brooke, Mr Douglas Hall, Ernest Langton, Col Rhodes, Col Francis, Dr Mellor, General Jack Seely*
1918–20	*Laura Simeon (widow)*	*Andrew Barton (steward at Swainston), Fred Fallick, Dr Hawkins, farmers*
1920–23	*Francis Mew (east shoot)*	*Commander Sauroun, Sir John Simeon (west shoot) Andrew Barton (head gamekeeper)*
1923–28	*Commander Sauroun (east)*	*Sir Godfrey Baring, Mr Allen, General Gupper, Major Saville, Captain Peto, Mr Grieg, Major Stewart, Mr Wykeham, Gen. Jack Seely*
1928–57	*Sir John Simeon (all)*	*Lord Mottistone, Mr Wykeham, Capt. Peto, Sir Hanson Rowbotham, Major Saville, Col Morrison-Bell*

Shooting Expenditure From Feb 1st 1918 To Jan 31st 1919	£	s	d
Keepers Wages	122	5	
Beaters "	35		
Licences	13	5	
Cartridges	59		
Retriever	5		
Dogs Food	53	8	6
Carriage of Game	5	13	10
Extras for Lunch	8	17	
Insurance		17	6
Glebe Rent	3	11	
Walters "	15		
£	321	17	10

Receipts re From Feb 1st 1918 To Jan 31 1919	£	s	d
Partridges 9½ P	46	12	4
Pheasants 12½ P	211	3	10
Rabbits	145	4	10
Hares	2	10	
Pigeons	1	1	4
£	406	12	4
Partridges Gave Away	15	7	6
Pheasants " "	31	9	
Rabbits " "	19	15	
Partridges Used at House	7	2	6
Pheasants " " "	18	10	
Rabbits " " "	25	16	
Woodcock " " "	5	8	
Hares	1	10	
Landrail & Pigeons	1	1	4
£	532	11	8

Swainston's game record and accounts for 1918–19, maintained by Andrew Barton, steward.

In 1932 most of the estate was sold to individual farmers, although shooting rights were retained for a further 21 years. The delicate relationship between keepers and farmers became even more strained, but at least most of the keepers had had plenty of practice! Much like the farming world itself, many keepers were born into the job, and two families in particular dominated the sport at Swainston for almost 100 years – the Bartons and the Fallicks.

In the early years the rearing of young birds appears to have been rather amateurish but improved rapidly during the 1880s, only to suffer a setback under the stewardship of the allegedly illiterate and unpopular Harry 'Beagle' Sanders. During his last season (1905–06) only 900 birds were shot on 5,000 acres of shoot. For most of the remainder of the period from 1850 until 1950, keepering was very much 'kept in the family'.

Fred Fallick often referred to 'the opposing forces'. Anything or anybody who might limit the success of the shooting season fell into this category – inclement weather, disaffected farmers, vermin, poachers and the Isle of Wight Hunt included!

As soon as the shooting season was over every effort was made for the next six weeks to reduce the level of vermin before the birds began to nest again.

The Swainston gamekeepers, 1920s. Left to right, standing: *Charles Fallick, Jim Birch;* seated: *Dave Angell, Frederick Fallick, Frederick James Fallick.*

Summary of Main Keepering Appointments

1850s *Charles Fallick head keeper at St Hubert's (Fred Fallick's great uncle).*

1871 *William Nunn head keeper at St Hubert's with sons Fred (18), Alfred (16) and James (14) as assistants.*

1881 *Luke Barton (57) head keeper at St Hubert's with son Charles (19). (Charles was cousin of Andrew Barton, later steward at Swainston).*

1886 *Fred Fallick appointed assistant keeper, Charles Barton made under-keeper at Highwood and North Park beats.*

1887 *Luke and Charles Barton and Fred Fallick walked to Pitt Place to re-apply for their jobs when Mr Seely took the lease of Swainston shoot.*

1888 *Five keepers in employment.*

1890 *Fred Fallick (19) put in charge of Three Gates beat (resident at Porchfield).*

1891 *Luke Barton died and Charles Barton was made head keeper.*

1892 *Walter Lambert appointed assistant keeper (died 1894 from influenza).*

1894 *Fred Fallick took North Park residency as second keeper.*

1895 *Harry Sanders appointed head keeper, Charles Barton lost job but placed as head keeper to Sir Walter Philimore at Reading, Mr Gulliver and George Cresswell appointed assistants and Tom Sanders as assistant to Fred Fallick.*

1896 *Dick Hayward and Honder Underwood appointed assistants, Tom Sanders took over Highwood beat, Fred Fallick resigned and obtained head keeper post at Hamstead for Mr Fred Tankard.*

1901 *Edward Sanders appointed as under-keeper.*

1906 *Fred Fallick invited back to Swainston as head keeper at St Hubert's after Harry Sanders was sacked, Jim Barton (Andrew's brother) appointed assistant, John Summerfield from Dorking appointed second keeper and Harry Smith (son of William the former carrier) appointed assistant keeper.*

1907 *Dave Angell appointed in charge of animals.*

1910 *Jim Barton as second keeper to North Park with Harry Smith as his assistant.*

1911 *Fred's son Charles Fallick appointed in charge of animals, Dave Angell takes over Walter's Copse beat as assistant, Charlie Barton (Andrew's son) appointed to keep birds out of cornfields.*

1916 *Dave Angell, Charles Fallick and Charlie Barton called-up (Charlie Barton did not survive the war).*

1918 *Fred Fallick the only keeper left.*

1919 *Dave Angell and Charles Fallick returned to their former jobs.*

1922 *Dave Angell took over Highwoods beat and Charles Fallick Elm beat and Yatlands beat.*

1924 *Charles Fallick moved into The Temple to take Highwoods beat, Dave Angell moved into North Park, Jim Birch taken on as assistant keeper.*

1930 *Leslie Shirlaw appointed as assistant keeper.*

1941 *Fred Fallick retired after 55 years keepering but still worked part time at Highwoods.*

1956 *Dave Angell and Charles Fallick retired.*

'Winged vermin' – jays, magpies, crows and hawks – were either shot or poisoned with bait hung high in the trees and bushes and coated in Rodene. 'Four legged' vermin were caught in plugged ground traps, often baited with rabbit meat coated in poison and carefully camouflaged. Pipe traps proved very successful against stoats, weasels, hedgehogs and rats, all of which would raid a nest for eggs or chicks – one weasel could account for 60 pheasant chicks, and hedgehogs were partial to young partridges. Most of the catch was removed to be buried, but keepers learned to leave hedgehogs whose carcases attracted blowflies. Their eggs produced maggots which appealed to black beetles which, in turn, attracted back further hedgehogs for the poisoning cycle to begin again! When young game was around, keepers also learned to distinguish the warning cries of the blackbirds; 'ching, ching, ching' when winged vermin approached, or 'put, put, put' when the four-legged variety was around. Foul-smelling Renadine (from Gilbertson and Page), placed near partridge nests or even painted onto the tail of a sitting hen, was sufficient to keep most of 'the opposing forces' away, including moles.

Many foxes encroached on to the shoot from Parkhurst Forest (badgers were comparatively rare) and gin traps accounted for many of them. The fox population varied and, when necessary, special efforts were made to cull them. In 1897 50 were shot in a period of six months, and again in 1930 all the keepers with Andrew Barton and Jim Arnold shot 50 in one day plus five litters, one containing 11 cubs. Some were also culled during a normal shoot when anything that moved was 'fair game', except on those occasions when Colonel Brooke, Master of the Isle of Wight Hunt, was in the party!

Not much corn was grown in the area but game birds had a liking for the young plants, so young boys straight from school were engaged as bird scarers at 1s. a week to keep the farmers happy. One farmer, convinced the birds were eating his beans, was shown a bird's crop full of 'leather jackets' (crane-flies) whereupon he invited the keepers to send more birds on to his land! Such were the wiles of the countryside!

Regularly, keepers invited farmers to special pigeon and rabbit shoots in the name of good relations. The best rabbit shoot was at Hebberdens Roughs where 20 guns shot 348 rabbits one day in 1918, 'Dusty' Miller collecting them with his horse and van and paying 6d. each for the good ones. Sometimes special wired-in warrens were established for the rabbits, such as that at Fleetlands Furzebrake on the banks of Causeway Creek, when the opportunity arose during the tenancy changeover between the Humbers and the Stricklands, around 1915. On one occasion here only two guns (those of Commander Sauroun and Fred Fallick) shot 102 rabbits, with George Hayward and Jessie Smith deploying the nets and ferrets. Later, in around 1929, the day's bag was 193 when Fred Fallick and Andrew Barton took the Simeon children ('Master John and Miss Betty'), and used George Hayward and Billy Prangnell and their dogs as beaters.

Around 1909 Frank Mew asked for a pigeon shoot to be organised at St Hubert's Lodge (St Hubert is the patron saint of hunting) for 30 local farmers, the keepers, and his friends Colonel Brooke and Ernest Langton. A total of 200 birds were brought in from Portsmouth and, to many people's surprise, the 1s. per head stake was won by William Smith from North Close Farm for shooting most birds.

Almost everyone owned a gun, or had access to one, and great pride was taken in shooting skills. As soon as he was employed in gamekeeping, Fred Fallick (aged 15) was given a single-barrel muzzle-loader to shoot anything that might threaten the game birds. His great-uncle, Andrew Fallick, persisted into the 1880s with his faithful old gun which used powder and a cask of shot, with percussion caps. He was an expert shot, always in demand as a loader for Sir John Simeon, and was noted in local census returns as 'living off garden and fowl'. Even his old gun was a distinct improvement on the flintlocks of earlier years which could only be fired when the flint could be persuaded to spark. According to Fred Fallick, flintlocks were the best excuse for missing that he had ever come across!

Poachers with guns posed a major problem for the keepers throughout the year, usually under the cover of darkness when the birds were roosting, or on Sundays when the keepers might be at chapel!

Poacher Walter Reynard allegedly threatened to shoot Fred Fallick when he and other keepers (Jim Barton, Harry Smith and John Summerfield) caught Walter and his accomplice Charlie Harvey poaching at Pump Copse in 1911. (Many years later he confessed he was only using a bluff that usually worked!) They were marched to Newport police station, arriving there at 3.45a.m., and were later sentenced to the maximum six months in prison. Soon after their release they were again caught poaching, this time by the three Smith brothers, Jessie, Albert and Percy, netting rabbits at North Close, and earned another six months 'inside'. At about the same date, Newtown Rifle Range and Camp was opened and a number of soldiers were caught poaching, one with a 2.2 rifle which Fred confiscated. Back in the 1840s Fred's grandfather Philip Fallick and his colleague Jacob Hayward were employed as 'night watchers' to warn poachers away, armed with bill-hooks strapped to the wrist. In the 1890s the Dunford family from Cowes were notorious for their activities on the Swainston shoot. Ironically, at about the same time, Fred Fallick was living in a cottage opposite the Locks Green smithy and almost next door to the local poacher, Thomas Downer, who lived at Corfe Heath Cottage just around the corner at Three Cocked Hat (sometimes called Boxiron Copse). Reportedly, Tom was of peculiar appearance, short and bent:

> *... with eyes like a fox and every bit as crafty. He always walked with his hands behind and appeared to be looking on the ground, but nothing ever escaped his eye. He had flat feet and turned the left one outwards and when walking whacked it down more firmly than the other. Everyone knew the sound of his footsteps.*

Tom never went to inspect his pheasant traps unless he knew where the keeper was. In some desperation to catch him, Luke Barton put a pheasant in Tom's gin trap, donned his best velvet coat and hat and drove his pony and trap past Tom's cottage as though making his regular trip to Newport. Within minutes Tom was out to his traps in The Firs, and straight into the arms of the waiting under-keeper! Confrontations sometimes turned nasty like that in 1888 when Fred wrestled a gun away from a stronger man (a weapon that turned out to be a kind of 'parish gun' which was shared among several poachers) and in 1891 when, with police assistance, another gun was confiscated near Corve [sic] Farm after a chase from Hebberdens. Many years later, in 1931, at the age of 60, Fred gave chase and caught his man, this one from Gunville, home to a good many poachers down the years.

'Opposing forces' of the poaching kind came in many guises ranging from young lads with catapults, to gun-slinging 'professionals', the 'thinkers' with their Heath Robinson traps, to Sir Godfrey Baring's butler complete with the gentleman's Rolls Royce! Even the trapping of rabbits carried a prison sentence unless you had special permission, like Henry Foss and Maurice Rogers who were allowed to trap those creatures that were damaging the banks around Newtown Marsh, which they maintained for the estate. They used snares set four fingers tall placed carefully in the middle of the rabbit's stride along its 'runs'. Henry was convinced that a young (August) rabbit, stuffed and roasted, tasted better than chicken. Likewise, Ted Barton obtained a contract to trap rabbits on Hebberdens Roughs, and boasted to his friends during the conviviality of a Saturday evening in Newport that 'I've earned enough to get a little Douglas motorbike!' He could often be spotted walking with his catch ham-strung on a long pole across his shoulder. (The hind legs of the rabbit were spliced and threaded onto the pole.)

Ted certainly did not have permission when, with his friend Herbert Foss, he took his whippet rabbiting most Sunday mornings at the 'vuzzbrake' alongside Old Vicarage Lane at Newtown. The dog would stand and quiver (much like a ferret does if a fox is about) and point its long nose at a rabbit in its 'squat' (tuft of grass), and respond instantly to the command 'Go!' They also set illegal snares on the Marsh below Town Copse. Most illegal catches of game were sold and there appears to have been little difficulty finding a cooperative businessman. A visiting 1920s fishmonger (Mr Barham) took a rabbit in exchange for a bloater and would hang it alongside others adorning his van. Some would be very 'ripe' by the time his weekly visit was due. Various butchers in Newport or 'the faithful 'Pester' Jackson, the fishmonger,' also took them. Writing of his childhood memories during the 1930s, Gordon Rickman described 'Pester' as deserving of his soubriquet. Frequently moving his fish barrow around the edge of St James Square in Newport (possibly in the absence of a licence to sell!), he harangued potential customers in a piercing voice.

Part of a cottager's staple diet, wild rabbit was often regarded as 'poor man's food'. During the 1920s, local men received only a penny ha'penny from Wapshott's in Lower St James Street, Newport, for each rabbit caught.

A good dog is crucial to success in many field sports. Pointers, setters and black retrievers were popular with the keepers, although Dave Angell's excellent dog, 'Bell', was a labrador. A good dog lasted ten years which meant that a fresh one was in training every five years or so. A well-trained dog could be trusted to sit untethered whilst 'tame' birds were fed, also to lie still under fired guns even when other dogs were working, and to retrieve winged birds ('runners') unharmed from the deepest thicket.

Fred Fallick's all-time favourite was Nell, a six-year-old retriever who could do the seemingly impossible. Frank Mew's wounded pheasant fell into a thicket at Parson's Roughs near the Newtown Vicarage and ran. Nell at first got entangled in a snare, managed to pull its plug, and returned to have the offending thing removed, but went in again eventually to fetch the bird which was still alive. On another occasion she was persuaded to return over a mile across the fields to retrieve a much-valued walking-stick that Fred had mistakenly left near London Heath. Such talent resulted from firm and patient training, and complete trust between man and dog.

The South of England retriever dog trials were held just once on the Island, based at Swainston in 1910 and using the Three Gates and Pump Lane area. A total of 21 dogs were put through their paces, including retrieving from across Clamerkin River at full tide. Three years later some international gun-dog trials were held at Three Gates offering a first prize of £50, a very considerable sum in 1913.

In great contrast to the retrieving dogs are the hunting variety – beagles, foxhounds and harriers – trained to track and kill their prey, originally deer, but more recently the hare and the fox. Until 1845, when the first pack of foxhounds was introduced to the Island, hare coursing with the Crockford Harriers was popular among the squirearchy. Harriers, like greyhounds, use sight rather than smell to track the

A shooting party of farmers from Swainston, c.1933. Left to right, standing: *W. Shotter, Mr Carr, ?, ?, B. Grace, B. Buckett, Geoff Barton of Harts Farm, George Mullet of Whippance Farm;* seated: *Mr Stainer, B. Hill, ?, ?.*

Left: *A gathering of countrymen in 1932, photographed by Sir John Simeon (junr).* Left to right: *Charles Fallick, Dave Angell, Frederick Fallick, Jim Birch, Wilf Barton, Frank Mew.*

Below: *A shooting party at Swainston with their dogs, c.1930.* Left to right: *William Prangnell with ham-strung rabbits, Percy Strickland and Ronnie Strickland both of Pitt Farm, Ted Barton and Geoff Barton both of Harts Farm, Joliffe Kingswell late of Noah's Ark dairy, Harry Cosh of Thorness Farm, Charlie Barnes of Clamerkin Farm, Jim Birch who was a keeper, Ted Strickland of Fleetlands Farm, Oliver Flux of London Farm, Mr Evans.*

hare so they tend to favour open country. The Newtown area, with its many woodlands, offers little suitable terrain. In addition, the damp ground of the area is not good hare territory. Hence, coursing in the district was always limited and most hares in the estate's Official Game Record were shot.

In the nineteenth century, fox-hunting largely replaced hare coursing on the Island, and the uneasy truce between the huntsmen and the keepers began. Until 1830, the only fox on Wight was tame (much like the Barton brothers' tame foxes at Harts Farm in the 1960s), but then Parson Fenwick's pet escaped and created havoc with the local chickens around Brook. The Harriers were persuaded to hunt it and the 15-mile chase that ensued so enthused some of the followers that in 1843 they smuggled the first wild foxes from the mainland and released them. The Isle of Wight Hunt was thus formed using hounds that are bred for their excellent sense of smell, their agility and their stamina.

The fox thrived and at Swainston became yet another 'opposing force'. Indeed, some of the leading 'guns' at the Swainston shoot were also keen huntsmen, a case, perhaps, of 'having your cake and eating it'! To the consternation of the keepers Mr Charles Seely, upon taking the lease of the shoot in 1887, immediately ordered 1,000 pheasant eggs and four foxes! And Colonel Howard Brooke, a regular 'gun' and great friend of Francis Mew, remained the longest serving Master of the Hunt (1894–1916) throughout its history. Around 1911 there were many foxes in the Newtown area and the keepers had their attention drawn to the tracks of a rubber-wheeled governess cart at a gateway at the top of Anley's Lane, and to the telltale lumps of straw where something had been released. The keepers suspected enthusiastic huntsmen had been releasing fox cubs but the Hunt denied all knowledge. Later, in around 1925, Commander Sauroun responded to the huntsmen's accusations that the keepers were killing too many foxes by offering £100 for the production of evidence. None was forthcoming. The shortage of foxes was probably due to the severe outbreak of fox mange in the early 1920s which persuaded the Hunt to introduce the first badgers to the Island in an attempt to dislodge the foxes from their diseased 'earths'.

The Hunt gathered locally at the New Inn, Shalfleet, resplendent in scarlet or black and with up to 30 hounds, and often made its way through Newtown attracting an enthusiastic following including the Gibson sisters, and royalty in the personages of Princess Beatrice and Prince Henry of Battenberg. But some local residents and farmers were less keen to find the hounds often pursuing their quarry across gardens and cornfields.

Hare coursing was revived in 1906 when the first Foot Beagles was formed, and by 1910 the ubiquitous sportsman Francis Mew had his own pack. His son of the same name was also a great supporter of the Foot Beagles all his life, hunting Signal Hill at Porchfield among many other locations. The Isle of Wight County Coursing Club (1950s) and the Isle of Wight Beagles (1970s) organised two or three meets each month in season, and the Beagles, based at Kingston at the time of writing, still account for around five or six brace of hare each year.

The hunting of game has never been a financially profitable pursuit and has, therefore, remained a sport for the privileged minority. Huge social divides marked the nineteenth century. Whilst, in 1851, Swainston Manor could employ 17 servants (governess, lady's maid, nurse, butler, footman, groom, stable servant, indoor servant, gardener, cook, two housemaids, two laundry maids, kitchen maid, scullery maid and a charwoman), as late as 1910 the head gamekeeper was paid only £1 per week plus his cottage, with its toilet a lantern-lit walk away into the woods! (In the year 2000, that cottage was on the market at an asking price of £285,000.) Even this bettered the lot of most labourers by some distance so it was not surprising that many viewed wildlife as a means of earning a few shillings or putting a little extra food on the table.

Aside from the poaching of game, the abundant wildfowl around local creeks became a target. Few migrant geese used the area until recent years and the main quarry was wild duck (the mallard) which was larger than wigeon or teal. Sadly for the likes of Clem Seagar, Herbert Foss and Gus Stark, ducks were comparatively rare and their favoured feeding grounds were at Locks Hard which was accessible only across private land. They could get 4s.6d. for each duck from Wapshott's in Newport, 2s.6d. for a wigeon, but only 1s.6d. for a teal. Herbert shot most fowl when they sheltered from an easterly under the banks at Brickyard Corner, lying in the long grass at the top of the bank and using the right barrel onto the mud-banks and the choke bore as they rose in flight. Winged birds often paddled across to North Close and had to be fetched with a boat. On one occasion he shot a swan, mistaking it for a goose, and furtively buried it before discovery!

Jim Arnold, who farmed at Clamerkin, had better access to Locks Hard and built several 'hides' of mud and furze alongside the river there. Never without a gun (tied to the handlebars of his bike if necessary) or his spaniel, Jim was an excellent shot and for many years the story went around the area of the time he shot 50 ducks in one night at Fleetlands. Never one to easily reveal his activities, he eventually admitted that it was actually 49!

The Barton brothers' hides were alongside the large lake at the northern end of the reclaimed Marsh. Ted Barton, in particular, was fond of shooting and one night took home a 'bag' of 16 wigeon. He favoured shooting on a still night when there was a moon in a light sky, and spoke of how he could hear

The hunt gathering at the New Inn, Shalfleet, around 1920 to enjoy the 'stirrup cup'. Included in the picture are: *Andrew Barton* (right) *and his cousin Charles, the former head gamekeeper* (standing alongside the garden wall of Andrew's cottage, now demolished), *Jack Barton* (sitting on the wall), *Mr Boville* (Master of the Hounds, on the grey).

The marshes around the creeks of Clamerkin River covered with sea lavender, c.1985.

Local farmers, c.1930. Left to right: *Reg Woodford (Corfe Farm), Maurice Rice (Elm Farm), William Holden (Upper Hamstead Farm), Bill Baker (Ningwood Farm).*

the steam trains going through, and the milk churns being loaded at Calbourne and Watchingwell Stations.

Most children in the early 1900s also made good use of the short mole-trapping season. They could get 2s. each for the best pelts (used for women's coats and gloves), caught mainly in January when the pelts were clear of the black spots they developed during the breeding season. Most of the traps were set underground in the fields or, occasionally, in mole 'runs' in gateways. The catch was skinned and the pelts pinned out on a board to cure before being sent by post to one of the several companies who advertised for them in the local press.

A sea change in attitudes toward game hunting and wildlife has driven these pursuits further from the public's favour. The great estates have been broken up and sold off, Hamstead in 1926 followed by part of Swainston in 1932 and much of the remainder in 1946. As part of the 'Regulations of Sale', shooting rights were retained at the Swainston sale in 1932 for a further 21 years (with rents payable to the new owners of 1s. per acre of open ground and 2s. per acre of copse), and were specified in detail in the sales particulars of certain plots ('The right to stand guns adjoining Yatlands Copse and Woodwax Copse is reserved' and 'The right to stand guns and beaters outside Crainges Copse is reserved'). The sales particulars for each estate also emphasised the high quality of shooting to be had, claiming in 1946 that Swainston was 'one of the finest sporting estates in the south of England' and 'well known for its high birds and partridge shooting.' As late as 1953 the sale of London Farm stipulated that 'The shooting will be in hand' and subject to a covenant of 1942 arranged on it by Sir John Walter Barrington.

The sport is still pursued into the twenty-first century, especially on the higher southern grounds of the former estate (Newbarn, Bowcombe and Ashengrove), but on a much lesser scale. Shooting rights are still in existence (held by Anthony Ball at the time of writing) and a syndicate uses the St Hubert's shoot. However, a greater concern for the protection and conservation of wildlife has emerged. Local resident Mercia Seabroke became a founder member of a committee which, in 1967, persuaded the Isle of Wight County Council to sponsor a nature reserve at Newtown and establish protective by-laws. The land of the reserve was loaned to a managing committee of interested parties, chaired by Mrs Seabroke for ten years. The Nature Conservancy, the Forestry Commission, local landowners, the Fisheries Authority and the National Trust were all represented. Much additional land has since been bought by the National Trust which has placed a ban on all hunting with dogs on its lands. Shooting is also forbidden on National Trust land, although there is the occasional boundary dispute regarding 'shoots' and 'stands'. Much of the area is designated as a National Nature Reserve.

Beleaguered field sports enthusiasts have become an endangered species! In late 2002, as Parliament prepared, again, to debate a bill to ban hunting with dogs, the Isle of Wight Hunt was served with a noise abatement notice by the Isle of Wight Council. Apparently, the hounds, housed at Gatcombe since 1927, were barking too loudly. The days of the hound and the gun seem to be numbered, as the urban majority has its say in the countryside. A gentleman's sport and a cottager's income could be the poorer for it.

An almost-forgotten rural scene at Swainston in 1911.

Epilogue

A unique combination of landscape, habitat and history makes Newtown an unforgettable place. Medieval street patterns and land divisions mark it out as one of the best-preserved examples of early town planning. Most of the area now constitutes a National Nature Reserve managed by the National Trust in partnership with English Nature, a landscape protected by at least six special designations. In addition, Brickfields Local Nature Reserve, at the time of writing owned by the Isle of Wight Council, lies to the north-east, and the Hamstead Heritage Coast, designated an Area of Outstanding Natural Beauty (AONB) lies to the north-west.

Five distinctive habitats (salt marsh, shingle, sand, woodland and pasture) provide homes to over 300 species of plants and almost 200 species of birds, including over-wintering shelter for thousands of waders and ducks ranging from brent-geese to the magnificent fish-eating osprey. The woodlands are home to such rarities as the red squirrel and the diminutive dormouse, and nesting sites for that superb songbird, the nightingale. The extremely rare Bechstine's bat inhabits the area, and the ground is carpeted with exotica such as green-winged orchids, devil's-bit scabious and adder's-tongue fern.

The area is attracting increasing attention from many quarters. As early as 1932, when the first sales of Swainston estate took place, properties were advertised as 'attractive cottages in Calbourne and Newtown suitable for weekend or countryside residences.' Now, the demand for residential property has pushed prices for modest cottages beyond the reach of many people. Second homes, unoccupied for much of the year, are becoming a feature. Since being given the Town Hall in the 1930s the National Trust has acquired much of the Haven and the surrounding farm land, copse and marsh, one of the most recent additions to their holdings being Clamerkin Farm, which was purchased in 1998 with the aid of the Neptune Fund. Trust policy is founded on the principles of protection and preservation. Visitor numbers are rising significantly as Islanders, tourists, sailors, bird-watchers and ramblers come to enjoy the quiet spaces and unspoiled vistas. Such numbers might eventually endanger those very qualities that attract them in the first place.

Laura, *an Itchen Ferry class sailing boat belonging to local residents, the Seabroke family.*

Historically, its remote location has tended to protect Newtown from over-commercialisation. Now, strict rules of land-use are enforced by the National Trust, local planning regulations are used to closely monitor proposed developments, and local residents are alert to any threat to the environment.

At the same time, commercial diversification has taken place in the district. Porchfield Business Park nestles unobtrusively across the fields near London Heath, accommodating such diverse enterprise as landscaping, boat building, furniture making and catering. Permission has been obtained for hi-tech hydroganic tunnel units at a nearby farm where a farm shop already does good business in high-quality dairy products. Another farm has established an equestrian centre, and another has converted redundant dairy units to holiday accommodation. Part of a further farm has been designated a Site of Special Scientific Interest (SSSI).

But the district's biggest business involves its visitors. They come in increasing numbers to enjoy an unspoiled landscape. The area has been fortunate to have had farmers like the Barton brothers at Harts Farm, the Prangnell family at Brickfields Farm and the Angell family at Locks Farm, all of whom retained farming methods scorned by other sectors of the farming community. Flora and fauna have not been destroyed by artificial fertilisers or over-grazing, and now retain a richness last seen in many places more than a century ago. Barry Angell, born and bred on Locks Farm, continues the tradition. Insisting on cutting his hay as late as July so that the green-winged orchids on the former village cricket pitch can seed successfully, he was unable to go in person to collect his English Nature award in 2002 for good farm management of ancient grasslands belonging to the National Trust and Ministry of Defence.

Hebridean sheep introduced to control weed growth on The Drove, an ancient highway that once led to Newtown's quay.

Public awareness of the unique nature of the district arose only just in time to protect it from commercial and residential development. Even so, the more remote corners of the Haven are invaded increasingly by marine traffic from Southampton and elsewhere, offering corporate hospitality functions and barbecues. Now, this special character has to be protected, partly by regulation, partly by education. Management requires intervention and control, and the National Trust, in particular, faces difficult choices between improving or controlling access for the public at large, and between permitting natural laws to determine the nature of the landscape or controlling that development with steeping (hedge-laying), coppicing, grazing techniques and the like.

The vulnerability of the village itself has been recognised, and the Countryside Agency and the Isle of Wight Rural Community Council are working to promote 'Wight Wheels' (an innovative approach to problems of rural transport), and a 'Vital Villages' programme. But, despite Newtown winning the Best Kept Small Village award in 2002, they work in the face of those commercial pressures that have driven the young away from Newtown in search of employment and affordable housing, and that led to the closure of its last Sunday School in 1972.

One of Newtown's last Sunday School groups in the late 1950s. Lily Mustchin is pictured with her pupils, left to right: Jane Chandler, Ann Mustchin, Elizabeth Mustchin, David Smith, ? Beazley, Rosemary Smith.

Porchfield Business Park sign, 2003.

Canada geese feed on the marshes of Causeway Creek overlooked by Lamb Cottage, the former rectory.

The broken embankment near Newtown Quay, in 1997.

Changing sea levels and increasingly frequent storms have destroyed the banks that once enclosed Newtown Marsh and are severely damaging the protective shingle-spits at the mouth of the Haven. There is some danger that the West Wight Coastal Defence Strategy Study, designed to contribute to the Shoreline Management Plan in 2004, will have come too late to prevent major landscape change. The local coastline has received an international RAMSAR designation for the protection of its wetland habitats, making it a Maritime Special Area for Conservation. In some ways the area is becoming more wild and driving back the mark of man around the Haven.

But a new kind of human endeavour is colonising the district. The Old Town Hall and its nearby visitor centre is already well established, as are two well-attended bird hides at the edge of the marshlands. Jersey Camp at Locks Green now hosts the 'Big Splash' Pond Warden courses run by the British Trust for Conservation Volunteers and sponsored by Southern Water, and groups of field studies officers use Newtown as a training base for education for a sustainable environment. School parties visit throughout the year. Nature trails have been established and guided walks are available. Visitor numbers are growing rapidly. Newtown is in fashion again.

For over 1,000 years the area has been subject to invasion of one kind or another – from plundering Dane and Frenchman to plague and land enclosure; from the incursion of the sea to migrating wildfowl. For more than a century pleasure-seekers have enjoyed the area's attractions. Now, it is easier for more people, with more time, to make the area their playground. There is some cause for concern, for such an invasion might overwhelm the area and erode its particular qualities. The National Trust, in its attempt to improve access, yet limit its effect, will need a sure touch.

An early invasion of day-trippers visit Stone Steps Tea Gardens, c.1910. Jim Griffin is seen standing sideways in the centre of the picture next to his wife, Clara, the daughter of Mr Jupe, who is wearing the bowler hat. Mr Flux is seated to the right of the flag, and Mr Loving, the chapel superintendent from Pallance Road, is seated in the centre.